THE CURSE OF CAIN

THE CURSE

The Violent

Legacy of

Monotheism

OF CAIN

REGINA M. SCHWARTZ

The University of Chicago Press • Chicago and London

The University of Chicago Press, Chicago 60637
The University of Chicago Press, Ltd., London
© 1997 by Regina M. Schwartz
All rights reserved. Published 1997
Printed in the United States of America
13 12 11 10 09 08 07   5 4

ISBN (cloth): 0-226-74199-0
ISBN (paper): 0-226-74200-8

Library of Congress Cataloging-in-Publication Data

Schwartz, Regina M.
     The curse of Cain : the violent legacy of monotheism /
Regina M. Shwartz.
          p.   cm.
     Includes bibliographical references and index.
     ISBN 0-226-74199-0 (alk. paper)
     1. Ethnicity—Biblical teaching.   2. Ethnology in the Bible.
3. Violence—Religious aspects—Christianity.   4. Monotheism—Controversial literature.   I. Title.
BS661.S35   1997
221.8′3036—dc20   96-43269
                                                           CIP

To my Father,
> IRVING LLOYD SCHWARTZ
> whose life defined heroism

and to my Mother,
> ROSANNE SCHELLMAN SCHWARTZ
> whose goodness is beyond definition

Contents

One day while I was teaching the Bible to undergraduates, a first-year student articulated a problem succinctly that I had to write an entire book to address. I was telling the class that the Exodus is the central event of the Hebrew narrative, asserting that this myth of liberation from slavery was deeply inspiring, especially in comparison to so many other foundational myths of conquest and plunder. This was, after all, not a myth that described the rich getting richer, but the enslaved getting freed. I added some remarks about class consciousness and liberation theology to make the story more contemporary, and lingered over the fact that this story has now come to have urgent political force in Latin America and South Africa as it had during the U.S. civil rights movement. Then, in the midst of this celebration, the student raised his hand and asked simply, "What about the Canaanites?" Suddenly all the uncomfortable feelings I had been repressing about the Bible for years flooded me. Yes, what about the Canaanites? and the Amorites, Moabites, Hittites? While the biblical narratives charted the creation, cohesion, and calamities befalling a people at the behest of their God, what about all the other peoples and their gods? Having long seen the Bible put to uses that I could not excuse—hatred of Blacks, Jews, gays, women, "pagans," and the poor—I now began to see some complicity, for over and over the Bible tells the story of a people who inherit at someone else's expense. And so, keenly aware that our deepest cultural assumptions are biblical and that they are not always attractive, I embarked on this book on monotheism and collective identity.

I make some strong claims. One is that through the dissemination of the Bible in Western culture, its narratives have become the foundation of a prevailing understanding of ethnic, religious, and national identity as defined negatively, over against others. We are "us" because we are not "them." Israel is not-Egypt. That is not to say that this way of thinking about identity is simply or originally biblical.[1] Ancient peoples conquered one another long before the Israelites wrote about it, and in philosophy, Aristotle's principle of noncontradiction established that for A to be A it could not be B, while Plato wrote of *polemos,* endless war against the foreign, the diverse, the "enemy." But it has been the biblical narratives, for better and for worse, that have wielded so much influence, even more than the classics, with the result that the Bible could be deployed against whatever "Canaanites" people wanted to loathe, conquer, or exile. And so, while I read the Bible in this book, I also read readings of the Bible: biblical narratives as read by biblical criticism and biblical narratives translated into secular myths of nationalism. My focus is on narratives in the Hebrew Bible, since this understanding of violent identity formation is articulated most clearly there.

Collective identity is linked to monotheism, the notion of exclusive worship, but there could be no cruder misreading of my argument than to attribute violence in identity formation to Judaism. Conquering the Canaanites was a fantasy of an exiled people; it could only carry force when it was adopted by groups who held the reins of power in Christendom.[2] Furthermore, what Reform Judaism gave me was less the understanding of Judaism as a separated identity than its strong stress on ethics; shedding traditional rituals and the trappings of group identity was accompanied by a renewed emphasis on being "a good person." While I know that distinction will not hold under close examination, it is this antiritualistic strain of Judaism that I inherited in my childhood, a latter-day version of Jeremiah inveighing against the hypocrisy of worshippers at the temple who were guilty of social abuses. Where the Bible both inspired and seemed to fail me, then, is on ethics: a moving accountability for the widow, the orphan, and the poor and commitment to liberation from oppression is joined to obliterating the Canaanites. And this is not just a contradiction, for when the narratives become preoccupied with Israelite identity, with defining Israel and non-Israelites, insiders and outsiders, that paramount definitional urge compromises the ethical imperatives. There is concern for the well-being of a neighbor up to a point, and that point is where the neighbor is regarded as posing a threat to the identity of ancient Israel— and that point is most often the very existence of the neighbor.

But why the violence? Why is claiming a distinctive collective identity important enough to spawn violence? I found an answer to this question in a principle of scarcity that pervades most thinking about identity. When everything is in short supply, it must all be competed for—land, prosperity, power, favor, even identity itself. In many biblical narratives, the one God is not imagined as infinitely giving, but as strangely withholding. Everyone does not receive divine blessings. Some are cursed—with dearth and with death—as though there were a cosmic shortage of prosperity. And it is here, in this tragic principle of scarcity, that I find the biblical legacy to culture so troubling. While I was heartened to discover that the Bible does offer glimpses of a monotheistic plenitude instead of scarcity— the heavens rain enough bread to feed everyone—those moments have not held the same command in our politics, in our culture, and in our imaginations that the biblical myth of scarcity has. Scarcity is encoded in the Bible as a principle of Oneness (one land, one people, one nation) and in monotheistic thinking (one Deity), it becomes a demand of exclusive allegiance that threatens with the violence of exclusion. When that thinking is translated into secular formations about peoples, "one nation under God" becomes less comforting than threatening.

Acknowledgments

Amid the moving generosity of most biblical scholars, there was only one who warned me not to write a book on the Bible, reminding me that the rabbis said, "It will burn your feet." With burning soles, I want to thank the many colleagues who did help and encourage, adding that they do not all agree with all that I've said, so that their souls need not burn.

The seeds of this work were planted twenty years ago by James Ackerman, my beloved mentor in religious studies, and were nourished most recently by John Milbank, who challenged as relentlessly as he listened. James Kincaid was my muse, sharing his courage and his tenacity for subverting our most cherished cultural assumptions. Raymond Collins knows how complete my debt to him is, for this and for the larger project. Ed Muir's incessant loving-kindness encouraged me daily. Bill Davis gave his strength. My friendships with Valeria Finucci, Barbara Fox, Carol Johnson, and Stephanie Sieburth gave warm support, both to the study and to me. Michael Lieb, Philip Blond, Kevin Hart, David Loewenstein, Eric White, Daniel Boyarin, Jonathan Boyarin, Sarah Beckwith, Toril Moi, and Stephen

Moore all encouraged the project at various stages with their active and helpful interest. I was also blessed with extraordinary students while I wrote this book, all of whom have since become professors: Barry Milligan, Glenn Wilmott, Sandra Gravett, and Ann Burlein. F. Volker Greifenhagen, also now a professor, tirelessly and generously assisted me with research. The students in my class on nationalism and religion at Duke kept me interested in the political implications of my thesis. Kenneth Hoaglund helped bring my rusty Hebrew back, adding his wise counsel. There are others whose influence on my thinking was less immediate perhaps but no less important. Robert Alter's work on the Bible has been pathbreaking for literary scholars; my debt to Mieke Bal's powerful work on violence against women in the Bible is palpable; William Kerrigan and Leopold Damrosch fueled my obsessions about God over the years; and I am also indebted to the insightful work of Herbert Schneidau and the brilliant observations of Harry Berger Jr. Among traditional biblical scholars, David Noel Freedman towers for his openness to new approaches even as his life has been devoted to historical–critical scholarship, as the editor of the multivolume Anchor Bible Commentaries, *The Anchor Bible Dictionary,* and a host of indispensable guides to the rich world of biblical expertise. I am grateful for the toleration that made him welcome my critique of the discipline and for his editorial expertise. I come to the Bible as an outsider, and have leaned heavily upon the learning and help of the experts, with the hope that they will forgive the mistakes an interloper inevitably makes. Finally, Freud's courage to write his *Moses and Monotheism* in the midst of Nazi persecution gave me strength to criticize the biblical legacy despite a continuing tragic climate of antisemitism.

While I was thinking through this project, I presented installments, often only early intuitions and tentative readings, to audiences who responded with invaluable suggestions and encouragement. Unable to name all of the colleagues and students who have contributed, I can acknowledge my debt to those respective audiences: at Cambridge University in England in the Theology and Postmodernism Lectures, at the University of California at Berkeley and Northwestern University under the sponsorship of their English departments and Religion programs, at the University of Chicago's Divinity School and Advanced Institute for the Study of Religion, at Wright State University and Virginia Tech where the applications of this study were so helpfully drawn out, and at sessions on "Theology and Ideology" at the Modern Language Association, and on "Ideological Approaches to the Bible" at the Society of Biblical Literature/American Academy of Religion, at a conference on "The Bible in Culture" at the University of California at Riverside, on "The Literary and the Bible" at Georgetown University, University of Colorado, Oxford University, and on "Covenants" at Bar Ilan University in Tel Aviv. Funding for a year's research came from the National Endowment for the Humanities, and Ron Butters, acting chair at Duke University, kindly enabled me to take my sabbatical at the Institute for the Advanced Study of Religion at the University of Chicago, where I profited from the atmosphere of a distinguished faculty. A version of chapter 1, "Inventing Identity: Covenants," was published as "Monotheism and the Violence of Identity," in *Raritan* 14, no. 3 (winter 1995): 119–40. Different early versions of chapter 4, "Dividing Identities: 'Nations,'" were published in *"Not in Heaven": Coherence and Complexity in Biblical Narrative,* ed. Jason Rosenblatt and Joseph Sitterson Jr. (Bloomington: Indiana University Press, 1991); *Semeia* 54 (1991): 35–55; and *Critical Inquiry* 19 (autumn 1992): 131–50. An early version of part of chapter 5, "Inscribing Identity: Memory," was published as "Joseph's Bones and the Resurrection of the Text: Remembering in the Bible," in *PMLA* 103 (March 1988): 114–24, and another in *The Book and the Text: The Bible and Literary Theory,* ed. Regina Schwartz (Oxford: Basil Blackwell, 1990), 40–59. I thank the respective presses for their permissions. Finally, Alan Thomas of the University of Chicago Press, who has assisted this and so many other publications with his astute judgment and keen intelligence, restores the old dignity and distinction to the hallowed vocation of Editor.

REBUILDING BABEL

At this point it seems impossible to think difference without thinking it aggressively or defensively. But think it we must, because if we don't, it will continue to think us, as it has since Genesis at the very least.—Alice Jardine

MURDER

O riginal sin. The wisdom of the ages tells us that all the miseries of the world—the injustice, hostility, pain, poverty, illness, violence, and even death—are the result of the first man and woman disobeying God. They ate a fruit when he told them not to. I have never been persuaded, and I have tried. I wrote a book about *Paradise Lost* to try to make sense of the idea but concluded that even Milton laid the blame elsewhere.[1] Now when I look at the tragic state of affairs in the world and then turn to that story of disobeying God for an explanation, it still doesn't square. But there is another foundational myth, one that follows on the heels of the story of Adam and Eve, that strikes me as especially appropriate for the violence that rends our world: the story of Cain and Abel. The first brothers committed the first murder, and unhappily I do think that the devastating legacy of Cain is very much with us. We are the heirs of Cain because we murder our brothers.

This original violence makes a more modest claim than original sin: we do not kill one another *because* Cain did; rather, we kill one another for similar reasons. While the story of Cain and Abel does not pause to offer anything like a full account of logical explanations or deep motivations, it is safe to say that it tells a story of sibling rivalry. It depicts a world that has just been created—a world that is virtually unpopulated—and in that world the first man and first woman give birth to the first brothers who immediately dramatize the first inexplicable rivalry. No friendly competition, it soon proves fatal. What are they competing for? Not, it seems, for the favor of their earthly parents, Adam and Eve, but for the favor of their heavenly Maker. In this cryptic narrative, each brother offers a sacrifice to God, but for some mysterious reason one sacrifice is deemed unacceptable while the other is well-received.

> Abel kept flocks and Cain worked the soil. In the course of time Cain brought some of the fruits of the soil as an offering to the Lord. But Abel brought fat portions from some of the firstborn of his flock. The Lord looked with favor upon Abel and his offering, but on Cain and his offering he did not look with favor. So Cain was very angry and his face was downcast. (Gen 4:2–5)

What we know about sacrifice can be gleaned from other biblical contexts. Its uses range from rites of expiation—including purification, exorcism, and scapegoating—to rites of communion and thanksgiving. The sacrifices of Cain and Abel suggest propitiation, that is, an offering to ward off divine wrath, to encourage the deity's favor, to invoke his blessings of prosperity. With the blessings or curses of the cosmos attached to divine pleasure or displeasure, God's rejection of Cain's sacrifice is no mere embarrassment. Not surprisingly, Cain is devastated: "Then the Lord said to Cain, 'Why are you angry? Why is your face downcast? If you do what is right, will you not be accepted?'" This sounds much like the unhelpful dictum from Exodus, "I will be gracious to whom I will be gracious and I will show mercy to whom I will show mercy." Yet however circular, God's response does suggest that Cain has already done something wrong (even before he has) since he has been rejected. In what follows, Cain earns that judgment retrospectively by murdering his brother. Cain has worked the soil, has offered the fruits of the soil, and when he kills his brother, the blood of Abel cries out from the soil. Then he is banished from the soil, condemned to wander beyond the presence of God in the land of Nod (land of wandering). "Hence you are banned from the soil which forced open its mouth to take your brother's blood from your hand. When you till the soil, it shall not again give up its strength to you" (Gen 4:11–12). In this story, the first brother, who is the first murderer, also becomes the first outcast.

Why did God condemn Cain's sacrifice?[2] What would have happened if he had accepted both Cain's and Abel's offerings instead of choosing one, and had thereby promoted cooperation between the sower and the shepherd instead of their competition and violence? What kind of God is this who chooses one sacrifice over the other? This God who excludes some and prefers others, who casts some out, is a monotheistic God—monotheistic not only because he demands allegiance to himself alone but because he confers his favor on one alone. While the biblical God certainly does not always govern his universe this way, the rule presupposed and enforced here, in the story of Cain and Abel, is that there can be no multiple allegiances, neither directed toward the deity nor, apparently, emanating from him. Cain kills in the rage of his exclusion. And the circle is vicious: because Cain is outcast, Abel is murdered and Cain is cast out. We are the descendants of Cain because we too live in a world where some are cast out, a world in which whatever law of scarcity made that ancient story describe only one sacrifice as acceptable—a scarcity of goods, land, labor, or whatever—still prevails to dictate the terms of a ferocious and fatal competition. Some lose.

When Cain's sad tale is retold in the Bible with another set of brothers, that uncomfortable rule of scarcity appears again. There is not enough divine favor, not enough blessing, for both Jacob and Esau. One can prosper only at the other's expense. When Jacob steals his brother's blessing, there are no blessings left for Esau: "Esau pleaded with his father, 'Do you have only one blessing, my father? Bless me too, my father!'" (Gen 27:38). The terrible cost of this scarcity of blessings is another Outcast: "Your home shall be far from the earth's riches." And again the Outcast becomes murderous:

> Esau harbored a grudge against his brother Jacob on account
> of the blessing that his father had given him. And Esau said to
> himself, "As soon as the time to mourn my father is at hand, I
> will kill my brother Jacob." (Gen 27:41)

In the Bible, these brothers are the eponymous ancestors of peoples: peoples whose enmity grows and is nurtured for centuries, peoples who define themselves and their prosperity in that close atmosphere of scarcity, peoples who conceive of the Other as cursed and murderous outcasts.

IDENTITY AND VIOLENCE

This book is about collective identity—the identities of groups, of peoples, of nations. It is a reminder, at a time when peoples are fighting fiercely to preserve their identities in places as far-flung as South Africa, Bosnia, the United States, and Ireland, that such identities are, after all, constructed—hence provisional and arbitrary—however stubbornly those identities are shored up with concepts of religion, ethnicity, race, or nationality. Nonetheless, in recent years, much energy has been devoted to defining and defending the borders of collective identities, and when the insight surfaces that their boundaries are provisional and constructed, it seems to have been more ineffectual than mobilizing. More has been achieved by digging in, claiming distinctive identities and gaining a hearing for them, particularly because the rights of those peoples who have been marginalized are often at stake.[3] But this ancient model of collective identity—as peoples set apart—may put such distinctive identities at another great peril, one that stems from its very oppositional character. The risk is not only further marginalization but more generally the fragmentation of humanity into clusters that must nervously defend their borders, both offensively and defensively. That danger is one we should heed from the example of nationalism in our modern world, where lines on the map are drawn and redrawn in blood, territories expand and contract, but the violence does not go away because that violence is in the very lines themselves.

This book is about violence. It locates the origins of violence in identity formation, arguing that imagining identity as an act of distinguishing and separating from others, of boundary making and line drawing, is the most frequent and fundamental act of violence we commit. Violence is not only what we do to the Other. It is prior to that. Violence is the very construction of the Other. This process is tricky: on the one hand, the activity of people defining themselves as a group is negative, they *are* by virtue of who they are not. On the other hand, those outsiders—so needed for the very self-definition of those inside the group—are also regarded as a threat to them. Ironically, the Outsider is believed to threaten the boundaries that are drawn to exclude him, the boundaries his very existence maintains. Outside by definition but always threatening to get in, the Other is poised in a delicate balance that is always off balance because fear and aggression continually weight the scales. Identity forged against the Other inspires perpetual policing of its fragile borders. History has shown that in the name of our identities—religious, ethnic, national, racial, gender—we commit and suffer the most horrific atrocities. This book argues that acts of identity formation are themselves acts of violence.[4]

I trace this notion of identity born in violence to the Bible, not because it is its origin (certainly earlier ancient peoples had such formations of collective identity) nor because the Bible advocates violence (it is much too heterogeneous to promote any single mode of forming group identity) but because of the enormous cultural

weight the Bible has had through its interpretations and dissemina-
tions, chiefly in Christendom and thence into secular thought and
institutions where it has forged contemporary notions of collective
identity. We secularists have barely begun to acknowledge the biblical influence, confidently, and I think mistakenly, believing that a
sharp division has been achieved between the premodern sacred
worldview and the modern secular one. But sacred categories of
thought have not just disappeared. They have lingered into the modern world where they are transformed into secular ones. As Carl
Schmitt, a political theorist who became an important ideologue to
the Nazis, well understood, "All significant concepts of the modern
theory of the state are secularized theological concepts not only because of their historical development—in which they were trans-
ferred from theology to the theory of the state, whereby, for example, the omnipotent God became the omnipotent lawgiver—but
also because of their systematic structure."[5] From a different political
quarter, the Marxist anthropologist Benedict Anderson reminds us
early in his important study of nationalism, *Imagined Communities,* to
seek the roots of nationalism in the cultural systems that preceded it,
those of the dynastic realm and the religious community.[6] While
nationalism assumed specific and distinct forms in the modern era,
with linguistic and cultural units often (but not always) overlapping
political ones and with the sovereignty of the state variously imple-
mented, these formations evolved from concepts of collective identity that had been in place for as long as there has been any notion
of "peoples."

The Bible encodes Western culture's central myth of collective
identity. Its narratives describe forging peoples, and it offers multiple
visions of what might be meant by "a people" (each of these will be
the focus of the chapters of this book): a group with a common deity
and cultic practices, a population who hold a territory in common,
a nation with a bureaucracy, a kinship group, an exiled community
united by a common literature. That is, most of the pages of the
Hebrew Bible are not filled with ethical precepts or Sunday-school
lessons in piety, but with stories detailing the processes of forming
collective identities. These include mythic tales about the epony-

mous ancestors of peoples and epiclike narratives devoted to describing the liberation of a slave class from its oppressors; stories that describe aspirations of self-determination and a communal pledge to a deity and his laws; tales of conquering and settling territory, of defending borders and establishing a variety of self-governing configurations—from tribes to judgeship to monarchy—stories of a nation divided and conquered, a people deported and their efforts to sustain an identity in exile, and finally the attempt to establish an identity, upon returning, as a province of another empire. Meanwhile, throughout all of these stories, there is an effort to forge identity by means of these very stories, to create the proverbial "people of the book."

Just before the advent of modern secularism, these biblical narratives devoted to formations of a people were disseminated in a way that was unrivaled in the history of their reception, indeed, in the history of reception of any book. Theologically, Protestantism had taken the Bible out of the hands of the clergy and put it in the hands of the masses. Materially, print technology had taken the Bible out of the hands of the scribal monks and put it in the hands of the masses. Europe acquiring literacy was Europe learning to read the Bible. Europe gaining print culture was Europe reading the Bible. "In the two decades 1520–1540 three times as many books were published in German as in the period 1500–1520, an astonishing transformation to which Luther was absolutely central. His works represented no less than one third of all German-language books sold between 1518 and 1525. Between 1522 and 1546, a total of 430 editions (whole or partial) of his Biblical translations appeared. In effect, Luther became the first best-selling author so known."[7] While the Reformation centered on Scripture reading in the vernacular, it also ushered in a transfer of legitimacy from the papacy to the state. Ultimately, the household became the temple, with Bible reading serving as the core of every family's self-government. And this Europe—filled with Bible stories about peoples—was also a Europe on the road to carving itself into new peoples, into nationalisms.

Despite the biblical preoccupation with collective identity and the vast cultural influence those notions of identity have inevitably wielded, the Bible has received scanty attention from scholars of modern and contemporary cultural and political theory. I have already alluded to one reason: the mistaken assumption that the Scriptures along with all things vaguely "religious" belong to a long dark age that ended with enlightened secularism. Another is to be found in the history of professional disciplines. Since the eighteenth century, the Bible has become the property of biblical scholars and theologians, with the less expert excluded. Biblical scholars have been busily charting the history of the composition and editing of the text rather than its reception, looking backward rather than forward. Theologians have been mining the Bible to authorize their own versions of the sacred. Falling between the disciplinary boundaries of biblical history on the one hand and theology on the other, the vast effect the Bible has had on our cultural and political lives has been left largely unexamined.[8] We may know, vaguely, that it was quoted extensively during the revolutions in France and the New World, during the civil wars in Great Britain and America, that the Bible was invoked both to justify slavery and to abolish it, invoked for missionary imperialism and revolutionary response, that its cadences were intoned at the birth of various nationalisms and its verses infused not only the rhetoric of Zionism and the liberation theologies of Latin America and South Africa, but also considerably less overt biblical polities. But what these superficial allusions belie is the much deeper influence the Bible has had on the way we think—about peoples, nations, religions, ethnic groups, and races—and that we even think in those categories at all we owe to the book whose chief preoccupation is imagining and forging collective identity. All this is to warn that, if we do not think about the Bible, it will think (for) us.

Interpretations of biblical narratives have also been put to any and every political purpose. When universalism was needed, Deutero-Isaiah's sentiment that Israel is a light to the nations was useful. When particularism was in order, Ezra's inveighing against the foreigner would do. Since it seems to contain all things, it has been useful for all ends. (In this, I am well aware that my own biblical interpretations and my explicit intention—to critique inventing group identity in violence—are very much a part of that history of purposeful and political biblical hermeneutics.) This long history has not been as innocent, as happily egalitarian, with conflicting interpretations merrily balancing each other out, as it might sound. Rather, those who have held the reins of power made sure that their interpretations were authoritative, that while they reigned their interpretations reigned, backed by the formidable and unassailable authority of God's word. Like the notion of the divine right of kings, biblical authority has functioned as a deeply conservative force, and if it has offered aid and comfort, it has also been used to sanction all manner of abuses.[9] Why we should need the Bible to "authorize" at all, why our ethics and our codes of conduct are not felt to be sufficiently compelling without the Bible's validation, may well be a complicated question (the mechanisms of projection? mystification?), but certainly the hazards of authorizing that text—*any* text—whether it is the Bible, the Qur'an, or the Protocols of the Elders of Zion, are palpable. The U.S. Constitution with its vast judicial afterlife offers compelling demonstration that when authority is vested in such documents they take on the power to threaten and to protect, to punish and to reward. To invoke the authority of the text is to claim the privilege of the highest court. However much biblical narratives themselves may caution against such authorization, offering critique after critique to unseat each of its own authorized institutions (judgeship, priesthood, monarchy, prophecy) and revising each of its covenant codes (Noachic, Mosaic, Davidic, prophetic), nevertheless, its interpreters have insisted upon canonizing, codifying, and authorizing, in short, in turning the text, despite itself, into a weapon. And in the violent tactics of identity formation, that weapon is most often wielded against the Other.

It could be otherwise. In addition to Cain's legacy of violent identity formation against the Other, the Bible has much to teach us about how difficult it is to designate the foreigner and how permeable the boundaries of any people are. Anyone with even the slightest familiarity with the Bible will know that it is far too multifaceted to be reduced to any single or simple notion of a deity, of religion, and especially of a people. However limited our knowledge of its composition, it is clear that the Bible does not conform to modern notions of authorship, composed as it was over hundreds of years in disparate socioeconomic, cultic, and political settings. Surely such a work cannot have "one line" on collective identity, one understanding of who the Israelites are or who the foreigners are. There were editors, presumably even final editors, who could have ironed out all these contradictions but who chose, importantly, not to resolve them, and in the process they bequeathed a text that foregrounds the many ways that "a people" is constructed. It was later interpreters who, grinding their political biblical axes, violated the editors' preference for multiplicity, simplifying the complexities of identity formation and flattening out the variegated depictions in order to legitimate claims for an identity locked in perpetual defense against the Other.

In addition to the powerful force the Bible has generally exerted on our commonplaces of group identity, a very specific historical circumstance accounts for the direct way in which biblical narratives have shaped concepts of nationalism. A key moment in the history of biblical interpretation occurred during that transition from the predominantly sacred to the largely secular worlds that spanned the seventeenth and eighteenth centuries. In fact, biblical interpretation itself helped to propel that shift toward secularism, with its so-called higher criticism.[10] Bible scholars of the period (many the rebellious sons of ministers) joined together in an effort to liberate minds from enthrallment to religious superstition. They asserted that the Bible was not the revealed word of God, but that it was written by individuals and schools in specific historical circumstances. With the aid of the burgeoning technologies of archeology and philology, the riddle of the Bible's composition finally could be unraveled, and the mysteries of this once sacred and inviolate text could be laid bare. But these erudite biblical scholars, for all of their commitment to objective scientific inquiry, could not escape their own historical setting and their own political and philosophical presuppositions. Whether Hegelian, romantic, pietist, or none of the above, they were imbued with nascent German nationalism. Could it really be coincidence that biblical higher criticism and the ideology of radical modern nationalism were born in the same period in the same place?[11] The

Bible's preoccupation with collective identity was read through the lenses of German nationalism—God's chosen people became the chosen nation—and read not only by scholars but also by the clergy and masses who became nationalized in the wake of reading translations of the Bible. Throughout all this reading and interpreting, then, German versions of biblical narratives of collective identity assumed their place in conceiving modern nationalism. With the archeologist's spade and the philologist's verb ending, miracles gave way to science, mythic origins to history, and the once sacred understanding of collective identity—as a people forged by the Deity—gave way to secular understandings of collective identity, including modern nationalism. In time, what had been a "covenant" became transformed into variations of a "social contract."

In a disturbing inversion, soon nationalism was authorized by the once-holy writ. A text that had once posited collective identity as the fiat of God ("I will be your God if you will be my people") came to posit collective identity as the fiat of the nation authorized by God ("one nation, under God"). Nationalism has stubbornly held fast to this legitimation by transcendence. Nations are the will of God. National borders are the will of God. National expansions and colonization are the will of God. National military confrontations are the will of God. Every nation is the one nation under God. In Germany, pietism was joined to the national cult: in 1784, Friedrich Carl von Moser asserted that "Pia Desideria" (true piety) was service on behalf of truth and the fatherland.[12] The German romantic nationalist Ernst Moritz Arndt said that Christian prayer should accompany national festivals, and his suggested monument to the Battle of Leipzig (where Napoleon was defeated by the Allies) was to be crowned with a cross, for such a monument "would deserve the highest praise, truly German and truly Christian." Even when German nationalism self-consciously tried to separate its cult from the Christian one, it could not hide the debt: "The Introitus, the hymn sung or spoken at the beginning of the church service, became the words of the Fuhrer, the 'Credo' a confession of faith pledging loyalty to Nazi ideology; while the sacrifice of the Mass was transformed into a memorial for the martyrs of the movement."[13] Where nationalism is not explicitly authorized by God, it replaces God. In France, Marie-Joseph-Blaise Chénier proposed in the National Convention on 5 November 1793 the establishment of a lay religion, that of la Patrie:

> Wrest the sons of the Republic from the yoke of theocracy which still weighs upon them. . . . Devoid of prejudices and worthy to represent the French nation, you will know how to found, on the debris of the dethroned superstitions, the single universal religion, which has neither sects nor mysteries, of which the only dogma is equality, of which our law-makers are the preachers, of which the magistrates are the pontiffs, and in which the human family burns its incense only at the altar of la Patrie, common mother and divinity.[14]

In the United States, symbols of nationalism are wedded to invocations of the deity from the dollar bill to the pledge to the flag.

We might expect that the nationalism born in the eighteenth century, a nationalism of the masses, would be eager to divest itself explicitly, first, of this ecclesial relic, for it was a reminder of the universalism of the great Holy Roman Empire beyond the bounds of nation, and second, of this monarchical relic, for kings had ruled by divine right.[15] Nonetheless, nationalism clung to these old vestiges for compelling reasons. Concentrating power in a supreme sovereign is clearly an effective way to fix identity and to galvanize loyalty, as the many soldiers who willingly sacrifice their lives for their human sovereigns attest, but an even more potent way to fuel nationalistic ambitions is to call down the omnipotence of the divine sovereign, to have Him, as if by miracle, confer that omnipotence upon the temporal authority. "On his national God the modern religious nationalist is conscious of dependence. Of His powerful help he feels the need. In Him he recognizes the source of his own perfection and happiness. To Him, in a strictly religious sense he subjects himself."[16] Once sovereign power is legitimated by transcendence, it is elusive and (unlike human sovereignty) inviolate. There is no check upon the will of a nation-God. Carl Schmitt understood this: "The concept of sovereignty in the theory of the state . . . and the theory of the 'sole supremacy of the state' make the state an abstract person so to speak, a *unicum sui generis* with a monopoly of power 'mystically produced.'"[17] Mystically produced and miraculously inviolate, the sovereignty of the divinely legitimated nation is, unlike its human counterpart, ultimately unimpeachable.[18]

Examples could be proliferated of social theorists speaking of nationalism as a religion, marshaling the rhetoric of the sacred to describe its adherents: "National awakening in early nineteenth-century Germany, and later in other countries was experienced as rites of intoxication and solidarity shared by an entire community." "Service, even death, for the sake of the nation's cohesion, self-assertion and glory are elevated by national rhetoric to the level of sacrifice and martyrdom." "In nationalism, [the nation's] value resides in its capacity as the sole, binding agency of meaning and justification. . . . this often has the radical consequence of transforming nationalism into a substitute religion. . . . The nation is consecrated, it is ultimately a holy entity."[19] In these pages, I intend to take such rhetorical flourishes seriously, showing how and why the following sweeping assertion holds—"in nationalism, the religious is secularized, and the national sanctified"[20]—by looking at the biblical legacy and the narratives that have bequeathed conceptions of collective identity. Needless to say, charting the complex inheritance of how those biblical ideas came to be translated into secular formations, that is, writing a complete history of the heirs of biblicism, would be virtually an intellectual history of the West—and such a project is well beyond the scope of this one. Here I can only point to some key intersections of biblical identity formations and later secular beliefs about collective identity, pausing over some of the moments in the history of the interpretation of the narratives that have been remarkably and often tragically tenacious.[21]

INVENTING IDENTITY
COVENANTS

I, Yahweh your God, am a jealous God and I punish the
father's fault in the sons, the grandsons, and the great-
grandsons of those who hate me; but I show kindness to thou-
sands of those who love me and keep my commandments.
—Exodus 20:5–6

Only you can make this world seem right,
Only you can make the darkness bright,
Only you and you alone can thrill me like you do
And fill my heart with love for only you.
—Buck Ran and Ande Rand

M any of us imagine that the secular world has freed us from the
encumbrances of religion, the rule of one deity and the authority of his priesthood, but the myth of monotheism continues to foster our central notions of collective identity. As a cultural
formation, monotheism is strikingly tenacious. Its tenet—one God

establishes one people under God—has been translated from the sphere of the sacred to nationalism, and thence to other collective identities. Most historians of nationalism concede that the concentration of power in an omnipotent sovereign was far too useful to divest at the birth of modern nationalism, and so allegiance to a sovereign deity in order to forge a singular identity became, in secular terms, allegiance to a sovereign nation to forge a national identity. That issued in such ironies as the following rhetoric from one of the architects of (secular) German nationalism: "He who does not love the fatherland which he can see, how can he love the heavenly Jerusalem which he does not see?"[1] In other words, the injunction of Romans 13:1—"let every person be subject to the governing authorities, for there is no authority except from God, and those authorities that exist have been instituted by God"— has been farther reaching than Paul could have ever imagined. In our nation's infancy, John Cotton advised John Winthrop of the Plymouth Colony that a "distinction which is put between the Laws of God and the laws of men becomes a snare . . . surely there is no human law that tendeth to common good but the same is a law of God."[2] And this has endured. In public school, I pledged my allegiance daily to the flag and the republic for which it stands, "one nation under God." Monotheism is a myth that grounds particular identity in universal transcendence. And monotheism is a myth that forges identity antithetically—against the Other.

But politics are not hardwired into theology, and the relation between monotheism and the social order is not simple. It can and has been variously conceived: as homologous, on earth as it is in heaven; as antithetical, the City of God versus the terrestrial city; as generative, divine kingship as the source of human sovereignty; or one category can subsume the other—depending on your persuasion, religious myths could mirror the social order or the sacral order design the state. Then too, figuring identity under a sovereign deity and figuring identity under a sovereign state could have a common source: some predilection for subjection, for imagining identity "under. . . ." In what can be called America's first constitution, the

Mayflower Compact, the Pilgrims promised "all due submission and obedience."

Before I launch into my critique of the system of thought broadly known as monotheism, I'd like to issue a brief note of caution. First, this critique should not be confused with an assessment of the scriptural religious traditions, all of which have some versions of polytheism in their rich and complex histories (I think of Calvin's frustration when Protestant women in labor insisted on calling upon St. Margaret, or of the rabbinic lore that makes Proverbial Wisdom a divine consort). Furthermore, although I will cite the Hebrew Bible because of the immense cultural influence its narratives have had through dissemination by Christianity and Islam,[3] there is, strictly speaking, no such thing as monotheism in it. Monotheism would make an ontological claim that only one god exists.[4] *Monolatry* or *henotheism* would better describe the kind of exclusive allegiance to one deity (from a field of many) that we find in, say, Deuteronomy 28:14, "Do not turn aside from any of the commands I give you today to the right or to the left, following other gods and serving them," but it sounds cumbersome, and since everyone uses *monotheism* to mean monolatry (thereby, with a sleight of vocabulary, turning allegiance to one god into the obliteration of other gods), I will stick to customary usage. Besides, even the monolatry variety of monotheism is not strictly synonymous with the theology of the Hebrew Bible.[5] To know anything at all about the Bible is to know that it is heterogeneous and that, in the history of biblical exegesis, the same text has been understood to convey widely divergent meanings, used to justify widely divergent theologies and policies, and used to justify the oppression of peoples and the liberation of peoples, often the same peoples, usually the same verse.

IMAGINING ISRAEL

Identities have of late come to be thought of as provisional, constructed, arbitrary, and one way to understand the biblical stories is to see them engaged in efforts to strengthen the precariousness of collective identity formations. In the Bible, the identity of ancient Israel is shored up with the myth that it is God-given.

> Then Moses went up to God; the Lord called to him from the mountain, saying, "Thus you shall say to the house of Jacob, and tell the Israelites: You have seen what I did to the Egyptians, and how I bore you on eagles' wings to myself. Now, therefore, if you obey my voice and keep my covenant, you shall be my treasured possession out of all peoples." (Ex 19:3–5)

Here collective identity is explicitly narrated as an invention, a radical break with nature and with the past. A transcendent deity breaks into history with the demand that the people he constitutes obey the laws he institutes, and first and foremost among those laws is the requirement that they pledge allegiance to him and to him alone. "Thou shalt have no other gods before me." A people are forged by their worship of one deity, Yahweh, and what makes others Other— Egyptian, Moabite, Ammonite, Canaanite, Perizzite, Hittite, or Hurrian—is their worship of foreign gods. When Israel is forged as an identity against the Other, it is figured as against other deities, and when Israel is threatened, it is not by the power of other nations, but by the power and wrath of her deity because she has wavered in her exclusive loyalty to him. Inclinations toward polytheism are repeatedly figured as sexual infidelity: "I am a jealous God, you will have none but me"; and Israel is castigated for "whoring after" other gods, thereby imperiling her "purity": "so shameless was her whoring that at last she polluted the country." Jeremiah's kinky confusion of idolatry and adultery condemns Israel for "committing adultery with lumps of stone and pieces of wood" (Jer 3:9).

These preoccupations with divine (and sexual) fidelity are part of that ideology of identity as someone or some people who are set apart, with boundaries that could be mapped, ownership that could be titled. "You are my own people, my very own." This people is to be the exclusive possession of the deity, and none other, and they are to have exclusive desire for this deity, and none other. The Other against whom Israel's identity is forged is abhorred, abject, impure, and in the "Old Testament," vast numbers of them are obliterated, while in the "New Testament," vast numbers are colonized (converted). This tying of identity to rejection runs counter to much of the drive that could be found elsewhere, both in the Bible and throughout religious myth and ritual, to forge identities through analogy, even identification. Instead of envisioning Israel as not-Egypt, in another biblical myth of origin, Israel is part-Egypt with a part-Egyptian Moses (born of one people, bred by another) leading the people out of Egypt, and in another story, Joseph, the son of Jacob/Israel, saves the Israelites by means of the high Egyptian status that is conferred upon him. Amid all the rich variety, I would categorize two broad understandings of identity in the Bible: one grounded in Negation (or scarcity) and another in Multiplicity (or plenitude). When biblical myths carve up humanity into peoples, they make assertions of collective identity in negative terms. To be Israel is to be not-Egypt; identity is purchased at the expense of the Other. But that is not the whole story. The logic of negation should be distinguished from one of multiplicity, a logic that sustains contraries without obliteration, that multiplies difference, and that foregrounds the provisional character of identity. The Bible conceives of Israel's relation with the Other in diverse ways. The spectrum runs the gamut from obliterating the Other to living peaceably with her, from welcoming her into the fold of God's people to demanding that Israelites "put away" their foreign wives, from distinguishing Israel from Egypt with clearly delineated boundaries to deriving Israel from that part-Egyptian Moses. Furthermore, even as biblical narratives establish a logic of negation, they also critique it by exposing its enormous cost. The degradation, suffering, and bloodshed of the Other are depicted graphically, so graphically that this sympathetic depiction of the outcast threatens to overcome sympathy for the insider. The abhorred are not abhorred by us.

Despite the Bible's efforts to shore up Israel's identity with the permanence and stability attached to notions like the "will of God," "natural" kinship relations, or territorial "inheritance," these constructs serve only to highlight the very precariousness they are meant to strengthen. Every effort to deny, repress, contain, and otherwise minimize how tentative the construction of Israel is has instead the effect of underscoring the vulnerability of that model.[6] The text seems engaged in establishing a nation ruled by a king even as it launches a powerful critique of the institution of monarchy. It narrates the origins of a kinship community that it completely undercuts. It asserts that the boundaries of land define the boundaries of a people but then insists that exile is the condition of their creation. It issues a call for a collective memory, but the memory and even the call for it are forgotten. It founds itself on the notion of a covenanted community and then takes pains to demonstrate how fragile, how easily broken, that is.[7] As the constructed character of identity comes to the fore, assertions of who the people are become unmasked as provisional. The commitment to negation begins to dissolve. Israel in opposition against not-Israel ends up being elaborated into a different understanding, of multiplicity rather than negation. The life and death struggles *between* Israel and Egypt give way to a another vision of Israel, not against, but *among* many nations: Moab, Ammon, Assyria, Philistia, Babylonia. If the poison is fixing collective identity in opposition to the Other, then this dynamism is one antidote, striking a hopeful chord in what often seems an intractable intolerance. When identity is mobile and multiple, the Other is difficult to name—and to hurt.

Plenitude is another antidote to the poison of forging identity in negation. The very idea that identity is constructed "against" suggests scarcity, as though there were a finite amount of identity itself, and so a space must be carved out for it and jealously guarded, like finite territory. If there were no identity shortage, if Israelites could be Egyptians too, for instance, there would be no need for aggressive or defensive gestures to protect their space. That is, singularity joins hands with scarcity, and both are given powerful expression in monotheism's emphasis on allegiance to one and only one god. The bargain is struck in Exodus, "I will be your God if you will be my people." Henceforth, a people must attach themselves to this principle, and all the biblical preoccupations with the creation and fate of the people, their political formations and their national aspirations, are tied to that deeper concern, monotheism. Just as foreign peoples are regarded as threats to Israel, so foreign gods are deemed threats to Yahwism, and when Israel suffers, its pain is framed as punishment for wavering in her exclusive loyalty to her deity.

CUTTING COVENANTS

Here I will investigate the way collective identity is forged in negation, and then underwritten by inviolable transcendence, by turning to biblical scenes describing the institution of Israel's identity in a covenant. The Hebrew phrase for "he made a covenant," *kārat bĕrît,* is literally "he cut a covenant," and the violence of that ostensibly dead metaphor is dramatized in each of the biblical ceremonies of the covenant: in the covenant with Abraham in Genesis where animals are cut in two and fire passes between them in a mysterious ritual, in the cutting of human flesh at circumcision—the so-called sign of the covenant—and in the covenant made at Mount Sinai where words are cut to inscribe the law in stone tablets.[8]

According to biblical scholars, severing an animal typically attended covenant ceremonies in the ancient Near East, but knowing that this was customary hardly helps to familiarize that bizarre passage in Genesis in which God first makes his covenant with the father of the Hebrew people.

> "Look at the heavens and count the stars—if indeed you can count them." Then he said to him, "So shall your offspring be." . . . "I am the Lord, who brought you out of Ur of the Chaldeans to give you this land to take possession of it." But Abram said, "O Sovereign Lord, how can I know that I will gain possession of it?" So the Lord said to him, "Bring me a heifer, a goat and a ram, each three years old, along with a dove and a young pigeon." Abram brought all these to him, cut them in two and arranged the halves opposite each other; the birds, however, he did not cut in half. Then birds of prey came down on the carcasses, but Abram drove them away. As the sun was setting, Abram fell into a deep sleep, and a thick and dreadful darkness came over him. Then the Lord said to

him, "Know for certain that your descendants will be strangers in a country not their own, and they will be enslaved and mistreated four hundred years. But I will punish the nation they serve as slaves, and afterward they will come out with great possessions. . . . In the fourth generation your descendants will come back here, for the sin of the Amorites has not yet reached its full measure." When the sun had set and darkness had fallen, a smoking fire pot, a blazing torch, appeared and passed between the pieces. On that day, the Lord made a covenant with Abram and said, "To your descendants I give this land, from the river of Egypt to the great river, the Euphrates— the land of the Kenites, Kenizzites, Kadmonites, Hittites, Perizzites, Rephaim, Amorites, Canaanites, Girgashites, and Jebusites." (Gen 15:5–21)

Ancient Israel is constituted in this scene, formed as a people and as a nation. Its history is also narrated, for in the Bible, collective identity is typically imagined historiographically. This history—of servitude and subsequent freedom from bondage, of building a great people in a mighty nation, of immense land acquisition, of establishing an empire—this entire foundational narrative of ancient Israel is framed by the account of severed pieces of animals. Why? In ancient Near Eastern rituals, the cut made to the animal is symbolically made to the inferior who enters into the covenant with a superior. An Aramaic treaty from the eighth century B.C.E. reads, "Just as this calf is cut up, so may Maltiel be cut up," and an earlier one describes how "Abba-an swore to Yarim-lim the oath of the gods, and cut the neck of a lamb saying, 'If I take back what I gave you,'" presumably adding a gesture indicating that his own throat would be slit. What must Israel's forefather do to avoid the fate of the severed animals? Why does a blazing torch pass between the pieces of animal instead of Abraham?[9] Does "cutting a covenant" create Israel's identity or destroy it? Must identity be forged in violence?

One possibility, the suggestion of Rene Girard in *La Violence et la sacre,* is that such violence is substitutive, directing the violence of the community onto scapegoats and hence away from the persons whose identity is being forged. "The sacrifice serves to protect the entire community from its own violence. . . . The elements of dissension scattered throughout the community are drawn to the person of the sacrificial victim and eliminated, at least temporarily, by its sacrifice. . . . The purpose of the sacrifice is to restore harmony in the community, to reinforce the social fabric."[10] Would that sacrifice could expiate violence. This logic of sacrifice is compatible with that illogic so evident in the "binding of Isaac" episode, where Abraham is willing to give up his "only" son to the sword in order to let his progeny live.

> Because you have done this and have not withheld your son, your only son, I will surely bless you and make your descendants as numerous as the stars in the sky and as the sand on the seashore. (Gen 22:16–17)

But I have abbreviated Girard's perception about sacrifice, for he also stresses that for identification in sacrificial rituals to work, the original object of violence must not be lost sight of in the substitution. Isaac is not fully replaced by the sacrifice of the ram; uncannily, the story has come down to us in English as "the sacrifice of Isaac." And in the covenant ceremony, Abram is not only *replaced* by the flaming torch and the severed animals, he is also *one* with them. Substitutive victims are victims nonetheless.

In the scene of the covenant at Sinai, where the covenant is made in stone rather than flesh and hence where we might expect substitutive violence to be in full play, something very different happens. The violence is not symbolized, it is literalized. And it is not deflected away from those who are part of this covenanting community, it is suffered by them.

> Moses went and told the people all the commands of Yahweh and all the ordinances. In answer, all the people said with one voice, "We will observe all the commands that Yahweh has decreed." Moses put all the commands of Yahweh into writing, and early next morning he built an altar at the foot of the mountain, with twelve standing stones for the twelve tribes of

Israel. Then he directed certain young Israelites to offer holo-
causts and to immolate bullocks to Yahweh as communion sacrifices. Half of the blood Moses took up and put into basins,
the other half he cast on the altar. And taking the book of the
Covenant he read it to the listening people, and they said, "We
will observe all that Yahweh has decreed; we will obey." Then
Moses took the blood and cast it toward the people. "This,"
he said, "is the blood of the Covenant that Yahweh has made
with you, containing all these rules." (Ex 24:3–8)

Moses does not refer to the inscribed commands as the "Book of
the Covenant" or the "Words of the Covenant," but as *dām habběrît,*
the Blood of the Covenant.

The demand of exclusivity proves an impossible demand, one violated even as it is enjoined. When Moses comes down from the
mountain, with the tablets in his hand that create the people as a
people with the stipulation that they must obey one deity, he dis-
covers them worshipping another. And the blood that flows next is
not the blood of bulls.

"Whoever is for the Lord, come to me," he said, and all the
Levites rallied to him. "This is what the Lord, the God of
Israel, says: 'Gird on your sword, every man of you, and quarter the camp from gate to gate killing one his brother, another
his friend, another his neighbor.'" The sons of Levi carried
out the command of Moses and about three thousand people
perished that day. (Ex 32:26–28)

Far from being a dead metaphor, *kārat běrît* is a loaded phrase, carrying all the resonances not only of making a covenant but also of
severing it and being severed by it. Yes, Israel's identity is instituted
by transcendent omnipotence, but that omnipotence threatens to
destroy the very identity it is called upon to establish. God is both
the guarantor and the threat to Israel. What was once the fragility of
identity has become outright violence, a violence made explicable,
perhaps even bearable, as the will of an omnipotent sovereign whose
wrath could be managed through obedience. A remark in the Book

of Jeremiah betrays how overdetermined this system is, for the people inevitably transgress the law: "I will make the men who have not observed the terms of the covenant made in my presence like the calf they cut in two to pass between the parts of it" (Jer 34:18).[11] When were they not cut in two?

How are we to account for this violence? How are we to distinguish it from the cutting so familiar from the discourse of "difference" with its celebration of discrete identities? How, that is, do we distinguish between the cutting that is an inscription of oppression and absolutism, and the cutting that is productive and proliferating? When is a cut in the name of heterogeneity, respecting differences, and when is it the violence of homogeneity, of totalizing, the violence that says, in effect, you will be in my system or you will not be?[12] When does cutting subvert (totalized) Identity and when does it destroy (particular) identities? Surely, power helps to distinguish: as we have seen, in the myth of monotheism, identities are underwritten by omnipotence, by the power to create and to destroy, to privilege and to disdain. A proliferating "difference" would cut into just such power, dispersing it until there is no position from which to posit a reviled Other.

THE BLOOD OF THE COVENANT

What, then, does it mean to say that *kārat běrît,* is not only to make a covenant but to break it and be broken by it? that the severings that create identity also destroy it? Does this mean that the price of a discrete identity must be violence, even obliteration? Exploring these questions in the context of ancient social treaties can help to defamiliarize biblical monotheism and to expose the ways that power is inscribed in a theological notion that has so long been surrounded by an aura of piety: the belief that collective identity is forged by a monotheistic "covenant." The Scottish Covenants of 1638 and 1643, the Covenantal Oath of the Afrikaners, even, according to some interpreters, the U.S. Constitution, are only among the most explicit political heirs of this notion disseminated by Calvin and various Calvinisms. "Covenantal communities" are among our most enduring political formations.[13] Nor are they only Protestant. The Proclamation of the Spanish Emancipation of the New World put the covenant to work in the demand that Indians convert, that they "recognize the Church as Mistress and Superior of the world and Universe, and the Supreme Pontiff, called Papa, in his name, and his Majesty in his name, as Superior and lord" *or else.*

> If so you do, you will do well, in what you are held and obligated to do, and his Majesty and I in his name will receive you with all love and affection. . . .

> If you do not do this, and maliciously set delays, I assure you that with God's aid, I shall enter with power among you, and shall make war on you on all sides and in every way I can, and subject you to the yoke and obedience of the Church and his Majesty; and I shall take your wives and children and make them slaves . . . and I shall take your property and shall do you all the harm I can, as to vassals who will not obey, and refuse to receive their lord, and resist and contradict him.[14]

Just as the biblical covenant came to be translated into secular forms, so it began its long life in a secular context. Biblical archeologists tell us that the written treaty between God and man is indebted to ancient social treaties between men. Surviving Hittite documents from the fourteenth and thirteenth centuries B.C.E. closely parallel the structure of the biblical covenant. The preamble introduced the speaker offering the treaty and told of his might. The historical prologue came next, describing in narrative how the lesser party was indebted to the greater party for past favors: "When your father died, in accordance with your father's word I did not drop you. Since your father had mentioned to me your name, I sought after you. To be sure, you were sick and ailing, but although you were ailing, I, the Sun, put you in the place of your father and took your brothers (and) sisters and the Amurru land in oath for you."[15] The rules followed, foremost among them the demand for the vassal's complete loyalty to the overlord (including military allegiance). A section devoted to blessings and curses completed the structure, with the overlord promising blessings of prosperity and peace in return for the vassal's loyalty and threatening complete annihilation should the vassal fail to fulfill the stipulations. That is, the greater party will destroy the lesser party if he should deviate from the terms of the contract, and he will destroy him should he refuse this deal. Historically, such treaties were made with a vanquished people by their conqueror. The treaty gave the conqueror the option of letting the vanquished people live, and in turn, they could choose to be subjected to the stipulations of the treaty instead of having obliteration chosen for them. In short, when we think of the prototype for the biblical covenant, we should not imagine a contract between two equal consenting partners; everything about the design of these treaties underscored their imbalance of power.[16]

The biblical debt to this Hittite treaty structure is not hard to discern. The covenant/treaty of Exodus 20, the so-called Ten Commandments, begins with a preamble to introduce the speaker and continues to a historical prologue: "I am the Lord your God, who brought you out of Egypt, out of the house of slaves." In this way, the contract establishes (if there were any doubt) that the Israelites owe their very existence to Yahweh, that he holds their "right of life and power over death." As the biblical scholar Gerhard von Rad succinctly put it: "The decalogue was the proclamation of the divine right over every sphere of life."[17] And this identity, granted by a greater power, continues to be radically contingent. The historical preface of the Decalogue defines the Lord as the people's protector and savior: "You yourselves have seen what I did with the Egyptians, how I carried you on eagles' wings and brought you to myself" (Ex 19:4). It also defines the vassal as the separate possession of the lord: "From this you know that now, if you obey my voice and hold fast to my covenant, you of all the nations shall be my very own" (Ex 19:5–6). The stipulations of the covenant follow, laws designed to regulate two spheres of relations: first, the community's relation to its deity (thou shalt have no gods before me), and second, relations among the members of the community (thou shalt not kill, steal, commit adultery). The connection between these two spheres has been the subject of biblical commentary from time immemorial. We are told that formulations like "love thy neighbor" are predicated on love of God, or in more sophisticated versions of the same sentiment, ancient Israel's theocracy is the enabling condition for its egalitarian sociality.[18] To put it differently, the laws that regulate the social order from On High displace the potential of violence from within the community to a violence vested fully in God. A less sanguine version of the theocracy-enables-democracy theory emerges: violence between men is deferred to violence between God and men; "Vengeance is mine, saith the Lord" (Deut 32:35, Rom 12:19).

The last formal feature of the Hittite treaties, the blessings and curses, promises of prosperity, and threats of horrific violence—to cut off, destroy, obliterate one and one's family for generations from the earth—were not appended to the treaty, but were part and parcel of its formal composition.[19] This seemingly innocuous formal detail has immense importance. Entering into the contract, agreeing to obey it in order to be protected, includes accepting the blessings and curses written into it—the covenant does not just list rules, it prescribes events, wonderful and dire events. Here are the blessings and curses from a Hittite treaty between Mursilis and Duppi-Tessub: "The words of the treaty and the oath that are inscribed on this tablet—should Duppi-Tessub not honor these words of the treaty and the oath, may these gods of the oath destroy Duppi-Tessub together with his person, his wife, his son, his grandson, his house, his land and together with everything he owns. But if Duppi-Tessub honors these words of the treaty and the oath that is inscribed on this tablet, may these gods of the oath protect him together with his person, his wife, his son, his grandson, his house, and his country."[20] In later treaties (that is, from the first millennium B.C.E.), the curses predominate, becoming more lurid and more elaborate. It is as though the liquidated damages clause overtook the terms of a legal contract.

In addition to the Ten Commandments, the Bible offers a covenant on a grander scale, the Book of Deuteronomy, which retells the Sinai story, framing it within a narrative told by Moses on the eve of the entry to the promised land. It includes the historical introduction that indebts the people to God for his past saving acts, and proceeds to the stipulations to be followed.

The Lord your God commands you this day to follow these decrees and laws; carefully observe them with all your heart and with all your soul. You have declared this day that the Lord is your God and that you will walk in his ways, that you will keep his decrees, commands, and laws, and that you will obey him. And the Lord has declared this day that you are his people, his treasured possession as he promised, and that you are to keep all his commands. (Deut 26:16–18)

If the people obey these laws, blessings of prosperity, fecundity, and security follow, and if they should fail, curses. But in the section in Deuteronomy devoted to blessings and curses, the curses threaten to overtake the blessings, with fourteen verses devoted to blessings and fifty-four to curses, and while the blessings are of generalized prosperity, the curses are graphic and specific. Among them:

The Lord will afflict you with madness, blindness and confusion of the mind. At midday you will grope about like a blind man in the dark. You will be unsuccessful in everything you do; day after day you will be oppressed and robbed, with no one to rescue you. You will be pledged to be married to a woman, but another will take her and ravish her. You will build a house, but you will not live in it. You will plant a vineyard, but you will not even begin to enjoy its fruit. Your ox will be slaughtered before your eyes, but you will eat none of it. . . . Your donkey will be forcibly taken from you and will not be returned. Your sheep will be given to your enemies, without anyone to help you. Your sons and daughters shall be given to another people, while you look on; you will strain your eyes looking for them all day but be powerless to do anything. A people whom you do not know shall eat up the fruit of your ground and of all your labors; you shall be continually abused and crushed, and driven mad by the sight that your eyes shall see. (Deut 28:28–34)

To these material and psychological tortures is added a generic curse for good measure: "You shall become an object of horror, a proverb, and a byword among all the peoples where the Lord will lead you" (Deut 28:37). Only after these horrific curses does the covenant formally conclude. "These are the words of the covenant which Yahweh commanded Moses to make with the Israelites" (Deut 29:1). The narrator might well have used Moses' apt phrasing instead: "this is the blood of the Covenant."

What is the magnitude of these terrible curses really about? What does breaking this "contract" threaten? What is at stake in the monotheistic covenant—with its demand of exclusive loyalty to the sovereign, its insistence on his complete possession of his subjects— seems to be the very identity of the community itself, whose fragile borders can be maintained only through the threat of such unimaginable (albeit luridly imagined) curses. The sermons of Puritan preachers vividly describing the hellfire awaiting the reprobate were intended to strike terror, indeed, and conformity into the hearts of the congregation. That is, joining the threat of conquest by physical violence is the threat of being colonized by spiritual violence, that is, the specter of a demanded conversion. In all cases, to cut a covenant with such power is to be utterly subjected to it.

The covenant at Sinai is given amid a huge display of such terrible power, with the full fanfare of fire, brimstone, thunder, and lightning: "At daybreak on the third day, there were peals of thunder on the mountain and lightning flashes, a dense cloud, and a loud trumpet blast, and inside the camp all the people trembled" (Ex 19:16). And the wide differential between the treaty "partners" is summarized succinctly in the description of their conversation: "Moses spoke and God answered him with peals of thunder" (Ex 19:19). "I am Oz, the great and powerful. Who are you?" "I am Dorothy, the meek and weak" begins the familiar parody of the Sinai theophany that exposes God as an inept hot-air balloonist from Kansas. Toto pulls back the curtain of the holy of holies, and we see the all too human wizard from Kansas generating his own *mysterium tremendum* at a microphone. But when the system of transcendent omnipotence is debunked, when God's ability to grant wishes, confer a heart, brain, and courage is exposed as not having a source in transcendence at all but in token symbols, it is only to be replaced by another system: nationalism. There is no place like home.

Again, politics are not hardwired into theology. Worship of one deity need not necessarily produce this violent notion of identity; but monotheism has been caught up with particularism, with that production of collective identity as peoples set apart, and it so happens that when the biblical text moves more explicitly toward polytheism, it also endorses a more attractive toleration, even appreciation of difference. "Let every people walk, each in the name of his god; but I will walk in the name of Yahweh my god forever" (Mic 4:5). Making Yahwism the defining feature of Israel's collective identity seems to have come rather late in the long process of biblical composition, late enough to fail to completely eradicate the traces of polytheism found throughout the Bible. According to several prominent biblical scholars, a minority movement beat back, in a fierce and long competition, the prevailing polytheism of ancient Israel. "The Bible records the biased view of the victorious party."[21] But its other views were not silenced, for it also records the bloodiness of exclusive monotheism. If, from one perspective, the myth of monotheism is a system in which identity depends upon rejection of the Other and subjection of the Self, from a different perspective, these same narratives offer a critique of just such a system by depicting the enormous cost of such identity. With its graphic depiction of violence against the Other and its sympathetic depictions of the outcast, the text invites us not to reject the rejected Other. In this way, the Bible may be critiquing, rather than endorsing, the very idea of covenant I have been elaborating. Who is to say?

When we try this idea on, when we reread all this bloodshed as a critique rather than endorsement of monotheism, other clues emerge. After all, rather than monotheism instituting some union of the people with each other and their God, the cutting covenant has cut the people off, from one another and from their God. And when we no longer tune our ears to the party line of the victorious monotheists, we can also become attentive to the brief, little-noted scene that forms the haunting sequel to the scene of the blood of the covenant.

> Then Moses took the blood and cast it toward the people. "This," he said, "is the blood of the Covenant that Yahweh has made with you, containing all these rules." Moses went up with Aaron, Nadab, and Abihu and seventy elders of Israel. They saw the God of Israel beneath whose feet there was, it seemed, a sapphire pavement pure as the heavens themselves. He laid no hand on these notables of the sons of Israel: they gazed on God, they ate, and they drank. (Ex 24:8–11)

The scene evokes another ancient ritual for covenanting besides the severing of animals and the not-so-implicit severing of the participants: the ceremonial meal. The Hebrew is so spare, just three verbs—"they gazed on God, they ate, and they drank"—three words that offer no hint of the violence of the covenant curses, but are prefaced instead by the explicit rejection of violence. Exodus tells us that just looking on God should be fatal—"no man can see the face of God and live"—but the story says "He laid no hand on these notables of the sons of Israel: they gazed on God."

Similarly, despite all its symbolic violence, the covenant with Abraham may be quietly subversive. An oath is made binding with the threat that its violator would be rent like the severed animals, but a flaming torch, symbolizing God, passes through the severed pieces. Yahweh swears an oath on himself to Abraham, thereby reversing the master/slave positions and, by extension, parodying the oath and its violence altogether.

In addition to these challenges to the very idea of constructing identity in violence, any single identity formation in the Bible is also challenged by another. Grounding identity in the myth of an originary covenant gives way to forming identity by kinship, which gives way to Israel's collective identity as a nation, which gives way to Israel defined with reference to the land, which gives way to Israel understood as not having territory at all but whose identity is forged by collective memory, with each system throwing into relief the provisional status of the other. Perpetually imagined otherwise, Israel is both one thing and so very easily another, and that dynamism is itself an antidote to the hardening of Israel's heart as a people against the Other. Instead of Israel being not-Egypt, it is a nation among the nations, Egypt, yes, but also Assyria, Babylonia, Philistia, Moab, Ammon. . . .

We are, then, the heirs of a long tradition in which monotheism is regarded as the great achievement of "Judeo-Christian" thought, holding out the promise of universalism and with it an endorsement of ethics and peace. But upon closer inspection, sometimes monotheism is entangled with particularism, with the assertion that this God and not any other gods must be worshipped, a particularism so virulent that it reduces all other gods to idols and so violent that it reduces all other worshippers to abominations. This tension in monotheism between the universal and the particular should come as no surprise. The One suggests both single and All, exclusive and complete. In contrast (and in theory), a genuine universalism would be tolerant of difference, even celebrate it, rather than reject and deny it. But the monotheism that strives for universalism instead of particularism runs another risk. The danger of a universal monotheism is asserting that its truth is *the* Truth, its system of knowledge *the* System of knowledge, its ethics *the* Ethics—not because, as in particularism, any other option must be rejected, but because there is simply no other option. The danger of universalism is that totalization will incorporate all difference. What needs to be imagined is neither a circle that includes everyone—a whole that submerges and subjects all individuality to itself, a totality that closes possibility— nor a part that reviles all other parts.

What is wrong with all of those constructs of the One and the Many is that they presuppose a kind of metaphysical scarcity. They imagine hoarding belief, hoarding allegiance, and even hoarding identity. Because there is a finite supply—of whatever—it must be either contained in the whole or protected as a part. Whether small or large, limited supplies suggest boundaries. But there have been other efforts to imagine monotheism. It has been seen as a principle that is not confining or totalizing, but opening and proliferating; as a principle that does not circumscribe limits, but endlessly transgresses all possible limits, a principle, as I prefer to think of it, not of scarcity, but of plenitude. Infinite potential and infinite arrival. This plenitude is frequently associated with creativity, with, indeed, the Creation, an idea (and it is an idea, after all) that seems close to infinite potential. Even when Creation involves circumscribing potential (binding chaos), as it so often does, still the aura of that plenitude hovers, as Plotinus imagined it saturating a newborn world, and as Wordsworth imagined it clinging to the newborn child.

Most systems of ethics are predicated upon the assumption of scarcity, the notion that there is not enough to go around. Such ethics are in general reactive, exploring how to behave in a world of limitations, obstacles, and dangers, and they typically endorse heroism: the ability to survive dangers, overcome obstacles, and exceed limitations. If a man's elder brother is all that stands between him and inheritance, how should he behave? If he has some property but wants his neighbor's, what should he do? In other words, ethics teaches us how to respond to various modes of scarcity. It is the combination of scarcity and its stepchild greed that gives rise to the ethical dilemmas of which life is made. But what would happen if we were to base our ethics on a utopian condition, one presupposing an ideal of plenitude instead of the world of scarcity we know too well? The law assumes that we cannot have what we want, and so we will covet, steal, or even kill our neighbor to get it. That is why there are prohibitions against those behaviors. But we could leave such prohibitions to the work of the law and let ethics do other work. With an assumption—albeit utopian—that there is enough for everyone, ethics would endorse, simply enough, generosity. Abundance dictates that goods are not lost or used up, they only circulate. A vision of plenty prompts ceaseless giving. Sometimes this vision of plenitude prevails in monotheism, describing a god who does not prohibit but gives. And when it does, it is accompanied by an alternative code, one that does not exclude, revile, violate, or even obsessively define the Other.

At key moments, the biblical narratives summon up moving visions of plenitude before they collapse into our more familiar world of scarcity. These are glimmers of a universalism that is neither fettered with particularism nor totalizing—even if those visions are difficult to sustain. Paradise is, of course, one such imagined plenitude: endless life, abundant food, gentle climate, hospitable nature. And amid all this abundance, there is peace. The lion lays down with the lamb. But then, a law intrudes into this paradisal plenitude that imposes the first limit, the first obstacle, and once the fruit of one tree is off-limits, the inspiring vision of plenitude utterly dissolves. God created a man of clay and introduced the law to test him: is he a worshipper or an idol? In the terms of a totalizing monotheistic order, there are no other options. Either he is loyal to the monotheistic order or he cannot be. With that prohibition a whole world of boundaries rushes in to the once-abundant garden: scarcity of food, pain in birth, sweat in labor, violence, and death, with that final limit completing all the others. From then on, comforts and resources are scarce and they must be competed for, like Cain and Abel's deadly competition for divine acceptance.

Again, in Exodus, before a whole host of laws are enumerated to curb the aggression induced by a world of scarcity, another moving version of paradisal plenitude is offered. It is, to be sure, a fallen paradise. This is the wilderness, not the garden, and the children of Israel are not as innocent as the children of Eden, having just escaped slavery in Egypt. When monotheism is not entangled with scarcity but with an ideal of plenitude, it offers a God who does not set limits but who provides. He rains bread from the heavens, manna in the wilderness, enough for everyone. And he asks the receivers to count on that sustenance, to rise to the challenge of living with the assumption, despite evidence to the contrary, that each will have his basic needs met. Furthermore, it is such glimmers of ideal plenitude—and not the prevailing scarcity—that are intended to school the ancient Israelites in ethics.

> "That," said Moses to them, "is the bread Yahweh gives you to eat. This is Yahweh's command: Everyone must gather enough of it for his needs." . . . When they measured in an omer of what they had gathered, the man who had gathered more had not too much, the man who had gathered less had

not too little. Each found he had gathered what he needed. (Ex 16:15–18)

Their failure to accept this divinely ordained distribution of wealth—each according to his needs—engenders greed. When they hoard their food, it rots and rots them.

> Moses said to them, "No one must keep any of it for tomorrow." But some would not listen and kept part of it for the following day, and it bred maggots and smelt foul; and Moses was angry with them. (Ex 16:19–20)

For forty years in the wilderness, the children of Israel eat manna, each according to his needs, and when they thirst, Moses strikes a rock to make water flow. But like the abundance of the garden of Eden, this vision of the perpetual satisfaction of need soon deflates into the familiar world of limitations, and with it collapses the ethics predicated upon an infinite rain of bread from the heavens. The pericope of the Decalogue follows the episode of manna, with all the Thou-Shalt-Nots that assume a world of scarcity—a world where lying, cheating, stealing, adultery, and killing are such tempting responses to scarcity that they must be legislated against. The vision of plenitude is difficult to sustain.

And so, for all of the violence associated with monotheism and its demand that devotion itself be limited, the Bible also continually offers glimpses of another vision of monotheism, one of plenitude. Deutero-Isaiah depicts a God without limits, beyond thought, who confers his boundless strength and fathomless understanding to humanity and who gives abundantly.

> For I will pour out water on the thirsty soil,
> streams on the dry ground.
> I will pour my spirit on your descendants,
> my blessing on your children.
> They shall grow like grass where there is plenty of water,
> like poplars by running streams.
>
> (Is 44:3–4)

This is not a god of original sinners prohibiting the bounty of trees but a god who gives trees bountifully.

> The poor and the needy ask for water, and there is none,
> their tongue is parched with thirst.
> I, Yahweh, will answer them,
> I, the God of Israel, will not abandon them.
> . . . .
> In the wilderness I will put cedar trees,
>   acacias, myrtles, olives.
> In the desert I will plant juniper,
> plane tree and cypress side by side.
>   (Is 41:17–19)

But even his vision of endless giving is caught up in that dark universalism that turns other gods into idols; he speaks of the makers of idols as "nothing" who fashion "nothing" or mere material bribes in contrast to the transcendent strength of the one God. It is as though the writer feared that his assertions of divine plenitude were not compelling enough and that he had to add, just for good measure, warnings to coerce singular devotion rather than simply invite assent to his ideal of boundless giving. The vision is difficult to sustain.

I wonder (much as Paul does in Romans) if the laws protecting men from violence against one another are not the corollary of conceiving identity in violence in the first place. It seems that defining ourselves against the Other sets in motion a cycle of violence that no legislation can hold. Perhaps when we have grown weary of asserting all of our differences, we will be willing to think more of likenesses, analogies, even identifications—not to forge totality, but to endlessly compose and recompose temporary and multiple identifications. I long to imagine, with the philosopher, "not only something that opposes the universal, but also some element that can be extended close to another, so as to obtain a connection. Such emissions . . . constitute a transcendental field without subject. The multiple become a substantive—multiplicity—and philosophy is a theory of multiplicities that refers to no subject or preliminary unity."[22] Not one, but many gods. This is not to endorse some kind of Nietzschean neopaganism; the idea is not to replace ethics with the rule of the strong. But some suspicion of the ancient biblical link between ethics and the myth of monotheism seems in order, along with some doubt about the wisdom of tying ethics to an understanding of identity that is agonistic by nature.

Finally, the Bible offers its own critique of the Wizard of Oz. For all of the appropriations of the discourse of monotheism by the rhetoric of nationalism, the Bible itself describes the origins of the nations as a punishment, the punishment for challenging the sovereign power of the heavenly deity, the punishment for building an idol heavenward. The story of Babèl describes all people joining together in a common project. The repetition of the Hebrew "let us" emphasizes the collective nature of their cultural enterprise.

> Now the whole earth had one language and few words. And as men migrated east, they found a plain in the land of Shinar and settled there. And they said to one another, come let us make bricks and burn them thoroughly, and then they said, come, let us build ourselves a city, and a tower with its top in the heavens, lest we be scattered upon the face of the earth. (Gen 11:1–4)

The deity smashes their tower, disperses them, and condemns them to speaking in different tongues so that they cannot communicate with each other and join together again in a project to overthrow him. The next time they make bricks, it will not be to their own glory, but in bondage to a human overlord. In this remarkable myth, the division of people into peoples is not in their interests, but in the interest of maintaining the power of a tyrannical, threatened deity jealously guarding his domain. How did the victorious monotheistic party miss that one, we might well ask? Or better, when can we stop perceiving it as victorious, and instead heed the sentiment of the prophet, "Let every people walk, each in the name of his god."

Owning Identity

LAND

Do not covet your neighbor's field.—Exodus 20:17

This land is your land; this land is my land
From California to the New York island
From the redwood forest to the Gulf Stream waters
This land was made for you and me.
—Woody Guthrie

POSSESSING LAND

Monotheism does not simply define a people as a covenanted community, however complex that definition turns out to be. It is in delineating a people another way, as those who belong to a land, that monotheism has left its deepest, most lasting, and undoubtedly its most troubling political legacy. In Bosnia, several peoples who conceive of themselves as having distinct identities lay claim to the same piece of land. Each believes that its right to that land is historically demonstrable and, in any case, more ancient than historical memory. Moreover, that claim is divinely sanctioned. God seems to have willed the same territory to be the unique inheritance of each of these peoples. In Israel, several peoples who conceive of themselves as distinct entities lay claim to the same piece of land. Each believes its right to that land is historical, ancient, and divine. Again, somehow God has willed the same territory to be the inheritance of each people. So achingly familiar, so ubiquitous, is the notion of possessing land that it is difficult to call attention to how odd it is, difficult to imagine, for instance, explaining to a civilization on another planet who live on it without any urge to carve its surface into pieces and label and assign ownership to them, why we earth creatures obsessively delineate territory, build walls, plant flags, and marshal our best technological resources to do so. Science fiction fails that imaginative effort, for it only projects the idea of possessing land onto whole galaxies, where futuristic territorial disputes are waged ceaselessly. And historical examples are rife. Whether the territory in question is big or small, the land is fertile or barren, or the impulse to possess it is long- or short-lived, horrific acts of human violence have been committed and continue to be committed in the service of what is after all an idea: the notion that a "group" (an imagined community) must "possess" (how can land be owned?) a "piece" (note how the earth is imagined in pieces) of land. The history of warfare since antiquity tells a complex story of a phenomenon that is not so very complex—territorial disputes—and in our century alone, two generations have been ravaged by world wars that were fought largely to reconfigure maps. As various borders contract and expand in these struggles, all that is consistent is that land is deemed more precious than life itself.

Is this border-obsession some extension of the borders of our personal identity? Is our skin not adequate border enough? Or does calling to mind another natural image, that of fields planted and fenced in, help to explain this madness? That is, do peoples fight er land rights because they are fighting over rights to the produce of the soil? How then would we explain the fact that the most devastating territorial wars have occurred in a global economy? Perhaps it is less the reality than the myth of scarcity that propels these disputes, the belief that resources are scarce, that there is not enough land, and so what land there is must be ruthlessly acquired, perpetually defended, and at all costs, fiercely possessed. But people do not possess land. Such a notion of land possesses them, for the land becomes soaked in the blood of the peoples who claim it.

We cannot really own anything, despite (or because, since desire is propelled by lack) of the overwhelming desire to do so. Objects of possession can be taken away by others. They can defy being owned on their own accord—they can break, wither, and die—so that despite persistent efforts to appropriate land, dwellings, women, and portable property, somehow all of them stubbornly resist being owned. Land is especially frustrating for those who would possess it because their territorial claims turn out to be, with more or less perspective, only temporary squatter's rights. And if the desire to own territory has its source in a desire to own the produce of the soil, the land can still fail to cooperate. It can seem willfully "barren" (a term also applied to women who are similarly possessed for their produce). And so, with land resisting both permanent conquest and a guaranteed yield of its fruits, it flaunts the lie of ownership in the faces of those who claim it.

With more and less subtlety, biblical narratives fully elaborate the notion that a defining feature of a people is its divinely ordained right to land. Despite the haunting protests that frequent the biblical narratives against Israel ever becoming a nation "like the nations," and despite the frequent celebrations of nomadism that punctuate the narratives, ancient Israel has bequeathed to later generations in far-flung climes the authoritative grand myth that will be used and misused by nations, ethnic groups, and religious communities for their own purposes. In this apparently compelling myth of identity, the divine promise of land to a people creates them as a people.

Despite this biblical obsession, the ancient Israelites did not invent the idea of defining a people by land. Their fortunes and misfortunes depended upon the movements of the much larger empires who filled the theater of the ancient Near East—Akkadian, Amorite, Assyrian, Egyptian, Persian, and Roman—empires that have left not just literary but monumental testimony to their wars of expansion. Those stones bear witness to how very strong the commitment to binding identity to land was throughout the ancient world—Assyrian reliefs carved with scenes of battle, Egyptian tombs recording victories on pyramid walls, Persian stelae devoted to the conquests of Cyrus, Roman arches sculpted with reliefs of the looting of Jerusalem—but it was through the accidents of religious history that the perishable book of a small persecuted people came to speak far more authoritatively about land to future generations. Its message has not perished. That book records the wish of a people in exile to be landed, of a homeless people to have a home, and it depicts their aspiration as synonymous with the very will of God. Monotheism has left a troubling legacy of the belief in land entitlement, one that continues to ghost territorial disputes.

The story of Israel proper begins with Genesis 12. After the primeval myths of Creation, Fall, Flood, and Babel—a prehistory that generally charts disobedience and disaster—the people of Israel are formed as a new start, to serve as an example to the peoples of the earth. But their existence is subject to a contract: their God demands loyalty from them and in return promises them numerous descendants, a mighty nation, and land. The ensuing story is devoted to the gradual acquisition of the promised land, the building of the nation in wars of conquest and defense, setbacks in that progress, and the destruction of the nation with the loss of the once-promised land. Throughout, these fortunes and misfortunes are not attributed to the strength or weakness of surrounding nations, but to Israel's obedience or disobedience to its God. Faith in the deity is the guarantee of a land grant.

> Yahweh said to Abram, "Leave your country, your family and your father's house, for the land I will show you. I will make you a great nation; I will bless you and make your name so great that it will be used as a blessing." (Gen 12:1–2)

And when Abram arrives in the land of Canaan, Yahweh tells him,

> Look all round from where you are toward the north and the
> south, toward the east and the west. All the land within sight
> I will give to you and your descendants for ever. I will make
> your descendants like the dust on the ground: when men suc-
> ceed in counting the specks of dust on the ground, then they
> will be able to count your descendants. Come, travel the
> length and breadth of the land, for I mean to give it to you.
> (Gen 13:14–17)

If in this passage the people and the soil are related by a simile—the
people are like the dust of the soil—elsewhere, that likeness deepens
into sameness. Man is actually made from the soil: "Yahweh fash-
ioned man of dust from the soil. Then he breathed into his nostrils
the breath of life, and man became a living being" (Gen 2:7). Again,
the biblical term for human, *'ādām,* is derived from the Hebrew term
for soil, *'ădāmâ.* To be human is to be made of land.

Adam is born into a garden irrigated by rivers and told to till and
tend it, and he is exiled from that garden when he is disobedient to
his God. The Israelites are promised a larger garden, the land of
Canaan watered by the mighty Jordan, and they are exiled from it
when they are disobedient to their God. Whatever other ideas about
collective identity are proliferated in the Bible—a kinship community, a community united by collective memory, a monarchy, a covenanted community—a people are "a people" by virtue of the promise made to them that they will possess a land, and promise is the
key word here, for that possession is elusive. The Israelites will lose
Israel. From promising beginning to bitter end, the narrative is preoccupied with Israel's identity as landed. Even as lack, land is defining.

As if anticipating the perils of the idea of attaching land to identity, the biblical writers have also included a critique of it. Their
alternative vision embraces the values of nomadism, is suspicious of
settled agriculture, and even idealizes the wilderness. A closer look
at that intimate etymological relation between man, *'ādām,* and land,
'ădāmâ, reveals that it is between human beings and all land. Man-

43

kind does not derive its etymology from the other biblical term for land, *'eres,* the term that signifies a political and national territory. This use of *'ădāmâ* marks a departure from the dominant idea that a people are specified by a particular land, for it suggests that if man is a creature of land, he is an "earth-creature" who is not tied to one piece of it.[1] Furthermore, it is likely that the Israelites compose this myth only after they are in exile. Only landless do they imagine themselves as a people who have inherited a land. And so, built into the very fabric of the logic that imagines Israel as a landed entity is also an Israel that is a landless entity. Lodged deeply in this nomadic ideal may be the admission that the very goal being upheld—possession, of land, of anything—is an impossible fiction, if by it we mean having exclusive rights to it.[2]

There is a dangerous consequence of attaching identity to territory: when a people imagines itself as the people of a given land, the obvious threat to its identity is loss of that land. Precisely that fear drives the plot of biblical narrative. While it depicts the people coming into possession (or conquering) the land, that triumph is undermined, surrounded as it is by accounts of losing land. In the first "loss," the Exodus, the people *choose* to leave a land. Enslaved and ill-treated in Egypt, their leave-taking is depicted as a victorious expression of freedom. In the next loss, the exile, the people are forced to leave the land, painfully exiled by the Babylonians. Joining the theology that God owns the land to this plot produces embarrassing complications. How can the people of Israel suffer exile from the land when their God has promised it to them and the land belongs to him to dispense as he chooses? In this most peculiar narrative, God saves the Israelites in the Exodus, enables the conquest of the land he promised, but then allows—even instigates—the defeat of the exile. Whether their God leads the Israelites out of Egypt or out of the promised land, his omnipotence is kept intact, and protecting that omnipotence is clearly paramount for the biblical writers. What, then, is the payoff for humanity to have an investment in transcendence? Or to put it another way, why bother subscribing to a myth of omnipotence when it still leaves one vulnerable to defeat?

When Israel was a child I loved him,
and I called my son out of Egypt.

In a touching image of paternal nurturing, the deity is imagined as bending down to lift his child, only to turn against him later, sending him to his Egyptian and Assyrian enemies; feeding an infant gives way to a devouring sword.

> I was like someone who lifts an infant close against his cheek;
> stooping down to him I gave him his food.
> They will have to go back to Egypt,
> Assyria must be their king,
> because they have refused to return to me.
> The sword will rage through their towns,
> wiping out their children,
> glutting itself inside their fortresses.
> (Hos 11:1–6)

The terms of the contract, complete obedience, have been violated.

> Let us have no rejoicing, Israel,
> no exulting like the other peoples;
> for you have deserted God to play the whore,
> you have enjoyed the prostitute's pay
> on every threshing floor.
> (Hos 9:1)

And so a God who once promised them a land flowing with milk and honey now threatens famine.

> Neither floor nor vat will nourish them,
> the new wine will disappoint them.
> They will no longer live in the land of Yahweh;
> Ephraim will have to go back to Egypt,
> and in Assyria they will eat food that is unclean.
> (Hos 9:2–3)

This is a strange myth indeed, of a god who offers a people liberation and grants them victory over their enemies only to turn into their deadliest enemy.

> Yahweh the God of Israel says this, "Look, I will bring disaster as to make the ears of all who hear of it tingle. . . . I will cast away the remnant of my inheritance, delivering them into the power of their enemies, and making them serve as prey and booty to all their enemies because they have done what is displeasing to me and have provoked my anger from the day their ancestors came out of Egypt until now." (2 Kings 21:12–15)

Having invested everything about a land in the will of the deity, the narratives concede that the will of the deity can take it all away. And they vividly depict him taking it away. He makes the prosperity of the land wither, he revokes Israel's possession of the land, and he threatens to tear Israel to pieces like a wild animal.

> Yet I am Yahweh your God since the days in the land of Egypt;
> you know no God but me,
> there is no other savior.
> I knew you in the wilderness;
> in the land of drought I knew them, and they were satisfied;
> once satisfied, their hearts grew proud,
> and so they came to forget me.
> Very well, I will be a lion to them,
> a leopard lurking by the way;
> like a bear robbed of her cubs I will pounce on them
> and tear the flesh round their hearts;
> the dogs shall eat their flesh,
> the wild beasts tear them to pieces.
> (Hos 13:4–8)

What appeared at first like a rather neat exchange of authorizations—ancient Israel projects its identity onto a deity who in turn sanctions Israel to take the land—becomes instead the source of Israel's vulnerability when radical monotheism unleashes its fury against pluralism. In the myth of monotheism, pluralism is betrayal, punishable with every kind of exile: loss of home, loss of the land, even alienation from the earth itself. The Lord giveth and the Lord taketh away; blessed be the name of the Lord.

Granted that collective identity and land, whether possessed or desired, are deeply implicated with one another, how does *transcendence* bear upon the question of land, that is, upon the *immanence* of the earth? In short, what does God have to do with it? God owns the land. It is only leased, with conditions he stipulates, not bequeathed, to the Israelites. Palestine was a tiny strip of land battled over in various times by Syrians, Assyrians, Philistians, Egyptians, Babylonians, Persians, and Romans, to name only the more familiar contestants, and yet it was a notably poor, drought-plagued land, leaving its inhabitants to struggle not only against invaders from without but against famine from within. In this unstable atmosphere, it is little wonder that the ancient Israelites came to conceive of the ownership of land as transcendent. Even the fertility of the land is subject to the will of God.[3] Egypt is watered by the fluctuations of the Nile, but Israel's rain falls at the behest of Yahweh.

> For the land that you are to enter and make your own is not like the land of Egypt from which you came, where you sowed your seed and watered it by tread like a vegetable garden. No, the land into which you are to cross to make it your own is a land of hills and valleys watered by the rain from heaven. Yahweh your God takes care of this land, the eyes of Yahweh your God are on it always, from the year's beginning to its end. And it is most sure that if you faithfully obey the commandments I enjoin on you today, loving Yahweh your God and serving him with all your heart and all your soul, I will give your land rain in season, autumn rain and spring, so that you may harvest your corn, your wine, your oil; I shall provide grass in the fields for your cattle, and you will eat and have all you want. (Deut 11:10–15)

Everything about the land—who lives on it, who tills it, whether it is watered, whether it yields its fruits—is divinely ordained.

Such transcendence would seem designed to protect Israel's land from either the might of marauders or the blight of drought (unless, that is, the Almighty willed those disasters). This omnipotence doubtless offered some yearned-for stability amid all the political and economic chaos in the ancient Near East, guaranteeing that the forces of history and of nature were not arbitrary. According to the biblical myth, whatever else we mortals do not understand about the powers of life, death, prosperity, famine, and war, we do understand what an eternal, immutable, omnipotent God requires of us: obedience.[4] Transcendence offers epistemological certainty. Yet in Israel's theology, that formidable condition of obedience is always attached to the comforting stability held out by transcendence.

> Take care your heart is not seduced, that you do not go astray, serving other gods and worshipping them, or the anger of Yahweh will blaze out against you, he will shut up the heavens and there will be no rain, the land will not yield its produce and you will quickly die in the prosperous land that Yahweh is giving you. (Deut 11:16–17)

In the end, this requirement of absolute allegiance to the One exposes the instability of the whole design: God and the people are meant to "belong to" or to own one another in some sense. Ownership is vested in divine possession of the people: "I will be your God if you will be my people." But when that ownership proves impossible (as it must), transcendence no longer safeguards Israel's identity nor its land.

> If you violate the covenant which Yahweh your God has demanded of you, if you go and serve other gods and bow down before them, then Yahweh's anger will be roused against you and you will quickly vanish from the good land that he has given you. (Josh 23:16)

The difficulty of holding onto the land, even land bequeathed in perpetuity by Permanence itself, is not solved by recourse to transcendence after all. Instead, that inevitable precariousness is woven into a biblical theology in which the land is in serious jeopardy if Israel does not obey her god. Fidelity to the one God persistently frames the discourse of land.

> If you are willing to obey,
> you shall eat the good things of the earth.
> but if you persist in rebellion,
> the sword will eat you instead.
>
> (Is 1:19–20)

The devouring sword of God will turn on Israel when the boundaries of her loyalty, and consequently of her identity, prove to be as fragile as those of her land.

What may seem like colorful prophetic metaphors (Israel as an exiled whore) or arcane Levitical law (obedience as the condition of having the land) becomes the stuff of narrative, arguably, our most potent cultural narrative, in the story of the Fall of humankind. It was that story that began this inquiry, and that story has now led us, not to sin, but to *land*. While later Christian exegesis lays heavy stress on the sexuality of the original sin, in the Hebrew narrative about the first parents, the emphasis is on land, from the opening pun on man's name—formed as we saw, from the land *('ădāmâ)*—to the conclusion of the curse: "from dust were you taken and to dust will you return." The fall of Adam and Eve is a story of becoming alienated from a paradisal land, of its fecundity made barren.

> Accursed be the soil because of you.
> With suffering shall you get your food from it
> every day of your life.
> It shall yield you brambles and thistles,
> and you shall eat wild plants.
> With sweat on your brow
> shall you eat your bread.
>
> (Gen 3:17–19)

Man is forcibly removed from the garden: "so Yahweh expelled him from the garden of Eden, to till the soil from which he had been taken" (Gen 3:23). He is condemned to exile for disobeying a rule, and as the myth tells it, being exiled from the land, from the community, and from God are virtually the same exile.

In the story of the fall of Adam and Eve, a particular people are not banished from a particular land; rather, humankind itself is condemned to a general exile from a perfect land. From Genesis on, the entire human condition is portrayed as one of exile from a mythical paradisal "home." The idea of exile presupposes that one is at home somewhere, with exile being the forced exclusion from that home. To be in exile is not to choose a place to reside but to be deprived of one's chosen place. Under the law of scarcity, that deprivation is conceived of as a punishment. But what is this at-homeness? Residing in a land temporarily or permanently? Owning the land? What is the difference between a sojourner and a stranger? From this universal perspective, exile is the hinterland devised for those who do not embrace monotheism, the no-man's land assigned to those whose identity is not single or singular in its devotion. Exile is the wilderness imagined by those who insist upon attaching a single circumscribed identity to a homeland. Yet it is the condition everyone inhabits. In addition to this universal curse, Adam's exile also foreshadows the particular exile of a particular people, the Israelites. The paradisal garden is an idealized, and lost, land of Israel. In this sense, "exile" is the condition of anyone who does not conform to a strict definition of what Israel is.

A system of thought that assumes that land is a desirable possession offers two alternatives: Home (Israel, Obedience) or Exile (outside Israel, Disobedience), and anyone who does not obey the law is condemned to Exile. "Yahweh is God. . . . Keep his laws and commandments as I give them to you today, so that you and your children may prosper and live long in the land that Yahweh your God gives you for ever" (Deut 4:39–40). But a third approach would imagine a very different relation to land. The assumption that land is never to be possessed at all, that land is an imagined idea that could be shed, would lead to an idea of sojourning, that is, of freely choosing rather than being condemned to wander over the earth. With no need to inhabit a specific territory, both home and homelessness would wither away as categories and "exile" would be refigured as nomadism.[5] One scholar has already explored how biblical narratives are driven by the conflict between the shepherd and the farmer, between the nomadic ideal and agriculturalism, and another has pointed out that to an exiled people, pastoral nomadism would be a logical ideal, for it imagines land that cannot be taken away.[6] Jerusalem will be captured by the Amorites, its population deported. In a remarkable passage, the pastoral alternative is brought into relief in the context of the failure of the land-holding paradigm.

> The word addressed to Jeremiah by Yahweh in the days of Jehoiakim son of Josiah, king of Judah: "Go to the clan of the Rechabites and speak to them; bring them into one of the apartments of the Temple of Yahweh and offer them wine to drink". . . . They replied, "We do not drink wine, because our ancestor Jonadab son of Rechab gave us this order: 'You must never drink wine, neither you nor your sons; nor must you build houses, sow seed, plant vineyards, or own property; but you must live in tents all your lives, so that you may live long on the soil to which you are alien.'" (Jer 35:1–7)[7]

In contrast to a system of thought in which people can become exiled, then, is another way of thinking that imagines them as perpetual sojourners.

> The land must not be sold permanently, because the land is mine and you are but aliens and my tenants. Throughout the country that you hold as a possession, you must provide for the redemption of the land. (Lev 25:23–24)

The ancient Israelites never lay claim to the land as natives; on the contrary, their story tells of a people who originate elsewhere. The father of Israel must leave his homeland and embark on a long journey in order to found the nation of Israel.

> Yahweh said to Abram, "Leave your country, your family and your father's house, for the land I will show you." . . . So Abram went as Yahweh told him. . . . Abram passed through the land as far as Shechem's holy place, the oak of Moreh. At the time the Canaanites were in the land. Yahweh appeared to Abram and said, "It is to your descendants that I will give this land." (Gen 12:1–7)

The prophets imagine the wilderness, not as a place of exile, but as an idealized place of innocence before the corruptions of the territorial state and a place to return to heal from those corruptions (Jer 31:2, Hos 2:14, Amos 5:25, Jer 2:2–3). The system of thought that conceives of the Israelites as forever sojourners and strangers in the land is incompatible with the one in which the people become exiles outside Israel. They were always sojourners, never exiles.

But in the end, biblical nomadism is contaminated by the dream of possessing land. The nomadic ideal fails as a genuine alternative to the corruption of the territorial state because one is always implicated in the other. The exile becomes the conqueror; the fugitive becomes the captor.[8] With the wilderness narrative literally wedged between narratives of exodus and conquest, narratives that presuppose the desirability of having territory, the nomadic ideal is encompassed by and therefore compromised by the land-holding ideal. Consequently, a forty-year period of wandering is framed, not as nomadism, but as purging, a punishment and a cleansing, in preparation for land acquisition. Wandering in the wilderness is filled with the expectation that the wanderers will hold land again and by the disappointment that they have lost land. What could be seen as a choice of pastoral nomadism is repeatedly imagined as a punishment. The ideal of a "home" assumes a central place within the whole nexus of thinking about monotheism, singular allegiance, and scarcity. Cain is cast out, Esau is exiled, and Moses is not allowed to enter the promised land. But perhaps instead of seeing Moses as a scapegoat for the sin of the people, we could re-imagine him as the great leader of the Israelites because he was the figure of their *desire* —one who looked but did not take possession of land—rather than of their *punishment* (as the narrative more overtly suggests).

> "My Lord, may I not go across and see this prosperous land beyond the Jordan?" . . . "Enough!" he said, "speak to me no more of this. Climb to the top of Pisgah; let your eyes turn toward the west, the north, the south, the east. Look well, for across the Jordan you shall not go." (Deut 3:25–27)

The belief that God owns all the land should work against this elaborate way of thinking about possession.[9] Owned by a transcendent, inviolable principle, the land is virtually "off the market" for human possession. That understanding of land as a trust or inheritance instead of a tradable commodity is dramatized vividly in the story of Naboth's vineyard.[10]

> Naboth of Jezreel had a vineyard close by the palace of Ahab king of Samaria, and Ahab said to Naboth, "Give me your vineyard to be my vegetable garden, since it adjoins my house; I will give you a better vineyard for it, or if you prefer, I will give you its worth in money." But Naboth answered Ahab, "Yahweh forbid that I should give you the inheritance of my ancestors!" (1 Kings 21:1–3)

When Ahab's queen, Jezebel, engineers the murder of Naboth to obtain the land, the crime is punished: "Thus says the Lord: 'Have you killed and also taken possession? . . . In the place where dogs licked up the blood of Naboth, dogs will lick up your blood'" (1 Kings 21:19). For the eminent biblical scholar Walter Brueggemann, "the god of Israel is a God who gives land, and Israel is a people that holds land in alternative ways. The core tradition is intended to promote an alternative to the imperial system of land known both in the Egyptian empire and in the Canaanite city states."[11] Signs of this alternative tradition are that boundary marks must be obeyed, "Remove not the ancient landmark that your fathers have set" (Prov 22:28), and that land must not be seized, "Do not remove an ancient landmark; do not enter the fields of the fatherless; for their Redeemer is strong; he will plead their cause against you" (Prov 23:10–11).[12] Such passages "articulate a theory of land division that assumes inheritance and the right to hold land, as in the case of an orphan without social power, simply because one is entitled as a member of the community."[13] In theory, the theology of the land as "inherited" protects its heirs against those who would seize it by force.[14] But in practice, Israel's attractive refusal to think of land as a tradable commodity is attenuated by its very understanding of community. Israel's inalienable inheritance secures its land *for* Israel and *from* outsiders. If the boundary markers are protected within the community of Israel, the boundaries designed to protect other peoples are not even recognized as such.

Instead of a belief in transcendence having the effect of removing land from the concerns of owning and losing, possessing land and being exiled from it, in the end, nowhere are those concerns more apparent than in monotheism. In biblical theology, the divine ownership of the land does not so much remove the land from the human sphere of contestation over property rights as it transfers land to another sphere, obedience to the divine order. As we have seen, the deity will bequeath the land as a gift to the people *if* they are faithful to him, and he will revoke it *if* they are not. A self-enclosed circular system is thereby instituted: to be "a people" is to be God's people is to inherit his land, and if they are not the people of God, they will not be a people, and they will lose the land. Any collective identity depends upon both: if they are not the people of the land or the people of God, they are not a people. In this formulation, identity is wholly dependent upon the notion of possessing the land— whether in promise, in realization, or in memory.

Even so, the same theology that stresses that identity is land-bound puts its emphasis on the *promise* of having land and the yearning for a return to land rather than on the middle term, actually possessing the land. That middle term is decidedly less appealing than the happier days of desire. Once it is possessed, the land does not yield what it should, its borders are perpetually threatened, but most important, the very possession of the land that should guarantee the identity of the people seems to prompt them to violate the terms of its possession: they are no longer faithful to their God. Possession of the land and idolatry go hand in hand. An opposition widens between prosperity and morality, with the nation depicted as luxuriating in moral corruption. The people love their God so long as they want something from him. When they get it, they invariably forget him. Moses' warning in Deuteronomy becomes a description:

Take care you do not forget Yahweh your God, neglecting his commandments and customs and laws which I lay on you to-day. When you have eaten and had all you want, when you have built fine houses to live in, when you have seen your flocks and herds increase, your silver and gold abound, and all your possessions grow great, do not become proud of heart. (Deut 8:11–14)

On balance, Israel's identity is tied less to possessing the land than to desiring to possess the land. They are not the "people of the land," but the "people of (frustrated) desire for land."

EXODUS AND CONQUEST

Possession implies domination. Defining identity in terms of territory produces two myths that are the two consequences of possessing (or dreaming of possessing) land: either a people take land from another people (conquest) or the land is taken from them (exile). Narratives of conquest and exile are the logical elaborations of a doctrine of land possession. But conquest and exile are not simply opposites. Exile also serves as a kind of retrospective justification for conquest. The logic runs something like this: because we were (or will be) made homeless, we can seize another's home; because we were (or will be) conquered, we can conquer. Domination is the price exacted for having been dominated. In such retributive thinking, reseizing the identical piece of land from the actual conquerors is unlikely—the peoples in question who inflict and therefore "deserve" pain are rarely the same—but historical memory is both so long and so dim that it is quite willing to confuse the identity of oppressors in order to allow the process of compensation (or revenge) to proceed. A Lebanese guerrilla fighter said in a recent interview that the Israelites had been his enemy for two thousand years, and a Serbian funeral oration praised the deceased for dying for Serbia just as his ancestors had died in the battle of Kosovo Polje against the Turks in the fourteenth century. Never mind the details of what must be repaired and who must make the reparation against whom. Substitution is the soul of revenge.

According to this hazy retributive logic, then, one way to read the haunting biblical myth of the Exodus, wherein ancient Israel is rescued from slavery in Egypt by her God, is to read it cynically, as a massive justification of ancient Israel's conquests. In the exodus narrative, Israel is held in captivity in a foreign land, released from that oppression through divine intervention, and then given a homeland by divine right, the land of Canaan, which Israel proceeds to seize by force, defeating her enemies (not Egyptians here, but Canaanites). In this sequence of events, the Exodus serves as the best of all moral justifications for the Conquest. With the captivity in Egypt and the Exodus from it positioned first, Israel is a victim before she is an aggressor. The Hebrews are a powerless group of people preyed upon by an evil mighty empire, and their deity offers them a homeland as a refuge from the terrors of history. The divine sanction of the conquest—these are Yahweh's swords and bows, not Israel's— makes it all the more justifiable.

> When you crossed the Jordan and came to Jericho, those who held Jericho fought against you, as did the Amorites and Perizzites, the Canaanites, Hittites, Girgashites, Hivites and Jebusites, but I put them all into your power. I sent out hornets in front of you, which drove the two Amorite kings before you; this was not the work of your sword or your bow. I gave you a land where you never toiled, you live in towns you never built; you eat now from vineyards and olive groves you never planted. (Josh 24:11–13)

If a vague sense that Israel is somehow undeserving of this land hovers over this passage—she lives in towns she did not build and eats from vineyards she did not plant, she vanquishes a people without her own sword or bow—so too does the sense that she is not guilty of the blood of the sword and the bow or of usurping the land. With the design and execution of her history all vested in a divine principle, Israel is not culpable.

The rhetoric of victimization—the land as a refuge, as a haven from aggressors—infuses much of the language of nationalism, a rhetoric that speaks more often of one's "homeland" in the sense of a safe place rather than a native land. It is a land that a people have fled to, not one of their birth. Serbians tirelessly invoke abuses sustained six hundred years ago to justify their seizure of land, Irish nationalists detail wounds inflicted by the British, Greeks remember every injury by the Turks. And this invocation of a persecuted past to legitimate present policy is not only a rhetorical tool used by small nations struggling for national autonomy; it is also the way in which mighty empires have whitewashed their consciences. As they invaded Ireland, the British rehearsed their freedom from French oppressors with Shakespearean eloquence; as they seized the natives' land, the American colonists erected a founding myth of liberation from the persecuting British; during its terrifying expansions, Nazi Germany rehearsed its injuries in World War I. And so it goes: conquest after conquest is justified by a myth of exodus.

And what about the biblical narrative? Should we hold it culpable for emblazoning this desire for land acquisition on its readers, inscribing deep into our culture the primordial myth of an exodus that justifies conquest? From one perspective—that of the history of the text—the conquest narrative is only a wild fantasy written by a powerless dispossessed people who dream of wondrous victories over their enemies, of living in a land where milk and honey flow, and of entering that land with the blessing and support of an Almighty Deity. But from another perspective—that of the text's political afterlife—there is another story that is less appealing and considerably less innocent, telling of creating a people through the massive displacement and destruction of other peoples, of laying claim to a land that had belonged to others, and of conducting this bloody conquest under the banner of divine will.

What determines the greater or lesser sympathy with which we approach these formulations, other than the greater or lesser attractiveness of the conquered and conquering subjects? Surely, there is all the difference between reading the conquest as an impossible fantasy of a disempowered people and reading it as an act of empowerment by an imperial people. And surely, a powerless people creating a myth of their liberation and subsequent conquest differs markedly from a powerful people justifying their real conquest with recourse to such a myth. But how? Are the dynamics of power always so clear-cut that the oppressed and oppressors are readily distinguishable? And if so, how is it possible that they both have had recourse to the same myth? That insight leads to the troubling implication that the narrative itself might assist one to become the other, that a strong cultural myth that links the Exodus to the conquest could help to turn victims into victimizers.

The relation between a given cultural inheritance and politics is not transparent.[15] Oppressed peoples write utopian myths of conquest. Peoples in exile write fantastic tales of land acquisition. But conquerors also pen celebrations of their conquests, and empires write of subject peoples as indeed subjected. While historical events give rise to narratives in complex ways, the historical afterlife of a given narrative is equally convoluted: Cromwell invoked the Exodus to describe the overthrowing of monarchy during the British Civil War, while Dryden invoked it to rally behind his monarch during the Restoration.[16] The widely divergent uses of the conquest myth in the official rhetoric of the United States demonstrates similar paradoxes. At the country's founding, the Exodus celebrated liberation during the American revolt against the British oppressors, while the conquest was invoked during the invaders' seizure of Native American land. During the Civil War, Lincoln's forceful invocations of the Exodus reemerged to free the slaves even as the South invoked the conquest in order to justify the perpetuation of slavery. The exodus/conquest story leaves itself wide open to both liberating and oppressive uses because it has yoked two opposing myths together, and the sheer durability of the narrative is such that they have become impossible to disentangle, lending our myths of domination the rhetoric of liberation and giving our myths of liberation the dark side of a fantasy of domination. Clearly, the consequences of overlapping and confusing the exodus and conquest paradigms are deeply troubling. As one Native American has phrased it, "As long as people believe in the Yahweh of deliverance, the world will not be safe from Yahweh the conqueror."[17]

Biblical narratives themselves offer two different explanations for taking the land of Canaan. Yahweh instructs Abraham to leave his home in Ur in order to go to "a land that I will show you." So, on the one hand, the conquest motif has its origins in a promise made to Abraham, a promise that is reiterated to his heirs, Isaac and Jacob, who continue the sojourn toward the land.

> To your descendants I give this land, from the river of Egypt to the Great River, the river Euphrates, the Kenites, the Kenizzites, the Kadmonites, the Hittites, the Perizzites, the Rephaim, the Amorites, the Canaanites, the Girgashites, and the Jebusites. (Gen 15:18–21)

A different version of the origin of the quest for land appears in the Book of Exodus where the promise to Moses is made out of the burning bush as a response to the suffering of the Hebrews in Egypt.

> I have seen the miserable state of my people in Egypt. I have heard their appeal to be free of their slave drivers. Yes, I am well aware of their sufferings. I mean to deliver them out of the hands of the Egyptians and bring them up out of that land to a land rich and broad, a land where milk and honey flow, the home of the Canaanites, the Hittites, the Amorites, the Perizzites, the Hivites, and the Jebusites. And now the cry of the sons of Israel has come to me, and I have witnessed the way in which the Egyptians oppress them, so come, I send you to Pharaoh to bring the sons of Israel, my people, out of Egypt. (Ex 3:7–10)

And then there is an extraordinarily clumsy passage that calls attention to these distinct traditions and self-consciously tries to collate them by harmonizing the promise to Abraham and the promise to Moses, the god of Abraham with the god of Moses, and the hope of conquest with the release of the exodus. It claims that the God of the exodus was unknown to the patriarchs by his name Yahweh, but he was the same deity nonetheless.[18]

> God spoke to Moses and said to him: "I am Yahweh. To Abraham and Isaac and Jacob I appeared as El Shaddai; I did not

make myself known to them by my name Yahweh. Also, I made my covenant with them to give them the land of Canaan, the land they lived in as strangers. And I have heard the groaning of the sons of Israel, enslaved by the Egyptians, and have remembered my covenant. Say this, then, to the sons of Israel, 'I am Yahweh. I will free you of the burdens which the Egyptians lay on you. I will release you from slavery to them, and with my arm outstretched and my strokes of power I will deliver you. I will adopt you as my own people, and I will be your God. Then you shall know that it is I, Yahweh your God, who have freed you from the Egyptians' burdens. Then I will bring you to the land I swore that I would give to Abraham, and Isaac, and Jacob, and will give it to you for your own, I, Yahweh, will do this!'" (Ex 6:2–8)

The passage begins with Yahweh asserting that he has disclosed himself in two different manifestations. He proceeds to invoke the memory of an ancient promise that was made by one version of himself to Israel's forefather; then, as this more recent manifestation, he acknowledges his earlier promise to free the distressed enslaved people, to adopt that people (you will be my people, I will be your God), and to deliver them and give them a land (the land sworn to their ancestors by the other Yahweh, El Shaddai). It concludes with a proud declaration of who will do all of these favors, the one powerful deity. In this editor's account, El Shaddai and Yahweh are thoroughly conflated, just as deliverance and conquest are thoroughly commingled. The nexus of exodus, conquest, monotheism, and possession and the intractable logic that binds them together are set in stark relief: a people are possessed, they are delivered from oppression, they are conferred a land, and all are a ringing endorsement of monotheistic omnipotence.

The appropriation of the myth of exodus/conquest for widely divergent purposes is replicated in biblical scholarship.[19] According to some scholars, the promises of the land are a late creation, dreamed of and written in exile when possession of the land was imperiled. Others argue that the promise of land should be dated earlier, that it was used to justify claims to the land made by settling Israelites. But this dispute only scratches the surface of a deep scholarly controversy over the conquest of Palestine, a subject that has been the chief preoccupation of biblical scholars for the last century. These scholars, skeptical of the biblical account of the conquest of Canaan with its boast of tearing down Jericho's walls at the blast of trumpets, of the sun standing still so that the Canaanites could be finished off, have developed alternative theories of the conquest of Canaan, ones that rely heavily on archeological data. But the data never seem to point in a conclusive direction; rather, the evidence becomes strangely compatible with the political biases of the scholars analyzing it. Marxists tend to produce theories of peasant revolts; according to their account, a large constituent of the so-called Hebrews were really oppressed Canaanites overthrowing the domination of their city-state overlords. Germans have tended to favor a theory of gradual settlement, maintaining that immigration and assimilation of Hebrews with Canaanites occurred because the seasonal migration of seminomads entailed agreements between herders and farmers. The dominant school of thought in the United States produced theories of invasion of the indigenous population in a massive conquest by outsiders—here, the destruction of key cities in the late thirteenth century offers archeological proof despite our not knowing who or what forces led to that destruction. But all of these historical versions of Israel's taking the promised land turn out to be less violent, less oppressive, and less morally repugnant than the version in the biblical narrative: "and when the Lord your God gives them over to you, and you defeat them, then you must utterly destroy them; you shall make no covenant with them, and show no mercy to them" (Deut 7:2).

Replacing this aggression with a more congenial version of the conquest certainly makes the Bible more palatable, but the historian's sleight of hand begs a question of ethical accountability. What happens to the cultural life of the narrative when experts rewrite it, relying on archeology? Does the cultural effect of the violent narrative really diminish? "People who read the narratives read them as they are, not as scholars and experts would like them to be read and interpreted. History is no longer with us. The narrative remains."[20] Narratives like the following:

> The people answered, "We have no intention of deserting Yahweh and serving other gods! Was it not Yahweh our God who brought us and our ancestors out of the land of Egypt, the house of slavery, who worked those great wonders. . . . What is more, Yahweh drove all those peoples out before us, as well as the Amorites who used to live in this country. We too will serve Yahweh, for he is our God." (Josh 24:16–18)

The story of an oppressed people overthrowing their overlords in a fantasy of conquest produces new difficulties: "If indeed the Canaanites were integral to Israel's early history, the Exodus narratives reflect a situation in which indigenous people put their hope in a god from outside, were liberated from their oppressors, and then saw their story of oppression revised out of the new nation's history of salvation. They were assimilated into another people's identity and the history of their ancestors came to be regarded as suspect and a danger to the safety of Israel. In short, they were betrayed."[21]

In other words, we need to take the ethics of these stories seriously because such stories are the cultural locus where, if anywhere, ethics are encoded. If at first it seems that reassigning the myth of conquest to a disempowered people makes it less offensive, on reflection, using history to rewrite, or write away, the violent narratives may be irresponsible. In the end, whether the people who generated the myth were empowered or disempowered—and making ethics contingent upon power makes a mockery of ethics as an independent court of judgment—whether they were conquerors or oppressed victims seeking liberation, they have bequeathed a myth to future generations that is ethically problematic at best, a myth that advocates the wholesale annihilation of indigenous peoples to take their land.

POLLUTING THE LAND

> Denounce your mother, denounce her,
> for she is not my wife

nor am I her husband.
Let her rid her face of her whoring,
and her breasts of her adultery,
or else I will strip her naked,
expose her as on the day she was born;
I will make a wilderness of her,
turn her into an arid land,
and leave her to die of thirst.

(Hos 2:2–3)

A stubborn emphasis on oneness asserts itself in preoccupations with purity. Whether as singleness (this God against the others) or totality (this is all the God there is), monotheism abhors, reviles, rejects, and ejects whatever it defines as outside its compass. "Defilement," writes the anthropologist Mary Douglas, "is never an isolated event. It cannot occur except in view of a systematic ordering of ideas. . . . the only way in which pollution ideas make sense is in reference to a total structure of thought whose key-stone boundaries, margins and internal lines are held in relation by rituals of separation."[22] Monotheism is just such a "total structure of thought" that legislates separation: "I am set apart and you must be set apart like me" (Lev 20:26). "Be Holy for I am Holy" is how that divine command is often translated. "Holiness," then, is literally set-apartness, and that which is set apart is also spoken of as pure or clean.

Classifying land as either clean or unclean is pivotal to this system. Leviticus asserts that the land must be kept undefiled or else its inhabitants will be ejected, "vomited" out of the land. The purity of the land is determined by its people following all the laws, especially the law of fidelity to one deity. When Israel is not monotheistic, it is filthy and it pollutes the land.

You must keep all my laws, all my customs, and put them into practice: thus you will not be vomited out by the land where I am taking you to live. You must not follow the laws of the nations that I expel to make way for you; they practiced all these things and for this I have come to detest them. I have told you already: You shall take possession of their soil, I myself

will give you possession of it, a land where milk and honey
flow. I, Yahweh your God, have set you apart from these
peoples. Therefore you must set the clean animal apart from
the unclean, the unclean bird apart from the clean. Do not
defile yourselves with these animals or birds, or things that
creep on the ground; I have made you set them apart as unclean. (Lev 20:22–25)

The things that are set apart are not only certain animals, specific
birds, things that creep on the ground, and God. All of these purity
laws are designed to set *Israel* apart, to create its discrete identity.

Speak to the sons of Israel and say to them, "I am Yahweh
your God. You must not behave as they do in Egypt, where
you once lived; you must not behave as they do in Canaan,
where I am taking you. You must not follow their laws. You
must follow my customs and keep my laws." (Lev 18:2–4)

Monotheism/monogamy/land become a nexus in a system of
ownership wherein Israel, women, and land are owned so they can
be delimited, and delimited so that they can be owned. Women must
be monogamous and Israel must worship Yahweh alone, or the land
will be polluted. Furthermore, foreign marriages defile the land; alliances with other peoples defile the land; syncretistic worship practices defile the land; and the land must be held in perpetuity—with
no pieces of it cultivated by foreigners—or it is defiled.

Be very careful, as you value your life, to love Yahweh your
God. But if you prove faithless, if you make friends with the
remnant of those peoples who are still left beside you, if you
form kinships with them and intermarry, then know for certain
that Yahweh your God will no longer drive these peoples before you; instead, they will be a snare and a pitfall for you, a
scourge to your sides and thorns in your eyes, till you vanish
from this good land which Yahweh your God has given you.
(Josh 23:11–13)

The stipulation that Israel retains the land only on the condition
of obedience is surrounded by "holiness codes," rules for observing

purity in sacrifice, sexual practices, social intercourse, and specific ritual laws for the priesthood.[23] Leviticus enumerates sexual practices considered so detestable that to commit them defiles both the offender and the land. In this remarkable passage, the wholesale ejection of foreign peoples is attributed to their unclean sexual practices. Israel is forewarned:

> Do not make yourselves unclean by any of these practices, for it was by such things that the nations that I have expelled to make way for you made themselves unclean. The land became unclean. I exacted the penalty for its fault, and the land had to vomit out its inhabitants. (Lev 18:24–25)

Sexual practices might seem a rather unusual justification for conquest until we delve deeper into the logic that binds sexuality and the land together in both biblical law and narrative, a logic committed to erecting carefully drawn boundaries of identity.

When Leviticus enumerates the violations that would result in being vomited from the land, it primarily specifies various understandings of incest.[24] The first is generic: "No one may approach a woman who is closely related to him, to uncover her nakedness. I am Yahweh" (Lev 18:6). Those relations are further specified: father, mother, father's wife, sister (mother's or father's daughter), daughter of son or daughter, daughter of father's wife, father's sister, mother's sister, father's brother or his wife, daughter-in-law, brother's wife, a woman and her daughter. Finally, homosexuality and sodomy are prohibited. For all of the many injunctions elsewhere against exogamy—you shall not marry a foreigner or she will be a snare, a thorn, and so forth—here the emphasis is curiously on regulating endogamy. Distinctiveness draws boundaries at both ends of the spectrum, exiling the Other and prohibiting the Same, and whether the foreigner or the close relative is off-limits, the principle holds: distinction making is the key to holiness. Incest is threatening because it blurs distinctions as surely as intermarriage does: if a son slept with his sister and she conceived, would their offspring be a sister or a daughter? In this light, it is interesting that homosexuality and sodomy are not listed with exogamous threats but with endogamous ones: both same-sex partners *and* animals are too close. Laws that take such pains to specify which sexual partners violate distinctive boundaries are trying to define an equally specific identity for Israel, one forged in that carefully delineated zone between the foreigner and the relative.

The link between sexuality and land pollution reaches a frenzied pitch in the obsession with that most heinous of offenses, prostitution: "Do not profane your daughter by making her a prostitute; thus, the land will not be prostituted and filled with incest" (Lev 19:29). A body/land analogy governs the rhetoric that describes women and land as possessions (of one man/deity), women and land as faithful or idolatrous, women and land as monogamous or adulterous, women and land as fertile or barren. But women and land are not only analogous; they become causes and effects in this system of monotheism/monogamy. When Israel worships a foreign deity, she is a harlot, the land is made barren, and she is ejected from the land. Yahweh speaks to Israel:

> Lift your eyes to the high places and look!
> Is there a single place where you have not offered your body?
> You waited by the roadside for clients
> like an Arab in the desert.
> You have polluted the country
> with your prostitution and your vices:
> this is why the showers have been withheld,
> the late rains have not come.
>   (Jer 3:2–3)

The laws collude with this metaphor of Israel as a subjugated and disobedient woman: in Leviticus 20:10 and Deuteronomy 22:22, both the man and the woman who engage in adultery must die; in Deuteronomy 22:20–21, a bride who cannot prove her virginity must be stoned to death. "Adultery in this larger context is understood not only as an aberration of personal behavior, but also as a social disorder with religious implications: adultery is a disturbance of the order of social relations established by God.[25] The "alien woman"—another man's wife—has forgotten the covenant of God

(Prov 2:17), and the link between such faithlessness and landlessness is overt: Those who go to the foreign woman "delight in the perversities of the wicked whose paths are crooked" (Prov 2:14–15).

> For her house bows down to death, and her tracks to the departed. All going in to her do not return, nor do they reach the paths of life. . . . For the upright shall live (in) the land; and the perfect shall remain in it. But the wicked shall be cut off from the earth; and the transgressors shall be rooted up from it. (Prov 2:18–22)

The biblical "alien woman" has been described succinctly: "she is an archetype of disorder at all levels of existence."[26] A word for the outcast, the Other, *zārâ,* is also used to refer to this alien woman.

This thinking about possessing land and women explains what otherwise may seem like an odd law stipulating that a divorced woman, once remarried, cannot return to her former husband without defiling the land (Deut 24:1–4). First, the familiar analogy: like the land, the woman must not be cultivated by foreigners; but analogy deepens into causation: because the woman is cultivated by strangers, she pollutes the land. Finally, analogy and causation deepen further into outright identification. The land itself must be faithful, or it will be disinherited as surely as King Lear's ungrateful daughter: "nothing will come of nothing."

> If a man divorces his wife
> and she leaves him
> to marry someone else,
> may she still go back to him?
> Has not that piece of land
> been totally polluted?
> And you, who have prostituted yourself with so many lovers,
> you would come back to me?—it is Yahweh who speaks.
>   (Jer 3:1–2)

My allusion to Lear is not incidental. In Jeremiah, it is not only the husband or lover who is betrayed, but also the father by his daughter.

A perceived scarcity of love—"I had thought you would never cease to follow only me"—issues in a scarcity of property.

> And I was thinking:
> How I wanted to rank you with my sons,
> and give you a country of delights,
> . the fairest heritage of all the nations!
> I had thought you would call me, my father,
> and would never cease to follow me.
> But like a woman betraying her lover,
> the House of Israel has betrayed me—
> it is Yahweh who speaks.
> (Jer 3:19–20)

And when Jeremiah envisions Israel returning from exile, it is as a disloyal daughter reformed and as a disloyal wife returning to her husband.

> Come home, virgin of Israel,
> come home to these towns of yours.
> How long will you hesitate, disloyal daughter?
> For Yahweh is creating something new on earth:
> the Woman sets out to find her Husband again.
> (Jer 31:21–22)

A disloyal son and an unfaithful wife: these are immensely reso-nant metaphors. Freud would have had a heyday with the family drama they are symptoms of: peacefully inheriting versus oedipal rivalry, the elevation and degradation of women, and demands of loyalty enforced with castigation. This intimacy between the biblical and Freudian family scenarios, one I elaborate in the next chapter, is no accident, for both rest on the same principle, the belief in scarcity. Psychoanalysis is not the only discourse that has tried to critique these monotheistic assumptions about property, women, and owner-ship, only to replicate them. Western culture is laced throughout with a variety of institutions, marriage laws, laws concerning the rights of so-called minors, sodomy laws, and a less overt but equally insidious bourgeois morality that specifies which sexual practices and partners are permissible as strictly as Leviticus. These institutions that reduce women to property—wives owned by their husbands, daughters owned by their fathers—are stubborn institutions that are the heirs of the monotheistic thinking about scarcity that have kept misogyny alive and well long after the biblical period, institutions that regard a sullied property—a land shared by a foreigner, an adulterous woman—and other variations of multiple allegiances (multiple gods, if you will), as anathema. The tentacles of the injunction "you shall have no other gods before me" reach throughout our social formations, structuring identity as a delimited possession with a remarkable grip.

WHORES IN EXILE

Ezekiel 16, the extended allegory of Israel as a whore, brings the relation between whores, exile, and monotheism (adultery, defiled land, and idolatry) into sharp focus. It is the story of a child being born and growing up wild and unloved in the field, and when she matures into puberty, of her being owned, sexually and materially, by Yahweh.

> And I passed by you and I looked on you and behold, your time was the time of love. And I spread my skirt over you and I covered your nakedness. And I swore to you and I entered into a covenant with you and you became Mine.

She is now washed, anointed, dressed, wrapped, covered, and adorned with silks, fine linen, embroidery, gold, and silver. "And you were very beautiful and you advanced to regal estate. And your name went out among the nations, because of your beauty; for it was perfect, by My Splendor which I had set on you."

But then young Israel commits adultery with the nations: with Egypt, Assyria, Canaan, Chaldea—with, not incidentally, all of Israel's enemies.

> At every head of the highway you have built your high place and have made your beauty despised, and have parted your feet

to all who passed by, and have multiplied your fornications. You have whored with the sons of Egypt. . . . You have whored with the sons of Assyria without being satisfied. You have multiplied your fornication in the land of Canaan.

But this adulteress has not, strictly speaking, been a harlot, for she has not taken wages; instead, she has done all the giving, even paying her lovers for their services. "The adulterous wife: instead of her husband, she takes strangers. They give a gift to all harlots, but you give your gifts to all your lovers, and bribe them to come to you from all around, for your fornication." Presumably, Israel the harlot would be superior to Israel the adulteress, for she would receive property instead of giving her property away, and that careful distinction offers a clue that, throughout this harangue against the adulteress, the issue is less sexual morality than ownership of property. The emphasis on property is underscored by the punishment of the adulteress. She will be stripped of her garments, of her wealth; Israel will be stripped naked and then brutally stoned and stabbed.[27]

> Because your lewdness was poured out and your nakedness was bared, in your fornications with your lovers and the idols of your abominations . . . therefore I will gather all your lovers with whom you have been pleased, even all whom you have loved with all whom you have hated, and I will uncover your nakedness to them, and they will see all your nakedness. . . . They shall also strip you of your clothes and shall take your beautiful things and leave you naked and bare . . . and they shall stone you with stones and cut you with their swords.

It is worth noting that the word for "uncover," *galâ,* also means "go into exile." No longer "covered," the adulteress is no longer "owned" from one point of view, no longer "protected" from another. Israel has become a whore in exile.[28]

A fascinating anthropological field study of Turkey relates a "monogenetic theory" of procreation—the idea that the male is the creator and the woman the vessel or medium of growth—to monotheism, exploring the symbolic relationship between procreation and creation, between genesis at the human and the divine level. Muslims characterize the male and female roles in the procreative process in terms of seed and field *(tehom ve tarla)*. "The man is said to plant the seed *(tohum)* and the woman is like the field *(tarla)* in which it is planted."[29] The Qur'an legitimizes this use: "Women are given to you as fields to be sown, so go to them and sow [your seed] as you wish" (Sura 2:223). The seed-soil theory of procreation is projected onto God where, "omnipresent and invisible," it justifies the dominance of men as the natural order of things. Men/god create. Women are the soil, or to be more precise, the field, and that distinction is important: soil is spoken of as either barren or fertile but is not otherwise demarcated; in contrast, a field is defined, enclosed, "covered" by ownership—like a woman who wears a head scarf is covered, closed, that is, under the ownership of a man, whether father, husband, brother, or son. "A woman who is uncovered is open, hence common property, promiscuous."[30] And an open field, like an open woman, requires closing or covering, that is, owning. At the heart of the extreme measures taken to "protect" women in Muslim societies—veiling, early marriage, seclusion, and clitoridectomy—are efforts to possess them. These are "various methods to enclose the human fields, like the earthly ones, in order that a man may be assured that the produce is his own."[31] "Monogenesis implies monogamy at least for women."[32] And projected onto divinity, it also implies monotheism.

Monotheism, then, is not simply a myth of one-ness, but a doctrine of possession, of a people by God, of a land by a people, of women by men. The drive to own property issues in the deep homology between possessing a woman's body and possessing land. Both are conquerable territory, it would seem, connected not only by the familiar fertility imagery of plowing and planting but also by the property images of boundaries and borders. In the Bible, this assumes the shape of a preoccupation with physical wholeness, with not allowing borders to leak even though they are everywhere open. A host of bodily emissions, from blood to semen, are considered unclean.[33] "A menstruating woman is considered impure for seven days and contaminates anything upon which she sits or lies during that period. Anyone who has contact with her or with anything she has contaminated is considered impure";[34] and notably, Israel is compared to a menstruating woman, considered unclean due to having foreign inhabitants (Ezra 9:11). In *Purity and Danger,* Mary Douglas has forcefully demonstrated the imaginative correlation between boundaries of the body and boundaries of society: "the threatened boundaries of [the] body politic would be well mirrored in their care for the integrity, unity, and purity of the physical body."[35] Nuancing this insight further by asking why some bodily emissions are contaminating while others are not, another scholar has concluded that, in ancient Israel, the impurity laws reflect what "poses a threat to the integrity of Israelite lineage." Incest, adultery, homosexuality, bestiality, and the prohibition against intercourse during menstruation are linked together as prohibitions because they threaten the clarity of lines of descent. "Concern that the social body be perpetuated was inscribed in worries over losses to the human body."[36] Sexual possession and prohibition are devoted to defining and delimiting the identity of a people, even a people who insist upon blurring lines of descent, that is, on participating in other identities.

But the effort to produce communities through possession and prohibition backfires. Rather than the peaceful exchange of intermarriage to forge cohesive communities, the impulse to define, to delimit, and to possess propels violence. Cognizant of the violence inhering in ownership, the ascetic tradition joins its commitment to peace to renunciation of sex and possessions. In contrast, the Serbs offer us a terrible modern example of the violence of binding collective identity to the conquest and possession of land and women. As Serbs have taken over territory inhabited by Muslims, they have murdered men and systematically raped women, holding them in captivity during their pregnancy in order to claim not only land but progeny. Still, the quest to own both land and women is perpetually frustrated, and when the impulse to own them is unsuccessful, that very frustration becomes a source of violence, against women and against the other men who claim them. It seems we kill in order to own and we kill because we cannot own. And this has been given legitimacy in religion: while biblical theology insists that Israel is the possession of the Lord, the narratives suggest that Israel cannot be so possessed. Even the Almighty kills his people because he cannot command their loyalty, cannot, that is, fully own them.

Later elaborations of monotheism sought to avoid this frustration by elaborating a version of loyalty that was not given (or exacted) under threat of violence, but made inevitable, planted in the very hearts and souls of the faithful. In the biblical prophets' efforts to reinvigorate Israel's identity through monotheism, they describe allegiance to Yahweh as an inscription on Israel's very heart.

> See, the days are coming—it is Yahweh who speaks—when I will make a new covenant with the House of Israel (and the House of Judah), but not a covenant like the one I made with their ancestors on the day I took them by the hand to bring them out of the land of Egypt. They broke that covenant of mine, so I had to show them who was master. . . . No, this is the covenant I will make with the House of Israel when those days arrive. Deep within them I will plant my Law, writing it on their hearts. Then I will be their God and they will be my people. (Jer 31:31–33)
>
> I will give them a different heart so that they will always fear me. . . . I will make an everlasting covenant with them; I will not cease in my efforts for their good, and I will put respect for me into their hearts, so that they turn from me no more. (Jer 32:39–40)

That covenant will not be in stone, but in the "fleshly tables of the heart." John Donne shockingly depicts such a physical inscription of divinity as rape, even if it is a bondage he relishes.

> Take me to you, imprison me, for I,
> Except y' enthrall me, never shall be free,
> Nor ever chaste except you ravish me.[37]

To be devoted to God, the poet and divine says, demands an act of violent identity transformation in which the individual will is made captive to divine will. The religious life is one of complete possession and utter subjection.

In the Book of Hosea, two completely contradictory images of Israel's relation to the land are elaborated. The land is depicted as both a prostitute and a wilderness: as a prostitute, because Israel worships foreign gods; as a wilderness, to reflect the nomadic ideal of wandering over land, rather than owning it. Both metaphors depict a margin—a social one in which a woman is not an exclusive possession and a territorial one in which land is outside the boundaries of possession. One image is reviled— the land as a prostitute violates the contract that Israel is the exclusive possession of Yahweh—while one is celebrated—the land as a wilderness depicts a nostalgic return to the birth of Israel. Born in the wilderness, the hope is that Israel will be reborn there. But we cannot plausibly read Hosea as a ringing endorsement of an unlanded ideal, for in the end, the period in the wilderness is cast as an interim, a precondition to reentering the cultivated land—the *owned* land—and when the woman is sent into the wilderness, it is hardly to acknowledge that she is not an object of possession. Instead, it is to purge her so that she can be more completely possessed.

> That is why I am going to lure her
> and bring her out into the wilderness
> and speak to her heart.
> I am going to give her back her vineyards,
> and make the Valley of Achor a gateway of hope.[38]
> Then she will answer there, as in the days of her youth, and as
> the day when she came up out of the land of Egypt.
> . . . .
> I will betroth you to me for ever.
> Yes, I will betroth you with righteousness and in judgment,
> with mercy and in compassion;
> and I will betroth you to me in faithfulness,
> and you shall know Yahweh.
> And it shall be in that day—it is Yahweh who speaks—I will
> answer.
> I will answer the heavens and they shall answer the earth,
> and the earth shall answer the grain, the wine, and the oil,

and they shall answer Jezreel.
I will sow her in the earth,
I will love Unloved;
I will say to No-People-of-Mine, "You are my people,"
and he will answer, "You are my God."
(Hos 2:14–23)

Psalmists, rabbis, priests, and theologians have all waxed eloquent about the moving sentiments contained herein. The notions of the "tenderness" *(ḥěsěd),* love, mercy, and compassion of God are the hallmarks of Hosea's prophecy as surely as his inveighing against Israel's whoredom is: nonetheless, all of these sentiments are in the service of an unrelenting ideology of possessive monotheism.[39] The prophecy of Hosea begins with God renouncing Israel, a rejection that is acted out symbolically by the prophet, who is told to marry a whore and then repudiate her and her children.

> When Yahweh first spoke through Hosea, Yahweh said this to him, "Go, marry a whore, and get children with a whore, for the country itself has become nothing but a whore by lusting away from Yahweh." So he went; and he took Gomer daughter of Diblaim, who conceived and bore him a son. "Name him Jezreel," Yahweh told him, "for it will not be long before I make the House of Jehu pay for the bloodshed at Jezreel and I put an end to the sovereignty of the House of Israel. When that day comes, I will break Israel's bow in the Valley of Jezreel." (Hos 1:2–5)

That first allusion to Jezreel refers to the place where the descendants of (the wicked) Omri were massacred by Jehu. But in a later passage Jezreel is invoked in a different context of forgiveness and conciliation in which Yahweh takes Israel back; there, the etymology of Jezreel, "God sows," is called to mind. Jezreel asks that God sow the earth, and the appeal he makes is now answered: "I will answer the heavens and they shall answer the earth, and the earth shall answer the grain, the wine, and the oil, and they shall answer Jezreel." This renewed divine commitment to Israel's prosperity issues in an exclusive eternal bond with Israel, "I will betroth you in faithfulness," and in the possession of Israel, "You are my people." And then, in that stark image of Yahweh taking Israel to him, the conjunction of the land's fertility to sexual possession is crystallized: "And I will sow her to me in the earth." A long and rich tradition of theological speculation idealizes love in Hosea, depicting it as a love freely given in contrast to one exacted, celebrating fidelity to God as the highest of human endeavors, but the distinction between a voluntary fidelity and being owned blurs troublingly when we note that it is only when Unloved says "My God"—acknowledging his possessor—that he is loved, and that this so-called love is manifest when Yahweh says to No-People-of-Mine, "You are my people." Israel must be the exclusive possession of her deity. Her identity is defined and her land is confined by that possession, and multiple allegiances are prohibited, are, in fact, the grounds for exile and even extinction. But the sexual possession so deeply entrenched in monotheism assumes its most explicit form, not in these metaphors of owning land and being exiled from it, but in another way of constructing Israel's identity, through kinship.

Natural Identity

KINSHIP

Them that's got shall get
Them that's not shall lose
So the Bible says
And it still is news
Mama may have, Papa may have
But God bless the child that's got his own!
That's got his own.
—Arthur Herzog Jr. and Billie Holiday

I would have you swear by Yahweh, God of heaven and
God of earth, that you will not choose a wife for my son
from the daughters of the Canaanites among whom I
live.—Genesis 24:3

Another way that the identity of Israel is constructed is as a kinship group. What is unique about this understanding of identity—what distinguishes it from, say, a group that defines itself as a covenanted community (chapter 1), or territorially (chapter 2), as a nation (chapter 4), or as a people who subscribe to a collective history (chapter 5)—is its claim to be "natural." According to kinship thinking, Israel's identity is shored up by nature itself, by blood and by seed, by genealogy, by brother and sister, father and mother, cousins and cross-cousins. All bespeak the nonarbitrary, nonprovisional, incontestable, that is, "natural," character of collective identity. Genealogies can be drawn, seed ascertained, and blood measured to determine who is an Israelite and who is not. According to this model, the people of Israel are a huge family that traces itself back to one father, Abraham, through a system of patrilineal descent that determines who belongs and who does not.[1] Hence, membership is not arbitrary. Or is it? The difficulty any discussion of kinship must address is that, far from successfully escaping the artifice of identity, kinship systems are themselves artificial. After long and tortuous debates about the significance and forms of kinship systems, anthropologists are now telling us that there is virtually no such thing as kinship.[2] There are *ideologies* of blood relations, *constructs* of brothers and sisters, but comparative cultural studies have shown us how diversely such notions are understood. There are no real blood relations.

The Bible itself hastens to point to the artificial character of kinship relations in many scenes: scenes where the right of inheritance does not pass to the firstborn but to the one who steals it cunningly, where the patriarch pretends his wife is his sister only to suggest later that his wife really is his sister, where a foreigner is not just adopted by Israelites but becomes the ancestress of the Davidic line, where brothers disown one another and an uncle treats his nephew and his daughters as foreigners. When Israel depends upon kinship to chart its identity, that identity is far from clear. In practice, the process of defining who is an Israelite and who is not takes on subtle distinctions. How foreign is foreign? How close is close enough? How far too far to qualify as an Israelite?[3] Not only is it difficult to ascertain who is a foreigner and who is not, but also those who are outsiders in one sense—excluded from marrying Israelites—are not always outsiders in another sense. The radical insider is also out of bounds in prohibitions against incest.[4] The very term Ezra uses as he prohibits marriage to foreign women, *niddâ* (unclean), is used in Leviticus for sleeping with a brother's wife. That suggests that the impure foreigner is also within. The prohibition against *exogamy* betrays an evident fear: marital alliances with foreigners incur the risk of contamination by foreign customs and by foreign worship, along with the risk of losing property. But when we take that logic to heart, what could possibly be the trouble with incest? This will be one of the puzzling and important contradictions that continually destabilize kinship as a way of imagining collective identity.

Basically, the problem of the foreigner has two distinct but interrelated aspects: how to identify her and what to do with her. The first—how to identify the foreigner—is broadly speaking a philosophical problem, one that requires inventing notions of the Subject and the Other, whether the specific discipline deployed is anthropology, psychology, or theology. The second—what to do with the foreigner—is a political problem: should you subjugate the Other or be subjugated by her, live peaceably with the Other or apart from her, try to destroy the Other or fear destruction from her, along with any of the many variations on these broad alternatives that can be endorsed by culture, legislated by authority, and enacted with more or less violence. But these two concerns, of definition and policy, are fully implicated in one another. On the one hand, the political realm is always thrust back to the problem of identifying the foreigner, and on the other, the question of definition is always politically charged. Who, after all, is empowered to define the Subject and the Other? In whose interest are such identities, who profits from these definitions and who suffers? If the most glaring difficulty that emerges from this invention called kinship is how to discern who is kin and who is not, that question quickly loses its academic character and takes on a destructive one when it is bent, as it so often has been in kinship thinking, on justifying exclusion. Kinship constructs become yet another way that identity is forged in violence.

The tragic requirement of collective identity that other peoples must be identified as objects to be abhorred is manifest in the violent exclusions in Israel's ancestral myths of kinship, assuming especially poignant expression in the story of the blessing of Jacob. Here the cost of granting a future to Jacob, that is, the cost of creating Israel (for Jacob is renamed Israel and his sons constitute the tribes of Israel) is literally the curse of his brother, Esau, the ancestor of the Edomites. Isaac has two sons, Esau and Jacob, and although they are twin brothers, they are also the ancestors of two different and rival peoples. The narrative describes Isaac as having grown old, with eyes dim, wanting to confer his blessing to his older son, Esau, before he dies. He asks Esau to prepare a meal for him for the occasion (ceremonial meals often accompany oaths in the Bible), but when his wife Rebekah overhears the request, she directs the younger Jacob (her favorite) to impersonate his older brother, even to dress as Esau in order to receive his blessing.

> Then Rebekah took the best clothes of Esau her older son, which she had in the house, and put them on her younger son Jacob. She also covered his hands and the smooth part of his neck with the goatskins. Then she handed to her son Jacob the tasty food and the bread she had made. (Gen 27:15–17)

The impersonation suggests what the narrative will soon make painfully explicit: a blessing cannot be conferred upon both of Isaac's progeny. Structures of inheritance, descent, and the conferral of symbolic property in the narrative are in the service of a system wherein identity is conferred at the cost of the (br)other. The Israelites and the Edomites cannot enjoy equally blessed futures. Like the divine favor denied Cain, there is not enough blessing to go around.[5]

There has long been consensus among scholars that this is an etiological tale of social and ethnic conditions—either the wish fulfillment of a beleaguered Israel that its powerful enemy, the Edomites, be brought low or (depending upon how the narrative is dated)[6] a description of Israel's domination over Edom for a brief period. And yet what is striking in a myth that is so evidently preoccupied with the fate of communities, with a sociological function, is its added psychological realism. Because there is only one blessing, the brothers must compete for it, and the pernicious principle of scarcity that offers only one prosperous future when there are two brothers is also expressed emotionally, as parental favoritism. The logic of scarcity even governs love. We have seen how in the case of land the principle of scarcity engenders violence, and this is also true of emotional scarcity where the consequences are equally devastating.

In a narrative that is otherwise terse and devoid of colorful adjectives, the writer suddenly evinces pathos dramatically (it is especially marked in the Hebrew) when he depicts Esau returning from the hunt to receive his father's blessing only to learn that it has already been conferred, on his brother. Overcome, Esau virtually stutters his pain.

> After Isaac finished blessing him and Jacob had scarcely left his father's presence, his brother Esau came in from hunting. He too prepared some tasty food and brought it to his father. Then he said to him, "My father, sit up and eat some of my game, so that you may give me your blessing." His father Isaac asked him, "Who are you?" "I am your son," he answered, "your firstborn, Esau." Isaac trembled violently and said, "Who was it, then, that hunted game and brought it to me? I ate it just before you came and I blessed him and indeed he will be blessed!" When Esau heard his father's words, he burst out with a loud and bitter cry and said to his father, "Bless me— me too, my father!" But he said, "Your brother came deceitfully and took your blessing." . . . "Haven't you reserved any blessing for me?" Isaac answered Esau, "I have made him lord over you and have made all his relatives his servants, and I have sustained him with grain and new wine. So what can I possibly do for you, my son?" (Gen 27:30–37)

And then Esau asks a profound question: "'Do you have only one blessing, my father? Bless me too, my father!' Then Esau wept aloud." When scholars speak of the "unilineal descent" structure that marks Israel's ancestral kinship patterns—the fact that the blessing and promise of a great nation passes from one patriarch to another in successive generations—what they do not always say is that in this process in every generation someone's future is cursed.[7] There is no blessed future for the Edomites.

> His father Isaac answered him,
> "Your dwelling will be away from the earth's richness,
> away from the dew of heaven above.
> You will live by the sword and you will serve your brother.
> But when you have grown restless,
> you will throw his yoke from off your neck."
> (Gen 27:39–40)

The vision emerging from this ancestral myth of Jacob/Israel, with its terrible answer to Esau's pointed question, opens toward an interminable future of subjugation, oppression, and violence between peoples, one that can only be overcome through more violence only to issue in renewed domination and further violence. "Have you only one blessing?"[8] Esau's grief is the grief of the ages, his are the tears of all subjected peoples. Would that there had been two blessings.

Esau's question succinctly expresses a conception of identity as something that is won in a competition, at someone else's loss, an identity born in the rivalry and violence that unravel from scarcity. But this understanding of identity is not first introduced here in the story of Jacob/Israel. In the Bible it is inaugurated, as we have seen, with the first human brothers, Cain and Abel. Significantly, the description of identity as a deadly contest is not limited to one people in particular; in the drama of the first brothers, it has been universalized to describe all peoples. According to the myth, long before there were any rival peoples, before there were "Israelites" or "Edomites," brothers killed brothers; originary universal siblinghood was fraught with universal sibling rivalry. Again, in that story, the parental deity inexplicably preferred one of the siblings to the other and favored one of their sacrifices over the other: "The Lord looked with favor upon Abel and his offering, but on Cain and his offering he did not look with favor." *Inexplicably.* That motiveless favoritism is precisely the point, for all we know is that, just as some unexplained scarcity makes a human father have only one blessing to confer but two sons to receive it, so some obscure scarcity motivates a divine Father to accept only one offering from two sons. The rejected son inevitably hates his brother. The biblical story of the first siblings becomes the story of the first favoritism giving rise to the first rivalry and finally the first murder. "And while they were in the field, Cain attacked his brother Abel and killed him." If the divine motive is unaccountable, the human one is clear. According to the biblical myth, the origins of hatred and violence among brothers is scarcity. If there is not enough to go around, then Jacob must literally impersonate Esau to get what is his, and Cain must destroy his rival to seek the favor that was Abel's. Scarcity, the assumption that someone can only prosper when someone else does not, proliferates murderous brothers and murderous peoples. And it seems that even God, the very source of blessings, does not have enough to go around: "Bless me, me too, my father! . . . Do you have only one blessing, my father?"

EXOGAMY, ENDOGAMY, AND THE FOREIGNER

Rules of exogamy, endogamy, and incest are among the chief ways cultures have expressed their tenets of identity and difference. If the incest taboo reflects fear of losing identity in the Same, the exogamy taboo expresses fear of losing identity in the Other. How close is too close, how far is too far, to forge collective identities through marriage alliances? Like Goldilocks, ancient Israel generally finds incest too hot, exogamy too cold, and something in-between—a relative but a distant relative—just right. But if Israel sets out to define itself in a very deliberate and narrow space between incest and exogamy, it had better be sure who is an insider and who is an outsider, who would constitute an incest partner and who would be a foreign partner. Is Sarah Abraham's sister or wife? Is cohabiting with a daughter-in-law, as Judah does, incest? How foreign is the Ishmaelite, the half-brother of Isaac and son of Abraham? How foreign is the Moabite, son of Lot, nephew of Abraham? How foreign is the Arab from the Jew, both sons of Abraham? The answers to these questions are not located in the realm of doctrine; instead, they are the work of narra-

tives that are so messy and contradictory that the categories themselves, "foreigner" and "Israelite," continually dissolve.

Women are the kink in the works of a patrilineal descent system;
if only the seed could pass directly from fathers to sons, it would
help keep the records straight. Which women are designated to become the wives and mothers of all those men? The patriarchal narratives in particular seem obsessed with the subject of who can marry
whom, offering a wide range of options along with a broad range of
judgments that are sometimes delivered none too subtly: "I'm sick
to death of Hittite women. If Jacob takes a wife from among the
women of this land, from Hittite women like these, my life will not
be worth living," opines Jacob's mother (Gen 27:46). In general, the
logic governing the marriages in Israel's founding ancestral myths
seems tautological, with Israel being constituted by endogamy and
the foreigner being constituted by exogamy. Abraham has one child
by his own half-sister Sarah and another by an Egyptian, Hagar; the
first incestuous marriage issues in Israel's lineage, the second exogamous relation issues in the Ishmaelites, the foreigners. His Egyptian
partner is expelled along with her son who, the narrative tells us
pointedly, marries an Egyptian. In contrast, Abraham has his servant
fetch the "perfect" mate for his other son, Isaac, from among his
own kin.[9] Isaac's sons take disparate paths: Esau marries Hittite wives,
compounding his foreignness, and Jacob marries his mother's brother's daughters.[10]

But the pattern breaks down when we look harder.[11] Jacob's marriages should offer the ideal model for the people of Israel—again,
not too close and not too far, cross-cousin marriage seems just right.
Presumably, marrying his mother's brother's daughters keeps inheritance, both symbolic and material property, all in the family.[12] But
even his exemplary marriages are less than exemplary. After the narrative goes to some length to establish Jacob's genealogical affinity
with his uncle, the story tells of their disputing rather than sharing
property, of Uncle Laban's deceitful efforts to retain Jacob's services
and of Jacob's elaborate animal husbandry to best him, culminating
in Jacob's "theft" of Laban's flocks and daughters. In short, an uncle's
and nephew's division of wealth is cast as a ferocious competition.

Why is there any suggestion at all of conflict, let alone theft, when Jacob and Laban and his daughters are in the same family—when Jacob was expressly sent to Laban to choose a wife from his own family—and the advantage of being in the same family is holding property in common? Yet, as Jacob steals away from his uncle, possessive pronouns proliferate, separating "them" from "us," "his" from "ours."

> Then Jacob put *his* children and *his* wives on camels, and he drove all *his* livestock ahead of him, along with all the goods he had accumulated as *his possession* in Paddan-Aram to go to *his* father Isaac in the land of Canaan. . . . Moreover, Jacob deceived Laban the Aramean by not telling him he was running away. So he fled with all that was *his*. (Gen 31:17–21, my emphasis)

Laban chases Jacob and catches up with him, asserting, "The women are *my* daughters, the children are *my* children, and the flocks are my flocks. All you see is *mine*" (Gen 31:43). With kinship relations no reliable measure of trust, with nephew and uncle so eager to designate what is *his* instead of what is shared, the story becomes more of a critique than an endorsement of endogamy. As Jacob's wives so aptly complain, "Do we still have any share in the inheritance of our father's estate? Are we not regarded as foreigners by him?" (Gen 31:14–15).

To ensure his own safety, Jacob does make a formal treaty with Laban—but then, that is how Israel would behave with foreigners, not with family. The contract stipulates that Jacob treat Laban's daughters well and that he must never marry other wives; ostensibly, the purpose of such a promise is to keep the wealth Jacob has taken/stolen/inherited from Laban all in the family. But in whose family? Is Uncle Laban a foreigner or a kinsman? In what sense, family? If the narrative preoccupation with who marries whom reflects an effort to delineate clearly who is a foreigner and who is an Israelite, surely that effort fails. But perhaps the project is more subtle, perhaps these stories are devoted to demonstrating just how difficult such definitions are, and that is why they proliferate ambiguities about kinsmen and foreigners.

The Book of Ezra depicts dispossessed exiles returning to the land that was once Israel; it is two generations after the Babylonian exportation from Israel, the Israelites are now under Persian rule, and they have reason to be anxious about what is Israel and who is an Israelite. Under those conditions, it is unsurprising that here the Bible reaches its most fevered pitch about rejecting the foreigner, with resolute prohibitions against exogamy. Paraphrasing a divine command, Ezra speaks:

> The land into which you go, to possess it, is an unclean land with the impurity of the people of the lands, with their abominations which have filled it from one end to the other with their uncleanness. Now therefore do not give your daughters to their sons. And do not take their daughters for your sons or seek their peace or their wealth forever, so that you may be strong and eat the good of the land and leave it for an inheritance to your sons forever. (Ezra 9:11–12)

Ezra wants to erect a virtual fence or a wall around Israel, to deem everything inside holy and everything outside polluted. The demand that those who have intermarried must put away their foreign wives is framed as his effort to purify Israel of its abomination. The images he marshals to describe this contaminated land are leaking bodies of both genders: the holy seed has intermixed with the foreigner, the land is a menstruating woman. Male or female, the body of Israel has been permeable, and now Ezra wants its borders closed.[13] This recourse to the Levitical category of purity is the most xenophobic utterance the Bible will make about drawing the borders of Israel by kinship. Here it is used to turn, not insects or certain sexual practices into abominations, but the foreigner himself who must be expunged and purged for Israel to maintain its purity.

But all the while that Ezra is trying to define the Israelite over against the foreigner, who is this foreigner? The land is unclean with the impurity of the people of the lands, but who are these "people of the lands" that he reviles and why does he name them so ambiguously?[14] Elsewhere in the Bible, people of the land (ʿăm hā ʾārĕṣ, singular) is mainly a reference to ordinary lay Israelites as opposed to those in the circles of royalty or the priesthood. A term that usually connotes class distinctions within Israel is used here to signify national or ethnic distinctions between Israel and some vague others, and oddly, the term is plural; it seems to refer to a heterogeneous group of outsiders. All this is confusing enough, but in addition Ezra himself has already offered a list of foreign nations invoking the expression "people of the lands": Canaanites, Hittites, Perizzites, Jebusites, Ammonites, Moabites, Egyptians, and Amorites (Ezra 9:1),[15] and that list includes peoples who no longer exist in his time. The list's function is essentially literary, alluding to another list in Deuteronomy that enumerates peoples the Israelites are enjoined not to marry. That list was supposed to have been given to the Hebrews who first entered the promised land, and alluding to it is doubtless intended to bolster Ezra's current policy with the returning exiles by referring to the first conquest of Palestine. But it has another effect. It gives the "people of the lands" a more mythological status as the Other, for they are a people who are not even specifiably there. When the "people of the lands" become a generic Other, that only further complicates the task of determining with any precision who is foreign—rendering Ezra's project of purifying Israel of foreigners impossible. Apparently, being intent on rejecting the foreigner does not simplify the task of defining him.[16] And not being able to define him makes him difficult to reject. Like kinship, purity is an impossible project.[17]

As though defining the foreigner were not difficult enough, biblical narratives are also inconsistent about what to do with him. If some passages forbid intermarriage with Ezra-like vehemence, others record it with indifference, and still others make a foreigner the key link in ancestral Israelite lineages.[18] There are further complications. We can never interpret the foreigner as equivalent to the non-native in the land, for Israelites are themselves, above all, such foreigners. Both of the biblical myths of the founding of the ancient Israelites, the call of Abraham and the Exodus, describe the people as originally coming from *somewhere else,* either from Upper Mesopotamia or from Egypt. We have also seen the pun at the heart of Israel's myth of human origins that makes all humankind essentially

a "people of the land." Again, the term is literally "ground," not
'*ereṣ*—a political configuration, the land of Israel—but '*ădāmâ,* the
very term for earth that gives rise to the earth creature, Adam, man.
"People of the lands" cannot be a designation for outsiders when all
peoples are peoples of the lands/ground.

Furthermore, if the biblical myths were intent upon establishing
a very distinct Israelite identity on the basis of kinship relations, we
might well ask why all of humankind share the same first parents in
Israel's founding myth of universal siblinghood. Then too, in stark
contrast to Ezra, Isaiah offers a vision of universalism.

> Let no foreigner who has attached himself to Yahweh say,
> "Yahweh will surely exclude me from his people." Let no eu-
> nuch say, "And I, I am a dried-up tree." . . . my house will be
> called a house of prayer for all the peoples. It is the Lord who
> speaks, who gathers the outcasts of Israel; there are others I
> will gather besides those already gathered. (Is 56:3–8)

But what happens to the foreigner who does not attach himself to
Yahweh? Universalism comes in different shapes, as an ideal of genuine toleration, as an effort to protect universal rights, and as a kind
of imperialism that insists that we are all one and that demands an
obliteration of difference. In a powerful study of the Inquisition,
Marc Shell demonstrates that a myth of universal kinship can be no
more conducive to universal love than one of particular kinship.
"The doctrine crucial to Christianity that 'all men are brothers'—or
'all human beings are siblings'— turned all too easily into the doctrine that 'only my brothers are men, all "others" are animals and
may as well be treated as such.'"[19] However narrowly or broadly
conceived, both Ezra and Isaiah are bent on delimiting community,
and whenever a "people" are circumscribed, someone is left out.
Violence is not, then, a consequence of defining identity as either
particular or universal. Violence stems from any conception of identity forged negatively, against the Other, an invention of identity that
parasitically depends upon the invention of some Other to be reviled.

While biblical narratives may be conflicting about the legitimacy of various marital relations and the deeper question of how foreign is the foreigner, they are remarkably consistent about presupposing scarcity. There are Israelites and there are Edomites, but there is only one blessing of prosperity to go around. This preoccupation with scarcity in kinship is grounded in monotheism, for presumably a foreign wife will lead one astray to worshipping foreign gods, to the (inevitable?) neglect of Yahweh. After all, Solomon's wives led him into establishing the "high places" of worship to Chemosh, Ahab's marriage to Jezebel with her prophets of Baal led him into apostasy, and that is also the threat posed by the "foreign woman" of Proverbs, who will lead the unwary down the wrong path. Prohibiting foreign wives because they will surely lead to the worship of foreign gods only defers the entire question of "the foreigner" to divinity itself, that is, to idols. When Ezra forbids intermarriage, he cites as his reasons the need to protect property and inheritance, but these, in turn, reflect his deep theological commitment to insisting on the worship of the one God.

> Therefore, give not your daughters to their sons, neither take their daughters for your sons, and never seek their peace or prosperity, that you may be strong, and eat the good of the land, and leave it for an inheritance to your children for ever. . . . We have broken faith with our God and have married foreign women from the peoples of the land, but even now there is hope for Israel in spite of this. Therefore let us make a covenant with our God to put away all these wives and their children. (Ezra 9:12–10:3)

The virulent particularism in Ezra's order to the returning exiles to put away their foreign wives and children springs from that special kind of particularism, zeal for monotheism. In his version of monotheism—as singleness—he impurity, abjection, and abomination of the foreign gods escalates to the sheer denial of their being. They are false gods, mere idols. Insistence on the singularity of God, then, is not necessarily an insistence on divine plenitude. All too often, scarcity governs the monotheistic narratives preoccupied with oneness: one elected son, one chosen priesthood, one anointed king, one conferred blessing, and one accepted sacrifice. Tellingly, the stories of rivalry, rejection, and murder that this singleness generates in humans are punctuated by a recurrent famine in the land, by natural scarcity: "In the days when the judges ruled there was a famine in the land" (Ruth 1:1).

The Book of Ruth dramatically associates the foreigner with the principle of scarcity. It tells the story of Ruth the Moabitess traveling with her Israelite mother-in-law into Israelite territory during a famine, being charitably fed by an Israelite who marries her, and bearing him a child who will be the grandfather of David. Fertility of the land and human fecundity are interwoven throughout the story, but these blessings flow in an atmosphere blighted with scarcity and barrenness.[20] The poor foreigner is given permission to glean in the fields of the prosperous Israelite, and the story celebrates his generosity, including his marriage to the poor foreign woman. The Book of Ruth seems to offer an alternative to the vision of constraints in Ezra. Ezra's fear of losing property was coupled to his demand to reject foreign wives, and that sense of scarcity, of land, of wives, was in turn joined to a particularist monotheism. In contrast, Boaz feeds the stranger and gains a foreign wife, thereby endorsing a vision of plenitude and of fullness in monotheism. When the vision of monotheism broadens, as it shows signs of doing in the Book of Ruth, then kinship expands too in order to include all those—even the dreaded Moabites—who attach themselves to it.

Yet even this vision of universal plenitude is compromised, ironically enough, by kinship, for the narrative takes pains to establish that in the end Ruth the Moabitess is not really a stranger after all, but a relative, so that Boaz's generous marriage that seemed to take in the poor foreigner is not fully to a foreigner. Boaz is a kinsman of Naomi, Ruth's mother-in-law; hence, when he fills Ruth's cloak with six measures of barley, telling her, "You must not go back to your mother-in-law empty-handed" (Ruth 3:17), he is providing for his kin, and metaphorically for the continuance of his kin. Furthermore, the enabling condition for his embracing the Moabitess is her prior embrace of monotheism. Only her adoption of the god of Israel allows the Israelites to fully adopt her. As so many commentators

have noted, the important vow in the Book of Ruth is uttered by
Ruth in a virtual betrothal to her mother-in-law, Naomi, and in it,
she binds herself to Yahweh.[21]

> Wherever you go I will go,
> wherever you live I will live.
> Your people shall be my people
> and your God my God.
>   (Ruth 1:16)

By attaching kinship to monotheism, the story of Ruth links a particular people to a particular god, thereby strengthening one system
of identity with the other.

RAPE AND THE OTHER

The relationship between Israel and the Other is brought into further relief in three episodes in Genesis known as the wife-as-sister
tales, stories that condense the problems of ascertaining who is eligi-
ble for marital alliances and who is not. In all three of the stories,
antagonism is the presumed state of affairs between Israel and the
foreigner. The Israelite must either enter, or pretend to enter, into
an alliance with the dominant foreigner or he will die at the enemy's
hand. The stories also presuppose that Israelite sisters could be exchanged with the foreigner in order to establish peaceful alliances.[22]
All of the plots turn on the foreigner's presumption of exogamy, of
acquiring the woman who is cast as desirable property, property that
will be forcibly seized if not peacefully given. In short, possessing a
woman polarizes the options of hostility or peaceful alliance between peoples.

> As he was about to enter Egypt, [Abram] said to his wife Sarai,
> "I know what a beautiful woman you are. When the Egyptians
> see you, they will say, 'This is his wife.' Then they will kill me
> but will let you live. Say you are my sister, so that I will be
> treated well for your sake and my life will be spared because of
> you." (Gen 12:11–13)

Pharaoh takes Abram's wife (thinking she is his sister) and he treats Abram well for her sake, showering him with wealth. But then the story takes a dramatic turn, for Pharaoh is afflicted with plagues.

> But the Lord inflicted serious diseases on Pharaoh and his household because of Abram's wife Sarai. So Pharaoh summoned Abram. "What have you done to me?" he said. "Why didn't you tell me she was your wife? Why did you say, 'She is my sister,' so that I took her to be my wife? Now then, here is your wife. Take her and go!" Then Pharaoh gave orders about Abram to his men, and they sent him on his way, with his wife and everything he had. (Gen 12:17–20)

The very idea of intermarriage is mocked here, for in the story, it is the foreign king's expectation of exogamy that becomes the instrument of his ruin, a ruse to lure him into adultery and punish him for it and the means by which Abram takes his leave of the once threatening foreigner. The episode foreshadows the Israelites' later exodus from Egypt:[23] the captive Sarai is freed by plagues from Pharaoh as a captive Israel will be freed by plagues from her Egyptian oppressor. It also makes a travesty of the very idea of alliance with the foreigner through marriage. Israel's sisters will not be Egypt's wives. That kind of peaceful alliance is impossible.

Antagonism between Israelites and foreigners does not always issue in plagues on the enemy. Relations do improve. Two other versions of this wife-as-sister ruse offer variations on Israel's relations with the Other. In one, the foreigner will be less easily hoodwinked, and in the other, Israel, less threatened, will also be less threatening. In the second story, Abraham and Sarah encounter the Philistines, and their host (the king of Gerar), also enamored of Sarah, is warned in a dream that despite their story, she is really Abraham's wife and not his sister.[24] He returns Sarah to her husband even without the prompting of plagues, telling Abraham to choose wherever he would like to live in the land. He also asks Abraham understandably, "How have I wronged you that you have brought such great guilt upon me and my kingdom?" and Abraham answers that he feared for his life; besides, he adds, Sarah really *is* his sister.

And Abimelech asked Abraham, "What is your reason for doing this?" Abraham replied, "I said to myself, 'There is surely
no fear of God in this place, and they will kill me because of
my wife.' Besides, she really is my sister, the daughter of my
father though not of my mother; and she became my wife.
And when God had me wander from my father's household, I
said to her, 'This is how you can show your love to me: everywhere we go, say of me, "He is my brother.""" (Gen 20:10–13)

In a dazzling condensation, the story tells not only of Israel refusing
to enter into a marriage alliance with the foreigner (again using de-
ception to make a mockery of the very idea of intermarriage); the
narrative also explains why: we cannot exchange our wives with you
because they are really our sisters. A people set apart, they keep the
people set apart through radical endogamy.[25] According to this bizarre story, exogamy is anathema for the patriarchs because they embrace incest.

In the third version, the foreign host is Abimelech of the Philistines again. Not at all fooled by the wife-as-sister ruse, he instructs
his people not to molest his guests (this time, Isaac and Rebekah),
and he goes on to initiate a peace with Isaac, who has become prosperous in the land: "Let us make a treaty with you that you will do
us no harm, just as we did not molest you but always treated you
well and sent you away in peace" (Gen 26:28–29). Here, a peaceful
alliance succeeds, but despite the commonplace that exogamy is society's chief means for establishing such peaceful relations, this alliance does not include connubial exchange. In fact, the peace is only
kept because there is no such exchange. The family borders of Israel
are kept intact (to the extent, that is, that those borders ever are
intact). In all of these wife-as-sister stories, the issue of exogamy is
also tied to a crisis of knowledge. Mistaken identity is the key to the
abuse, and conversely, when the host is not deceived, both peoples
fare better. From that perspective, the stories serve as cautionary tales
about the importance of definition; you had better know who is
available for exchange and who is not, who is ours and who could
be yours, or you could suffer . . . well, plagues, for instance. Peace

seems to depend upon clean separatism enabled by clear definitions even as the stories also show just how tricky that is.

To offer a really fair test of the aptness of the theory that exogamy turns hostile relations between peoples into friendly ones,[26] we would need an instance of exogamy that is not overlaid with adultery, one in which a *sister* of Israel, and not a wife posing as a sister, is exchanged with a foreigner. Genesis 34 offers us just such a circumstance. This story tells of an invitation to reconfigure Israelite identity by opening up Israel's kinship borders to the Other. But the story of the sons of Hamor and the sons of Israel demonstrates once again that Israel is constituted over against the Other. The invitation turns out to be cynical, and it is accepted in bad faith.

The story begins with an act of aggression by foreigners against the Israelites. Shechem, son of Hamor the Hivite (a Hurrian) and ruler of the area, rapes Jacob's daughter Dinah, and afterward he purportedly falls in love with her and wants to marry her. "His soul was drawn to Dinah and he loved the girl and he spoke to her heart" (Gen 34:3).[27] So Shechem's father proposes matrimonial alliances with the sons of Jacob.

> My son Shechem has his heart set on your daughter. Please give her to him as his wife. Intermarry with us; give us your daughters and take our daughters for yourselves. You can settle among us; the land is open to you. Live in it, trade in it, and acquire property in it. (Gen 34:8–10)

The sons of Jacob accept on the condition that the sons of Hamor be circumcised.

> We can agree only on one condition, that you become like us by circumcising all your males. Then we will give you our daughters, taking yours for ourselves; and we will settle among you and become as one people. (Gen 34:15–16)

But while the sons of Hamor are still smarting in pain from their circumcision, the sons of Jacob attack them, killing every male, plundering the city of Shechem, and taking its women and children. In the end, an offer of matrimonial alliance is scorned with violence;

instead of women being exchanged, they are seized as plunder. An offer to share the land is scorned with violence; instead, the land of the Shechemites is seized. An offer to reconfigure identity, to become "as one people" is scorned with violence; instead, they will remain two peoples, only one of whom can survive. In this story, the very mark of Israel's corporate and corporeal identity, circumcision, becomes a weapon against the Other, one that proves once again that, far from incorporating the Other into the body of Israel, the pain and exclusion of the foreigner is the condition of Israel's existence. The story illustrates what the sad tale of Esau and Jacob suggests: that identity is forged at the expense of the foreigner.

Nonetheless, we would greatly oversimplify the implications of this narrative to read it as only a tale of constructing one identity by destroying the Other. In fact, Jacob himself (who is renamed Israel) does not endorse such foreign policy.

> You have brought trouble on me by making me odious to the inhabitants of the land, the Canaanites and Perizzites; my numbers are few, and if they gather themselves against me and attack me, I shall be destroyed, both I and my household. (Gen 34:30)

But Jacob is not given the last word on how to deal with the foreigner in this story. It is reserved for his sons. "Is our sister to be treated like a whore?" The sons of Jacob justify their violence against the Shechemites with the reminder that the son of Hamor began by stealing Israelite property (their sister) and that he only wanted to legitimize it as "exchange" after that theft had occurred. Their sister was not treated as a wife but as a whore, and one whose services were not bought but stolen.[28]

We are given further reasons not to trust these Shechemites. When the narrative reports Hamor speaking to his own people, we overhear him planning to institutionalize the exploitation of these Israelite squatters on Shechemite land instead of the version he announced to the Israelites, with its hope to become "as one people."[29] His speech opens with the sweet sound of a generous alliance: "These people are friendly with us; let them live in the land and trade in it, for the land is large enough for them; let us take their daughters in marriage and let us give them our daughters" (Gen 34:21). But it soon turns sour with cynicism: "Will not their live-stock, their property, and all their animals be ours? Only let us agree with them, and they will live among us." Having seized Israel's daughter, do they now plan to seize everything of Israel's? This reading produces, not a story of virulent particularism, but a story of justified rebellion against a violent oppressor. The reminder at the story's end and beginning that a son of Hamor has raped a daughter of Israel casts a dark shadow on the effort by the sons of Hamor to establish a more universal identity, to be "as one people." And the foreigner's abuse of power contaminates his rhetoric of universalism which like so many universalisms looks suspiciously like a virtual imperialism.

In this complex story, the tide of distrust overwhelms both peoples. On the one hand, a small and defenseless group are depicted as eking out survival in the land of a prosperous dominant people. Their daughter is taken forcibly, and her defenselessness becomes an image of theirs. The hegemonic group seeks to make reparations by offering their land and wealth and peaceful settlement to the Israe-lites—but they take the daughter, as they plan to take the Israelites. Another version is also offered here, of a people who may well want to establish a peaceful alliance with the Israelites in order to ex-change commodities (livestock and sisters) with the newcomers and to become as "one people." In that story of universalism sought, particularism is upheld. The sons of Jacob "seized their flocks and herds and donkeys and everything else of theirs in the city and out in the fields. They carried off all their wealth and all their women and children, taking as plunder everything in their houses" (Gen 34:28–29). In that passage, Israelites do not sound like an abused people liberating themselves from the oppressors but like the oppres-sors themselves, and the distastefulness of their aggression is sealed when they take wives and children forcibly as Shechem had taken Jacob's daughter. Is this self-defense? From the Shechemites' per-spective, when we try our best to join Israelites—get circumcised, marry their daughters—we are murdered. If the effort toward universalism should not have been so spurned and the sign of the covenant, circumcision, not so abused, it is also the case that Shechem raped Israel's daughter. There are no good guys or bad guys and there is no solution when identity is forged in violence. If anything emerges with clarity from this confusion, it is that this story is the site of a long struggle to define Israel's relation with the Other, that Israel comes into being in a dangerous political arena, one that presumes that one people must be dominant, the other subjected, and that their contest for power will issue in a winner and a loser. The ideas of living together on the land, of sharing property without exploitation, of peaceably exchanging wives rather than raping women, and of expanding the borders of identity in order to dispense with the entire Israel/Other distinction amount to, at best, a very painful joke.

Fictions of collective identity have stubbornly vested themselves in the metaphor of the body, even if it is too simple to blame the division of subject and Other on embodiment (we would need to back up and inquire into how consciousness makes itself the object of itself, and then challenge a body/consciousness division). What all of these tales of seizing, exchanging, and stealing women suggest is that when a people's identity is figured as a body, it is a body that is sexualized and then traded or hoarded, as a whole or in parts, and, as we will see, it is also a body that is fed, starved, and violated. Those who have thought long and hard about gender have undertaken the heroic labor of disentangling social constructions of gender from nature. But collective identity has similarly become naturalized in the impossible fiction of kinship, and that dangerous fiction needs also to be disentangled. Whatever communities are, they are not a body, and imagining corporate identity as corporeal—as defined by blood and by seed—has served racial, ethnic, and religious hatred all too well throughout history.

INCEST IS BEST

We have to take into account a remarkable retelling of the story, before we rest too confident that the Shechemite's rape of Israel's daughter and the Israelites' subsequent theft of the Shechemite women underscore the theme of hostility between Israel and the foreigner, demonstrating that at the formation of identity, someone—either Israel or the foreigner—must be sacrificed.[30] A daughter of Israel will be raped again. The episode will even self-consciously allude to the rape of Dinah—inverting it—for just as the rapist of Dinah suddenly (and improbably) came to love her and "to speak tenderly to her," so Amnon, the rapist of Tamar who had been obsessed with desire for her just as suddenly and improbably comes to hate her: "the hatred with which he hated her was greater than the love with which he had loved her" (2 Sam 13:15). Verbal repetitions between the stories abound, notably the description of the rape itself, the judgment upon it, and the responses of the men after the rape.[31] But the key difference between these parallel stories is that this rape of a daughter of Israel (the daughter of King David to be precise) is not an exploration of exogamy, but of incest. In this retelling, the victim is raped by her brother and the dialogue deliberately stresses that relation.[32]

> And Tamar took the cakes that she had made and brought them into her brother Amnon into the inner room. And she brought them near to him, and he lay hold of her, and said to her, "Come lie with me, my sister." And she replied, "No, my brother, do not humble me, for it is not done so in Israel. Do not do this foolishness. And I, where should I cause my disgrace to go? And you, you shall be as one of the outcasts in Israel. But now, please speak to the king; for he shall not withhold me from you." But he was not willing to listen to her voice, and was stronger than she, and raped her. And Amnon hated her with a very great hatred, so that the hatred with which he hated her was greater than the love with which he had loved her. (2 Sam 13:10–15)

Incest is difficult to think about without imposing the context of our own cultural taboos; however, the biblical story does presume that marriage between Amnon and Tamar, half-brother and half-sister, is permissible. That is, Amnon's obsession with Tamar could have led to marrying her instead of raping her, a legal response to his passion that she poignantly offers, defending herself from her attacker: "speak to the king; for he shall not withhold me from you." Just as the rape of Dinah led to the proposal of an exogamous marriage between Israelites and the Shechemites, and its rejection, so the rape of Tamar includes a proposal of an incestuous marriage, and its rejection.

Why? Wouldn't the very logic that makes the foreigner dangerous make the brother safe, that views the foreigner as a threat to Israel's distinct identity regard marriage to the brother as strengthening that identity? If the concern were losing property to the outsider, wouldn't marriage to the brother keep it intact? Because the foreigner was feared and reviled and exogamy spurned, then incest, maintaining the strictest possible cohesion of the family, holding property, and strengthening the lineage, should be the most desirable condition.[33] Certainly the Egyptians thought so, for despite the grand mythmaking of Claude Lévi-Strauss and Sigmund Freud to account for what is supposedly a universal incest taboo, it is not universal. Evidence abounds that incestuous marriages were institutionalized in the ancient world.[34] And even though biblical law strictly forbids it, biblical narratives equivocate. In two stories, incest is an abomination committed by foreigners: Ham cohabits (or does something with) Noah, and Ham's heirs, the Canaanites, are differentiated from the Semites and cursed; Lot's daughters cohabit with their father to give birth to the Ammonites and Moabites, peoples who are forbidden from entering the sanctuary of the Lord to the tenth generation (i.e., forever). But in another narrative, where once again the threat of complete extinction forms the backdrop to sexual encounters, Judah's incest with his daughter-in-law (though presumably a foreigner) issues in the celebrated lineage of David. For that matter, the first marriage in the Bible is radically endogamous—incestuous to be precise—not only father/daughter (since Adam begets Eve) but brother/sister. Woman came from man, from his flesh, and returns to man. They cleave to one another in marriage: "bone of *my* bone, flesh of *my* flesh." No exogamous union here.

In the story of the rape of Tamar, the body of Israel is neither violated by the Other nor, as in the paradisal ideal of Adam and Eve becoming one flesh, is it reunited as the original body. Extraordinarily, the body of Israel is self-violated. And that internal violence perpetuates itself. After a brother rapes his sister, a brother will murder his brother in retaliation and thereby murder the heir to the throne; an effort by the murderer to usurp the throne from his father will follow, and soon Israel will be self-divided in civil war. In the context of biblical patrilineage, the story of the rape of Tamar implicates the men she belongs to, her father and her brother. Her father, King David, is notably silent about the matter (in the previous chapter he has just taken Uriah's wife Bathsheba, so perhaps he does not feel himself to be on high enough moral ground to rebuke his son). But Tamar's full brother, Absalom, takes her violation as an affront, and he chooses to avenge the insult. Absalom's retaliation mirrors the offense. Under the pretense of requesting a meal, Amnon raped Tamar; under the pretense of offering Amnon a meal, Absalom murders his brother. Throughout, this allusion to a meal is evocative, for a meal should conjure up a covenant ceremony, a symbolic gesture of cohesion, instead of a bloodbath. Within what should have been the secure relations of trusted family members—a brother's love for his sister and a brother's love for his brother—a rape and a murder have been committed.

Looking at this narrative of compounding violence in contrast to the story of Shechem's rape of Dinah, where a daughter of Israel was raped by the Other, not by the brother, invites us to rethink what the notion of "foreigner" might mean. If the borders of Israel are defined by kinship, Tamar's violator is no longer *outside* of Israel's borders. Yet Tamar tells her brother Amnon that if he commits this rape, he will be an outcast in Israel, thereby alluding to another category, not Israelite or non-Israelite, not outsider or insider, but the "outcast within." According to one interpreter, this position mediates between the impossible contradiction of the rule of endogamy (with its impulse toward social and religious cohesion) and the injunction against incest (with its impulse to ally with foreigners).[35] But this foreigner-within category only deepens the crisis of contradiction, frustrating all categories of foreignness and with them all rules of endogamy and exogamy. Broadly speaking, to figure incest as a rape that issues in murder and compounding violence poses a serious challenge to the idea that Israel's identity can cohere as a kinship group, for along with incest, this story critiques the wisdom of trusting one's brother. As I have already indicated, an emphasis on internal dissension weaves its way through biblical narratives, from Cain's murder of his brother Abel, to Esau's murderous designs on Jacob, through the Joseph story where the Egyptians are more hospitable to him than Joseph's own murderous brothers, to the story of the traveling Levite who naively insists to his servant that they do not "enter a town of foreigners, of people who are not Israelites; we will go on to Gibeah instead" (Judg 19:12), only to face far worse violence from Israelites than any foreigner presumably would have dealt him.

In the story of Amnon and Tamar, the brother's lust for his sister raises not only the familiar problem of whom do you marry, an insider or outsider, and the corollary problem of definition, who is an insider and who is an outsider (in this case, who is your brother and who is your enemy), but also the value (if there is any left) of "kinship" as a category that can usefully distinguish safe harbors from dangerous waters. Under the thin surface of a tale of incestuous rape is the deeper familiar theme of fraternal rivalry. In turn, that rivalry rests upon the assumption that both property and symbolic property, including parental love, are scarce. A peaceful bond with a brother, like a peaceful alliance with a foreign people, is only desirable if there is a sense that no one is lessened by it, that is, by the conviction that there is enough to go around. But from among King David's sons, only one will inherit the kingship, and there are so many brothers. This scarcity is further dramatized on the emotional level. If the intensity of David's grief for Absalom is any indication of the strength of his attachment, his desperate lament for Absalom is of a different order from his mourning for the elder Amnon: "O Absalom, my son, my son Absalom, would I had died instead of you, my son, my son" (2 Sam 18:33). One senses that King David loved his son Absalom best. Perhaps—and I readily acknowledge this as speculative—here lies the unhappy motive in Amnon's desire for his sister, a desire that is at bottom desire for what is his brother's, a desire to *be* his brother and thereby receive that paternal love. Being enamored of Tamar, raping Tamar, and then turning her out seem like expressions of wanting to have or to *be* Absalom and subsequently to abuse Absalom. And if so, then Amnon's initial love turns so quickly into rivalry because the hope of attaining the love from his father that is reserved for Absalom fails—uniting with Tamar fails to transform Amnon into Absalom—and henceforth the very sight of her is a reminder of that failure. Amnon cannot bear to look at her. The desire to merge into one—the identity of incest—quickly flips into the horror of there being two—that is, into rivalry. Overvaluing kin inverts into undervaluing kin, with neither model accommodating a valuation that can acknowledge and honor difference. Hence, Amnon's confusion of hatred and love (psychoanalysis has dubbed this "conversion") is manifest so explicitly in his emotional reversal: "the hatred with which he hated her was greater than the love with which he had loved her." Incest gives way to rivalry, and love to hatred, for insiders as well as outsiders in the biblical world when it is governed, as it so often is, by principles of scarcity. In any event, the story responds to one of the deepest of riddles about kinship in the Bible. When ancient Israel rejects the foreigner as vehemently as it often does, why would it also make the love of the insider, the nearest of kin, taboo?

KINSHIP, RACE, AND PROPERTY

The idea of kinship is in the service of property. The logic runs like this: once you know who is who, then you know who gets what. This (il)logic is reciprocal: you want to know who gets what because you want to keep property in the family, but you construct the family to determine who gets what. A fiction that begins by attaching property rights to inventions of bloodlines comes to use those bloodlines to justify exclusion from property. The reasoning is circular: kinship directs inheritance and protects property so that those who are not designated to share in the wealth are seen as nonkin. Extreme inequity, like the creation of a servant class, often reclassifies those exploited as another family of man altogether. At various junctures in

European history, Jews and Catholics have been conveniently designated as "races" in order to justify excluding them from the distribution of wealth, and colonial discourse is filled with descriptions of
the imagined inferiorities of natives, often deemed not only a separate race but even a separate species, subject to inhumane treatment
justifiably because, after all, they were not regarded as fully human.
The more people were victimized by the institution of slavery in
the United States, the more persistent became the cultural effort to
imagine them as another "race," that is, another "family of man,"
and often worse, as a subhuman species.

Among the many pivotal moments in the history of interpreting
narratives of the Hebrew Bible are two that have allowed it to be
used to endorse racism. It is unfortunate to have to say this, but
readers who want to use the Bible to authorize racism have made it
necessary: the Bible itself is not "racist," although many people who
read/interpret it have put it to such service. My own readings are
intended to draw out how contradictory biblical narratives are on
the subject of group identity, on who is a foreigner and who an
Israelite, and on whether in the end these categories lose meaning
altogether. That is, it should be apparent by now that what I have
been exploring here is not a single view of the Other that is somehow "in the Bible," but instead pursuing a strategy of reading the
Bible that makes any single consistent ideological viewpoint difficult
to defend. Such a strategy makes it difficult to use the Bible as a
political club. Even more to the point (the point being the relation
of the Bible to contemporary political urgency), a work composed,
assembled, and edited some two to three thousand years ago in an
altogether remote cultural context is unlikely to address current
political crises directly, whether apartheid in South Africa, ethnic
cleansing in Bosnia, or racism in the United States. All that having
been said, however, it does remain true that millions of people imagine that biblical narratives do just that—function as direct commentaries on their immediate lives—and they claim the Bible has the
authority to do so.

The answer to the riddle of how this authority came to be is not
to be found in the Bible, but in history: the history of religions, the

history of institutional power, and the history of interpretation. We know that Christianity's emergence from Judaism was a gradual process. When the early Christian church referred to the "Scripture," it meant the writings of the Hebrew Scriptures (which had been translated into Greek in the Septuagint), and they were invoked, ironically, in the service of promulgating faith in Jesus, with special attention to reading select passages as messianic prophecies. The ramifications of electing to interpret the "old" covenant as a prefiguration of a "new" one have been far-reaching in the history of reception of the narratives of the Hebrew Bible, for it meant that the first testament was adopted and supplemented by Christianity, rather than replaced or deleted.[36] As the Christian Old Testament, those narratives were invoked wherever Christianity took hold: by the monarchs of Europe, by crusaders, by colonizing missionaries, by Protestant states, and by antebellum preachers in the U.S. South. Through the growth and dissemination of religious traditions, then, interpretations of a text that was collated in the first centuries A.D. in Palestine came to inform later interpretations and thence the political life of the antebellum South of the United States. A genealogical construct for a people became, in the rhetoric of antebellum preachers, explicitly racist. From their pulpits, they turned to a brief narrative in Genesis that they erroneously labeled "the curse of Ham" and performed remarkably pernicious feats of translation and hermeneutics on it to justify the institution of slavery.[37] The original narrative describes a curse of Canaan, not of Ham:[38]

> Accursed be Canaan. The lowest of slaves will he be to his brothers. Blessed be the Lord, the God of Shem. May Canaan be the slave of Shem. (Gen 9:25–26)

But that did not deter the preachers from substituting Ham, the progenitor of Africans who spoke Hamitic, and making him the forebear of a cursed dark-skinned people. As Josiah Priest, among others, read it,

> Accursed be Ham. He shall be his brothers meanest slave; blessed be Yahweh God of Shem, let Ham be his slave. May

God extend Japheth, may he live in the tents of Shem and may
Ham be his slave.

According to the primitive racial biologism of these antebellum
theologians, universal humankind was re-created after the flood by
the family of Noah. His children, Japheth, Shem, and Ham were the
progenitors of the white, red, and black races.[39]

> God, who made all things, and endowed all animated nature
> with the strange and unexplained power of propagation, super-
> intended the formation of two of the sons of Noah, in the
> womb of their mother, in an extraordinary and *supernatural*
> manner, giving to these two children such forms of bodies,
> constitutions of natures, and complexions of skin as suited his
> *will*.[40]

Josiah Priest's conflicting imperatives—on the one hand, to assert
the universalism of all humankind as one family descended from
Adam and, on the other hand, to establish the separation of distinct
races—produces the remarkably convoluted logic whereby something wholly unnatural had to occur. A child was made black in the
womb of Noah's wife. In his bizarre logic, an unnatural event produced "natural" differences by a supernatural decree.

> Those two sons were Japheth and Ham. Japheth He caused to
> be born white, differing from the color of his parents, while
> He caused Ham to be born black, a color still farther removed
> from the red hue of his parents than was white, events and
> products wholly contrary to nature, in the particular of animal
> generation, as relates to the human race. It was therefore, by
> the miraculous intervention of the divine power that the black
> and white man have been produced, equally as much as was
> the creation of the color of the first man, the Creator giving
> him a complexion, arbitrarily, that pleased the Divine will.[41]

When the infamous Supreme Court Dred Scott decision made it
illegal for even freed slaves to own property, it became painfully clear
that another class of humans was being constructed to keep the

wealth all in the family, a white family, to be sure, one whose "universal" values were guaranteed by the Constitution and one whose Bill of Rights protected the life, liberty, and pursuit of happiness of all its family members, the citizens.

> The question is simply this: Can a negro, whose ancestors were imported into this country [an immigrant white population points out that Blacks were nonnatives] become a member of the political community formed and brought into existence by the Constitution of the United States, and as such become entitled to all the rights, and privileges, and immunities, guaranteed by that instrument to the citizen. . . .
>
> We think . . . that they are not included, and not intended to be included under the word "citizens" in the Constitution, and can therefore claim none of the rights and privileges which that instrument provides for and secures to citizens of the United States. On the contrary, they were at that time considered as a subordinate and inferior class of beings, who had been subjugated by the dominant race, and whether emancipated or not, yet remained subject to their authority.[42]

In his sensitivity to the economic basis of racism, the philosopher Etienne Balibar speaks of two incommensurable humanities, a humanity of destitution and one of "consumption," one of underdevelopment and one of overdevelopment, based on the distribution of goods.[43] However, behind the question of the apportionment of goods lurks another presumption: that goods are scarce. A perceived scarcity of property necessitates the distinctions: inheritors and outcasts, kin and nonkin. And it is not only goods that are in short supply. If the biblical stories about guarding hegemony are any indication, there seems to be room for only one at the top of the power heap. And up there, identity itself is also imagined as scarce.

GOD THE FATHER AND HOMOSEXUALITY

What is going on in the allusive story of Noah's curse? What is that terrible curse—"he shall be his brother's meanest slave"— about?

When Noah was drunk and "uncovered his nakedness," Ham "saw his father's nakedness" and these expressions vaguely suggest a sexual act. Plenty of commentary has been devoted to cleaning it up, but no one has been able to completely rid this odd story of its suggestion of incest, of homosexual incest, father-son incest, to be precise. The fury of Noah's curse could suggest that he believes some terrible crime has been committed, and the strong legislation against homosexuality and incest in the Bible lend corroboration: "you must not uncover the nakedness of your father or mother" (Lev 18:7); "you must not lie with a man as with a woman. This is a hateful thing" (Lev 18:22). In Genesis, Sodom is scorched to the earth, and in the Book of Judges, a host deems it preferable to allow his guest's woman to be gang-raped than to expose the man to the advances of other men. There is more. Noah's curse is one of two stories in the Bible in which Israelites are differentiated from other peoples on the very basis of incest: in the story of Ham's incest with his father, the Semites are distinguished from the universal humankind descended from Noah, and in the story of Lot's daughters seducing their father, the Israelites are further distinguished from the Moabites and Ammonites. In both cases, Israelites are defined as the people who do not commit incest. The virulence of this biblical abhorrence should make us wonder what it is about incest that ancient Israel finds so threatening—and so compelling. Again, what is going on in the allusive story of Noah and his curse?

The peculiar curse condemns Ham's son to be subordinate to his brothers, a curse that does not, on its surface, address an incestuous transgression by Ham against his father. But the story of Noah's curse does seem to address another fear, the fear of the father being displaced by his son. It may well be that Ham's desire for his father is a desire to become his father, and that Noah senses in his son's desire to dishonor him a naked wish to displace him. His curse to set the brothers at enmity makes those sons unable to threaten him. Presumably, if the brothers had banded together, if they had joined Ham to look upon the nakedness of their father, in doing so, they would have borne witness to their own challenge to paternal authority. But with the curse that subordinates one brother to another, patriarchal authority is confirmed by means of sibling rivalry. Noah's curse enforces a hierarchy that would keep his dominion intact.

Ham's (homosexual) encounter with his father is presented as a transgression of filial piety. Oddly enough, while the Bible celebrates loving the father, sex with him is anathema. Why? Why does the son's love of the father not issue in incest with the father? Why does the Bible regard them instead as so deeply contradictory?[44] That question takes us further into the complex workings of identification and desire. Identification produces emotional ambivalence, prompting both love for the object of identification and fury toward it because the identification is never wholly successful. For the son to successfully become his father, the father must cease to be, and so desire prompts both identification with the father and the wish to destroy him. This is what Freud referred to as the emotional ambivalence of father complexes, and it is what led him to assert in *Totem and Taboo* that "the violent primal father had doubtless been the feared and envied model of each one of the company of brothers: and in the act of devouring him they accomplished their identification with him, and each one of them acquired a portion of his strength."[45] According to this thinking, piety would be only the excessive solicitude that thinly masks love/hate. "The occurrence of excessive solicitude . . . appears wherever, in addition to a predominant feeling of affection, there is also a contrary but unconscious feeling of hostility—a state of affairs which represents a typical instance of an ambivalent emotional attitude. The hostility is then shouted down, as it were, by an excessive intensification of the affection."[46]

In the biblical version of the incestuous wish for the parent (as opposed to the Greek), sex with the father impinges on his authority. Ham insults his father's authority, and in an odd displacement, Ham's son must be put in his place—desire and power are thereby separated.[47] The punishment, as we saw, is not to be made subservient to his father or to be castrated by his father, but to be enslaved to his *brothers* to offset the danger that, bonding together, they will threaten the father, like Freud's primal horde. "United, [the brothers] had the courage to do and succeeded in doing what would have been impossible for them individually."[48] Division, dissension, disparity, and domination: all are paternal responses to a perceived threat to authority, responses, that is, to a desire that is confused with degradation, to a love that is confused with aggression. The hazards of identification are confirmed again when all of these themes recur in the last of the so-called primeval narratives, the story of Babel, where the sons join together in imitation of God, an identification that is punished, once again, with division and domination. While humanity's heavenward aspiration seems like a predictable enough effort to imitate their ideal, that mimetic desire is received, oddly enough, as threatening to the deity. And so in order to secure his position, the Almighty disperses his children. Introducing linguistic difference that prevents them from communicating with one another to forge a common culture, God sees to it that nations are born, but culture—signified by their communal tower project—is destroyed, and along with it their hopeful ambition has been reconfigured as presumptuous and disobedient. In this story, radical Otherness is introduced as a punishment for imitating the deity—as a guilty ambivalent imagination would project it, the people are punished for vying with the envied and feared omnipotent deity. Monotheism is figured as the oppression of the father, and Otherness becomes the effort to paralyze any imitation with its threats of displacement and desire.[49]

By now, the theme of sibling rivalry is achingly familiar, winding its violent way through the entire primeval and ancestral history of Israel. Beginning with the world's first brothers, in every generation, brothers are enemies. Cain and Abel are pitted against each other instead of against their father. Ham's sons are condemned to enmity. In the story of Babel when the children of God do cooperate, their cooperation only confirms the parental fear of displacement; together, they build heavenward to become "as the gods." The pattern continues in the patriarchal narratives where the stories of Isaac and Ishmael, Jacob and Esau, and Joseph and his brothers are all stories of cursed, murderous brothers. In the later history of the monarchy, Absalom's enmity with his brother Amnon diverts him, for a while, from his competition for his father's throne. Conversely, the intimate love between David and Jonathan is the key to David's success at succeeding Jonathan's father, King Saul. "And may Yahweh be with you as he used to be with my father. . . . once again Jonathan swore the solemn oath to David because he loved him as his own soul" (1 Sam 20:13, 17). And David laments Jonathan:

> O Jonathan, in your death I am stricken,
> I am desolate for you, Jonathan my brother.
> Very dear to me you were,
> your love to me more wonderful
> than the love of a woman.
>   (2 Sam 1:26)

Together with Noah's curse, this relationship offers a vital clue to the Bible's prohibition against homosexuality: it seems that there is a palpable fear that when men love one another, they will overthrow their fathers. And so the biblical norm of paternal dominance deliberately promotes rivalry, not love, among brothers. Sibling rivalry is in the interest of the parent. Favoring one son, blessing one son, receiving one sacrifice with favor—all of this has the effect of setting brothers against one another and keeping the authority of the f/Father inviolate. In such an atmosphere, the son's love of the father is figured, not only as love, but also as a dangerous challenge to his authority, even, as in the case of Ham seeing his father's nakedness, as aggression.

According to Freud, rivalry with the father springs from competition for the mother, competition that issues in the guilty wish to murder the father to attain her. We all know that story. What is noteworthy about it here is that Freud had to turn to a Greek myth to find it. The Hebrew Bible wouldn't yield the narrative of slaying the father. It insists instead on honoring the father. Even when, at the end of his life, Freud does imagine a Hebraic version of slaying the father in which the followers of Moses rise up against him and kill him (and cover up their guilty crime with the invention of monotheism),[50] he still finds it so unthinkable that the father of the Hebrew people is slain that he goes to great pseudohistorical and philological lengths to demonstrate that this slain father, Moses, was not Hebrew after all, but Egyptian. Given his deep commitment to the myth of the son slaying the father, it is all the more remarkable that Freud insists that the symbolic father of the Hebrews is not their natural father. We could reasonably have expected Freud to put the narrative of the victory of the primal horde at the beginning of his own cultural story, for instance, to invent a tale of the murder of the father of the Israelites, Abraham, by his sons, or better, the murder of Jacob/Israel by his sons who become the eponymous ancestors of the twelve tribes in order to seize their father's name, Israel. But instead, in *Moses and Monotheism*, Freud chooses to tell the story of the murder of Israel's Other, the Egyptian. And in this, his convoluted-seeming logic is deeply biblical after all, for the Bible insists that you slay your *Other* to forge your identity—not your father.

Not so very far beneath the complex displacements that include Freud's explicit assertions of oedipal longings, what he is implicitly but persistently expressing is not desire for the mother at all but, like so many biblical narratives, desire for the father. In both *Totem and Taboo* and *Moses and Monotheism,* where his biblicism is most in evidence, women recede into a shadowy explanation-at-hand for the subject that truly fascinates Freud: the ambivalent desire, both admiring and hostile, of sons for their father. A closer look at Freud's account of desire, then, would replace an oedipal desire with a homosexual one but continue to retain all the attendant horrors of guilt, ambivalence, and projected fears of punishment. While he sublimates that love for the father into something else altogether, into a universal oedipal wish, this male desire for the father is far more culturally specific, deeply embedded, as it is, in biblical kinship thinking. As Noah's terrible curse of his son belies and as the general biblical hysteria about homosexuality suggests, the son's desire for the father is also primary in biblical traditions. Only this desire— denied, repressed, suppressed, and punished—explains both the ferocity of biblical injunctions against homosexuality and the ferocity of the deity's determination to punish his children, to stomp out their desire with its threat of parricidal displacement.

In Freud's own preface to the Hebrew translation of *Totem and Taboo,* he describes this book on incest, exogamy, and holy dread as a study "which deals with the origins of religion and morality, though it adopts no Jewish standpoint and makes no exceptions in favour of Jewry." His extreme protestations only suggest a latent association that soon becomes overt, for he also insists (on the same page) that despite his apparent lack of interest in Judaism he has embraced "its very essence" and that essence becomes "the totemic system [which] was, as it were, a covenant with their father, in which he promised them everything that their childish imagination might want from a father—protection, care, and indulgence—while on their side they undertook to respect his life, that is, to not repeat the deed [murdering the father] which had brought destruction on their real father.[51] What Freud began describing as totemic religion—which he defensively asserts has nothing whatsoever to do with Hebraic thinking—finally does burst out as his description not only of Judaism but of *all* religion. Religion itself "arose from a filial sense of guilt [for wishing to slay the father], in an attempt to allay that feeling and to appease the father by deferred obedience to him. All later religions are seen to be attempts at solving the same problem.[52] And this desire encompasses not only human sons for human fathers but the children of God for their divine father. In his convoluted way, Freud has intuited the core of biblical thought on kinship: its deep preoccupations (and explicit horror) with homosexuality and incest joined to its advocacy of filial piety and a solicitude so extreme that it issues in monotheism's chief tenet: "Thou shalt love the Lord thy God with all thine heart, and with all thy soul, and with all thy might."

Freud reinscribes the Bible in a secular key for our time. It is the story of sibling rivalry, of scarcity, of goods that must be competed for—women, wealth, whatever—of fear of the potency of the father, of desire for him, of a guilty wish to displace him accompanied by the anxiety of dismemberment and the excessive solicitude that is the response to that fear. While this rewriting of the Bible is implied throughout his writings—and he knowingly asked, "Why did it take a godless Jew to discover psychoanalysis?"—at the end of his career, in *Moses and Monotheism,* he declares his debt to the Bible with resounding, if inventive, explicitness. In the end, not only religion and psychoanalysis, but culture itself must be traced back to Moses, to his relation with his heavenly father and his mortal sons. Monotheism condensed what was all along the primary relationship: "Now that God was a single person, man's relations with him could recover the intimacy and intensity of the child's relation to his father."[53] In *Moses and Monotheism,* the dramas he had once classified as infantile are enacted historically (or in biblical prehistory to be more accurate) and at several removes; hence, it is important to Freud to assert that Moses was not a Hebrew but an Egyptian. (Before he turned Moses into an Egyptian, Freud had to turn to the Greeks, to the triumph over Kronos, in order to elaborate his parricidal story.) In Freud's rewriting, Moses is slain, but for him, this is not the father of the Hebrew people who is slain, but the fate of the *Egyptian* Moses, and thereby Freud is able to preserve intact the biblical precept of filial piety. At the core of monotheism is the mandate that the Hebrew father cannot be slain, and that is why the excessive solicitude masking that very desire seeps from the pages of the Bible. Freud's sweeping explanation that civilization itself is founded on efforts to appease guilt for the parricidal wish begins to sound less ludicrous when it is seen in the context of that suspiciously pious and deeply solicitous biblical injunction of monotheism: "Thou shalt love the Lord thy God with all thine heart, and with all thy soul, and with all thy might." Why does this love have to be commanded? And why does it so often fail?

Throughout the Bible, an ideal of filial piety is promulgated, of sons for fathers, of man for God. While Greek and nonbiblical ancient Near Eastern myths tell of the usurpation of the father, of new generations overturning the old, in the Hebrew stories, authority and power are typically *bequeathed* to the next generation, not *seized* by them. The story of the first man and woman is a warning of the terrible consequences of disobeying the paternal command. Unending guilt, eternal pain, universal strife, and death—a death that does not come soon enough to alleviate those curses—result from defying the paternal order. Indeed, such a violation was not even imaginable to the first man; the story needed the Other, the Woman, to think of transgressing the paternal law, and even then she had to be tricked in order to do it. (While she is made the agent, the image of the original male impulse to defy the father still lurks in the image of the serpent/phallus that is cast as the source of the entire rebellion.) No small part of the punitive parental deity's response is to condemn the man, the woman, and the serpent to eternal alienation from one another, like the curse on the sons of Noah and like the divisions imposed at Babel, lest they rise up again in concert. Because Adam and Eve colluded in their disobedience "and she gave him the fruit and he ate," they are punished with divisiveness. Once equal partners, now the woman is subjected to the man.

The next story about fathers and sons tells not of defying the father, but of trying to *please* him. As we have seen, both children, Cain and Abel, offer appeasing sacrifices, but the deity likes only one, fueling the hatred that leads to the first fratricide and thereby inaugurating the principle of competition that continually resurfaces with each generation of Israel's patriarchs. This first sibling rivalry protects the deity from an affront like that dared by the first parents. The Noah story is the first narrative of a human father with his sons, and it combines the themes of the first two narratives: defying the father and fraternal strife. When one son commits some affront to his father, he is cursed with subjugation to his brothers. The "Table of Nations"—a detailed account of the fragmentation of universal humankind—immediately follows. Fragmenting humankind is also, as we have seen, the punishing deity's response to the boldness of building a tower of Babel heavenward. Children divided ensure that parents are unassailable. In contrast, when they do cooperate with one another, they mount an open rebellion against their God the father (or is it mimetic love?), who responds, not by entering into a competition with them (how can there be serious competition with the Father, after all?), but by imperiously forcing them into rivalry.

The son's desire for his father is expressed in efforts to become like the father (in his image), in yearnings to build heavenward, yearnings to become "as the gods," yearnings not only for the father's blessing but for the father's mantle, yearnings to enter the presence of God as Moses does and to be transformed into radiance by his glory, and even yearnings to *be* God, as in the case of Christ. Throughout, the desire for the father and the efforts to become like him are attended by massive guilt and fear of displacing him. Biblical narratives figure man's mimetic desire for God as threatening, both to the desired God and to the desiring man. If man does become God, it will be not to join him but to displace him. Such thinking emerges from a regime of monotheism that presumes scarcity. Primeval biblical narratives tell of God punishing man with mortality for his aspiration toward godhead (Adam and Eve), of God crippling man's will to be deified, of God crushing man's heavenward ambitions and punishing him with divisiveness (Babel), and of God punishing the sons of God with mortality for cohabiting with the daughters of men: "My spirit must not forever be disgraced in man, for he is but flesh; his life shall last no more than a hundred and twenty years" (Gen 6:3). And so the pattern in the ancestral history of Israel of siblings being prompted toward rivalry against one another—instead of against their father—emerges as another expression of the priestly interest in protecting the preserve of divinity. The entire nation of Israel is punished, overrun in stages by conquerors who exile and murder the Israelites at the instigation of an angry Father. While the anger may seem to abate when man does succeed at becoming God in the New Testament, the price of Christ's deification is horrific suffering and death. And the relish that religious traditions have taken in the passion of Christ suggests that the punishment has not been appeased; rather, it has been focused, contracted from exiling the children of God to the sacrifice of one son—with whom all the faithful identify.

The entire scheme I have just delineated—I may as well call it the "Noah complex" to distinguish it from the Freudian oedipal one—in which love/hate for the father with whom the son identifies issues in intolerable guilt for that incestuous desire, a guilt projected onto an omnipotent monotheistic deity who punishes, maintaining his preserve at the price of his sons' dissension, turning the brother into the reviled Other—is thoroughly predicated upon the supposition of scarcity. Scarcity imposes sibling rivalry: a shortage of parental blessings and love yields fatal competition for them. Scarcity imposes parental hostility: it presumes that in order to imitate the father successfully, he must be replaced, not joined. Scarcity imposes hierarchy: the short supply of prestige or power or whatever must issue in an allocation of those resources, and some will invariably get more than others. Scarcity imposes patriarchy: the hegemony of the father's position must be secured since even authority is scarce. Scarcity imposes monotheism: one god must maintain his singleness defensively, against the difference of other gods. Scarcity imposes transcendence: it guarantees the inaccessibility of God to man. All of the injunctions against iconoclasm that attend monotheism are designed to enforce the separation between the Creator and his Creation. These include prohibitions against graven images and against looking upon God that have long been interpreted as philosophically sophisticated innovations about transcendence in the ancient world. But a tradition that dictates that "no one can see the face of God and live" keeps that God's position secreted, separated, sanctified, and above all, secure, much as the inner chambers of a king secure him by denying access to any but his most trusted servant. In one tradition, even Moses is denied such entry.

> The cloud covered the Tent of Meeting and the glory of Yahweh filled the tabernacle. Moses could not enter the Tent of Meeting because of the cloud that rested on it and because of the glory of God that filled the tabernacle. (Ex 40:34–35)

Moses covers his face because he is afraid to look at God, and when he does look, he peers through a narrow chink in a rock only to see his backside—like Ham's wise brothers, Shem and Japheth, who "took a cloak and put it over their shoulders and walking backwards, covered their father's nakedness; they kept their faces away, and did not see their father's nakedness" (Gen 9:23).[54]

The scarcity at the heart of the legacy of biblical monotheism is also part of Freud's biblical legacy of psychoanalysis. Freud only imagined one breast. Moreover, the competition/identification with the father that issues in excessive solicitude toward him presumes, like the biblical scheme, that the father must be replaced, not joined. Both Freud's emphasis on emotional ambivalence and his understanding of piety as excessive solicitude also presuppose scarcity.

Hostility is only joined to affection (and confused with it) when there is such a shortage of models—and emotions—that they must be contracted together. Piety is only false when latent hostility implies competition for power, a competition that suggests that such power must be in short supply. When there is only room for one at the top, sons cannot grow up to become their fathers, man cannot become God. We have seen that the stories that are aptly referred to as the patriarchal narratives in Genesis are characterized by validating hierarchy rather than subverting it. Any notion of an intergenerational conflict—whether the successful Greek prototype of Zeus's rebellion and castration of Kronos, or the failed Hebrew one of Adam and Eve being punished with death for disobeying the paternal law—always presupposes that there is not enough to go around. Moses is kept well below his God; he is no classical hero who leads the people out of Israel, his God the father does the work. Moses asks, "But who am I to go to Pharaoh and brings the sons of Israel out of Egypt?" and his omnipotent guide responds, "I shall be with you" (Ex 3:11–12).

There is another possible dynamic between fathers and sons, neither Greek usurpation nor biblical obedience, neither a successful nor a failed intergenerational conflict, but a vision of no conflict at all. If the complex (oedipal or Noachic) were grounded in plenty rather than scarcity, if there were room for more than one at the top, the motive for competition would disappear. Hierarchy would wither, and the ambivalence that harbors hostility for the father could give way to uncompromised love. In this vision of plenty, imitation would not be a replication of the Same, the identical, but a proliferation of nonidentical repetitions (as repetition was for Kierkegaard) that open up the Same into endless difference. When identification is nonidentical, there is no motive to displace. An understanding of mimetic desire that presupposes scarcity suggests that once you start loving, either you lose your identity or else the loved one does: someone loses. But if repetition is never identical, new creations, new possibilities, signal new identities, rather than rivalry for the Same. Plenitude proliferates identities without violence. And when such plenitude is figured as a God, it is as a God who gives and goes on giving endlessly without being used up, and certainly without jealously guarding his domain.

This vision of plenty is embedded in the same Bible where the rule of scarcity has been so dominant. Feeling burdened by the weight of carrying Israel alone, Moses complains, and God offers to take some of his spirit and distribute it among the seventy elders who will share in the administrative burdens (Num 11:14–25). Then, in a critical encounter between the two worldviews, Moses levels an eloquent challenge to the paradigm of scarcity.

> Two men had stayed back in the camp; one was called Eldad and the other Medad. . . . These began to prophesy in the camp. The young man ran to tell this to Moses, "Look," he said, "Eldad and Medad are prophesying in the camp." Then said Joshua the son of Nun, who had served Moses from his youth, "My Lord Moses, stop them!" Moses answered, "Are you jealous on my account? If only the whole people of Yahweh were prophets, and Yahweh gave his Spirit to them all!"

Moses perceives no competition; he wants a kingdom of prophets.

Fraternal rivalry disappears along with intergenerational strife, with its violent assertions of paternal authority. And so, while one tradition prohibits Moses' access to God, another depicts Moses looking on God face to face (Num 12:8). While one tradition describes Moses as too slow of speech to be able to liberate the enslaved Israelites from Pharaoh without the assistance of the Almighty, another describes prophets as not merely the obedient inferiors of God, but authorized to speak the very words of God. That tradition depicts God as a father inspiriting his children with his own strength, not punishing them for their mimetic desire.

> He does not grow tired or weary,
> his understanding is beyond fathoming.
> He gives strength to the wearied,
> he strengthens the powerless.
> Young men may grow tired and weary,

youths may stumble,
but those who hope in Yahweh renew their strength,
they put out wings like eagles,
they run and do not grow weary,
walk and never tire.
(Is 40:28–31)

This vision of plenitude also gives rise to narratives in which a God who could kill his sons elects not to, a Father who could wield a knife on their manhood chooses not to take it away, circumcising rather than castrating, and a sacrifice that could be demanded of the son of Abraham is not exacted. Circumcision, the very mark of the identity of this people, signals that these sons are not engaged in intergenerational strife with their father.

The jealously protected monotheism that so powerfully sums up the scarcity paradigm in the first commandment of the Decalogue, "I am the Lord thy God, thou shalt have no other gods before me," is not the first commandment of the Bible. The first command, "Be fruitful and multiply and fill the earth," is a blessing of plenty, not a warning of scarcity. The many curses—of Adam, of Eve, of Cain, of Canaan, of Esau, of Babel—are countered by the blessings, of fecundity, of prosperity, along with the imperative that man should imitate the creativity of the deity without peril of competition. And while the heavenward builders of Babel are scattered, "lest they become as gods," in the beginning God created man "in his image." Having been made in the image of God, man is ordered to reproduce that image, not to secrete it away. Hence, these narratives do offer glimpses of another kind of deity, a God of plenitude, of generosity, one who need not protect his turf because it is infinite. And this vision of One, as plenitude, not as particular, would have made exclusive monotheism wither if it could have been sustained. Israel would have longed to be not only a kingdom of prophets or priests, but a kingdom of Gods. Apparently the vision was difficult to sustain.

DIVIDING IDENTITIES
"NATIONS"

Proclaim his salvation day after day,
tell of his glory among the nations,
tell his marvels to every people.
Yahweh is great, loud must be his praise
he is to be feared beyond all gods.
Nothingness, all the gods of the nations.
—Psalm 96:2–5

America, America,
God shed his grace on thee
And crown thy good
With brotherhood
From sea to shining sea.
—Katherine Lee Bates and Samuel A. Ward

Having lingered over the ideas of "a people" as a covenanted
community, a territory, and a kinship group, here I would like
to return to that complex version of collective identity, the

nation, that introduced this study. My hope is to separate the idea of nation in the biblical narratives that span the Book of Judges through 2 Kings (the so-called Deuteronomistic history) from the nineteenth-century nationalism read into these narratives by biblical scholarship. Of course, to allude to nations of the ancient world in the modern sense of "nation-state" is anachronistic, but the Hebrew Bible does imagine communities as nations in a different sense, as dynasties with separate geopolitical and religious boundaries, demarcated by the worship of different deities. The Ammonites are those who worship Milcom, the Moabites those who worship Chemosh, Egyptians those who worship Pharaoh, Canaanites those who worship Baal, et alia. It is in this ancient sense of nation that Genesis produces a "Table of Nations," and it is in this sense of nation that the Bible urges, in a strain running its entire length, that Israel should never become a geopolitical dynasty, never become, that is, "like the nations." When the identity of ancient Israel is constructed antithetically against Egypt, it is expressed as Yahweh versus Pharaoh.[1] The true nation worshipped the true God; the false nation worshipped a false god.

The modern nation-state reflected this ancient understanding of nation-deity. In theory, Christendom seemed to incorporate many nations under one God, with the spread of Christianity's monotheism creating one holy empire. But in practice, when more or less secular nations were carved out of that empire, each had its version of a tutelary deity: instead of one God who spoke Latin, the French God spoke French, the German God spoke German, the English God spoke English (with an Oxbridge accent), and the U.S. God spoke English (with a southern accent). Nonetheless, these nations were still under recognizably the same God, despite his various linguistic, cultural, and national manifestations—the God of the West—and he was differentiated from the pagan deities of the East. (There are further differentiations: recently, Christian countries seem to recognize their God more readily in Israel than in the Muslim world, contributing to the mutual Western-Arab distrust.) My point is that the persistence of national identity formations around some version of divinity has continued in the framing of the modern nation, and not just as a faint relic, and until we unmask the monotheistic commitments of nationalism, we will be hard-pressed to understand such seeming conundrums as the violence stemming from Islamic fundamentalism, the wars in South Africa and in Bosnia, and the proliferation of other violent clashes about identity commitments throughout the globe.

As it turns out, the founders and leaders of modern Israel itself have not thought about their new nation without invoking the ancient one. Their rhetoric is heavily laced with biblical citations. In his opening remarks in Middle East peace talks in Madrid in 1991, Yitzhak Shamir intoned the psalmist's "If I forget thee, O Jerusalem, let my right hand lose its cunning" and the haggadah's "Next year in Jerusalem," and he began with an assertion of the complete continuity between the biblical nation and the present one: "Distinguished co-chairmen, ladies and gentlemen, I stand before you today in yet another quest for peace, not only on behalf of the State of Israel, but in the name of the entire Jewish people, that has maintained an unbreakable bond with the Land of Israel for almost 4,000 years [he is dating the birth of Israel to Abraham]. . . . For us, the ingathering of Jews into their ancient homeland, their integration in our society and the creation of the necessary infrastructure are at the very top of our national agenda."[2] The ancient homeland blurs into the national agenda. And because the Bible did not think to specify the establishment of the modern state of Israel explicitly, reading such nationalism into it requires specially tinted lenses. These lenses have been tinted not so much by religious interpretation—many orthodox Jews hold that the New Jerusalem is utopian and the "return" will be ushered in only by the messianic age—as by nineteenth-century German philosophy and historicism. And the presuppositions of those disciplines were, in turn, forged in the climate of German nationalism. Reading biblical narratives through the lenses of German nationalism helped to disseminate notions of modern nationalism (supposedly authorized by holy writ) that—with tragic irony—can inform the modern nation of Israel. But holy writ is not definitive about either the meaning of a nation or its desirability; hence, it is difficult to use as a weapon in Middle East conflicts.

As for scripture authorizing politics, first we have to specify who authorizes scripture in whose interests and what is this "scripture" that is so authorized. I may as well confess at the outset that my lenses have been tinted epistemologically by contemporary approaches to history rather than by the nineteenth-century German historicism that forged biblical scholarship, and that they are tinted politically by a deep suspicion of exclusive national identities.

The Bible has been authorized by the West, then, not only as a spiritual guide and a handbook of truth, but also as a manual for politics. As though all this authorizing of scripture doesn't make biblical interpretation hazardous enough, the authority attached to the Bible has also bled onto the discipline of biblical studies and the political assumptions that have formed it. Biblical scholarship is preoccupied with history—not the same history that the Bible constructs, but a history that the Bible offers clues to, the political and religious history of the ancient Near East. I think it is crucial to make distinctions between those projects, that is, to make distinctions between the writing of history in the Bible and the writing of history in biblical scholarship, especially because they are so often, and so dangerously, blurred. Dangerously, because confusing beliefs that are read into biblical narratives with a positivist historian's understanding of "real events" can turn what should be the founding fictions of Western culture which demand critique into "facts" that seem formidably unassailable. Dangerously, because the German historicism that gave birth to biblical scholarship is no mere positivism (as if there were such a thing); rather, every archeologist's spade and every philologist's verb ending is deeply inscribed with politics. Dangerously, because that very politics, once read into the Bible through the backdoor of something as seemingly innocent as historical-critical scholarship, can offer people "evidence" for justifying the oppression of other people. It is too late in the day and our understanding of narrative is too advanced to allow any pernicious notions of "biblical truth"—including those of biblical higher criticism—to continue to stick.

NATIONALISM IN THE DISCIPLINE

"Traditional history," as Michel Foucault characterizes it, "retracing the past as a patient and continuous development," strikes me as an apt description of the major pursuit in biblical studies for the past two centuries. The project that has dominated the field is the historical reconstruction of the biblical text. As de Wette prescribed in the nineteenth century, "the subject matter of biblical introduction is the history of the Bible."[3] This project is marked, first, by its quest for origins: the origin of a given passage, the origin of a cultic practice, the original setting of the text. Next, it includes a deep commitment to charting development, whether the formation of the text (what is the extent of the documents attributed to the J and E writers and when did they come together?), the development of the ancient Israelite religion (what are the earliest signs of Yahwism?), or the development of political organizations in ancient Israel (how did the tribal confederacy become a monarchy?).[4] Much biblical scholarship has been devoted to ascertaining sources—even though the Bible has unhelpfully obscured its sources—and many of the historical reconstructions of ancient Israel have been markedly teleological—even though the Hebrew Bible depicts a history that stubbornly resists any notion of fulfillment or completion.[5] If quantitatively the One can suggest scarcity, temporally it suggests linear development, with a single imagined goal. In contrast, a temporal version of multiplicity would include multiple moments, implying discontinuities and ruptures. Even when the Bible embraces multiplicity and even when its version of history is marked by disruptions, biblical scholarship, informed by the nineteenth-century predilection for development, has insisted upon establishing continuity.

These projects have their own history. In the nineteenth-century, historical-critical biblical scholarship saw itself as part of a larger Germanic historiographic tradition. Among other scholars, Robert Oden has recently asserted that this is not just a question of influence; "rather, the broader historiographic tradition shared the same methods, the same goals, the same prejudices, and the same world of understanding as biblical scholarship."[6] The chief assumptions of that tradition—that history charts development, that its focus should be the development of the nation (the German nation in particular), and that the nation should be understood as an individual entity with its own unfolding spirit, its own internal laws of development—will govern biblical interpretation. The influential historian Johann Gustav Droysen summarizes the thought: "'The moral world, ceaselessly moved by *many ends,* and finally, . . . by the *supreme end,* is in a state of restless development and of internal elevation and growth.' . . . With every advancing step in this *development* and *growth,* the historical understanding becomes wider and deeper" (my emphasis).[7] And when he writes of the idea of a "divine order," of "God's rule of the world," he adds the insistence that a divine plan is working itself out in Prussia in particular.[8]

Droysen's philosophy of history is indebted to that of Wilhelm von Humboldt, who may sound at first surprisingly at odds with the prevailing notions of coherence and continuity. "What is apparent," he writes in "On the Task of the Writer of History," "is scattered, disconnected, isolated," but then he explains that it is the historian's task to take what is "apparent" and show the hidden coherence: the historian "takes the scattered pieces he has gathered into himself and work[s] them into a whole."[9] This theme of "cohesive-hidden-order-that-informs-seeming-chaos" soon came to design a very special consistency from the seemingly chaotic Bible. For just as Humboldt and Droysen discovered that the inner logic in the randomness of events is the course of national development, so for the founder of biblical higher criticism, Julius Wellhausen, the inner logic of the Bible became the development of ancient Israel. With history called on to narrate the ideals of the German nation, its various "progresses"—moral, military, political, religious—and the story of ancient Israel written by historians who were also thinking about, even writing, the story of Germany, it is no wonder that the two stories were often confused. All that development so faithfully outlined in the growth of the German nation was easily, too easily, found in the growth of ancient Israel.

We can see this confusion at work in Wellhausen's introduction to his magisterial *Prolegomena to the History of Ancient Israel:* "It is necessary to trace the succession of the three elements [the Jehovist, the Deuteronomic, and the Priestly] in detail, and at once to test and to fix each by reference to an independent standard, namely, the inner development of the history of Israel."[10] With this commitment to charting such "inner development," he cannot help but find it. Familiar nineteenth-century organic metaphors govern his discourse: innate tendencies "grow," a seed "flowers" into a nation. The metaphors he uses to discuss his theory of the literary composition of the Books of Judges, Samuel, and Kings, are symptomatic:

> We are not presented with tradition purely in its original condition; already it is overgrown with later accretions. Alongside of an older narrative a new one has sprung up, formerly independent, and intelligible in itself, though in many instances of course adapting itself to the former. More frequently the new forces have not caused the old root to send forth a new stock, or even so much as a complete branch; they have only nourished parasitic growths; the earlier narrative has become clothed with minor and dependent additions. To vary the metaphor, the whole area of tradition has finally been uniformly covered with an alluvial deposit by which the configuration of the surface has been determined.[11]

He shifts from the metaphor of a plant with a new branch to a plant that has only parasitic growths; next it is overgrown with accretions, and then he dresses it (the plant wears "minor and dependent" clothes), only to proceed to drop the plant altogether to opt for geologic history; now the biblical text comprises layers of alluvial deposits, and presumably scholars can take out their spades and dig right through it. Whether as the growth of an organism or the accretion of geologic deposits, this is the picture of history that he quickly applies not only to the development of the text, but to its plot, that is, to the biblical narrative's own account of history. Deftly, almost without our noticing, the story of Germany becomes the story of Israel.

Finding this presupposition of development in one too many places, I frankly began to be suspicious. If biblical scholars reconstructed the *text* that way because the whole discipline of textual studies (including philology) was permeated by the assumptions of German historicism, so be it.[12] But how did they find that development in, say, the story of David, when that story is so marked by discontinuity and ideological conflict? How were biblical scholars going to reconcile the drive for finding continuity and development with this messy tale? They did it by fragmenting the narrative, by chopping it up into different documents, first into big pieces, then into smaller ones, and when they were finished, they had taken the amorphous, heterogeneous story we have been given and separated it into strands, each governed by the predictable criteria of development and continuity. Here is just one of the prominent source theories: a historian or historical school wrote a large strand of the biblical story according to the coherent principle that Israel's fate was determined by its responses to the law. It is rewarded for obedience and punished for disobedience. One version has it that this part was written in exile, from the point of view of a collapsed hope for a nation of Israel, as an explanation of that failure.[13] Still, amid all of the stories describing the failures of Israel, there was also a recognizable drive to idealize David, and this contradiction, between the pessimism of the account and the optimism about David, is resolved by separating the documents. To retain coherence, one document must espouse one conviction (that Israel is continually going astray from the law and must be punished for its sins) and the other document must espouse another (that David is the ideal of kingship and kingship is the ideal for Israel).

To a surprising degree (surprising because most of us assume that these decisions about sources were based only on linguistic data), the criterion of a consistent sympathy or idea or the plot continuity of a narrative, whether pro- or anti-monarchy, pro- or anti-David, or pro- and anti- whoever or whatever the critic chooses to focus on, has been a determining factor in separating strands of narrative and ascribing them to different authors. Sources have even been named for the character the biblical writer ostensibly sympathizes with— the "Saul source," the "Samuel source"—and when two basic sources did not resolve all the contradictions, more narrative strands had to be isolated to account for them, and when these were not named for a character, they were named for a continuous thread in the plot; hence, we have the "ark narrative," or "the rise of David narrative." Note how blithely the erudite scholar who wrote the impressively learned Anchor Bible commentaries on 1 and 2 Samuel can take for granted in his introduction that *his* demand for coherence is also felt by his readers: "Numerous internal thematic tensions, duplications, and contradictions stand in the way of a straightforward reading of the story." What does he mean by a "straightforward" reading of the story? Whether he is suggesting that reading forward and reading straight means reading straight for the goal, reading for development, or he is defining "straightforward reading" in his sentence tautologically to mean the kind of reading we do when there are no "thematic tensions, no duplications or contradictions" (and I know of no such reading), he sets out to rectify the problem, rewriting the Bible into coherent stories, and the difficult one we have in our Bible is either neglected or, worse still, "solved." Along the way, central ideological conflicts are ironed out, a leveling that has long and wide cultural repercussions.

NATIONS IN THE BIBLE

Michel Foucault distinguishes traditional history from "effective *[wirkliche]* history." If traditional history is devoted to searching out sources, establishing continuity, finding resemblances, and charting development, "effective history" turns to ruptures and discontinuities, to disrupting the fictions of unity and coherence, and to breaking the commitment to seeking origins and ends. "History becomes 'effective' to the degree that it introduces discontinuity into our very being—as it divides our emotions, dramatizes our instincts, multiplies our body and sets it against itself. 'Effective' history deprives the self of the reassuring stability of life and nature, and it will not permit itself to be transported by a voiceless obstinacy toward a millennial ending. It will uproot its traditional foundations and relentlessly disrupt its pretended continuity. This is because knowledge is not made for understanding; it is made for cutting."[14]

The Hebrew Bible can be read as depicting history as a series of ruptures in which various identities are cut and recut, formed, broken, and reformed, rather than as a continuous process in which a unified entity called Israel develops. We saw that, in Genesis 15, Abraham is told to cut three animals in half for that mysterious covenant ceremony in which fire passes between the pieces while the Lord promises the patriarch a future nation.

> When the sun had set and darkness had fallen, a smoking fire pot, a blazing torch, appeared and passed between the pieces. On that day, the Lord made a covenant with Abram and said, "To your descendants I give this land, from the river of Egypt to the great river, the Euphrates—the land of the Kenites, Kenizzites, Kadmonites, Hittites, Perizzites, Rephaim, Amorites, Canaanites, Girgashites, and Jebusites." (Gen 15:17–21)

Did that cutting create Israel's identity or destroy it? Or both? Animals are not the only entities severed here. Abraham's descendants are to be separated from their home, "sojourners in a land not theirs," as a stage of the process of creating a new home, and yet Yahweh will threaten that Israel's inheritance, the new home, will be cut off. Israel is already "cut off" in that it is separated from the other nations; that separation is defining, and it means that not Israel, but its enemies have been "cut off" before it (2 Sam 7:9). Other forms of rupture characterize this history. *Cutting* is joined to an emphasis on *tearing away* and *breaking,* and what is broken is not always Israel's enemies, nor, for that matter, is it always Israel. When David defeats the Philistines, he rejoices that Yahweh has "broken through" his enemies, comparing this bursting or breaking to the breaking of waters (2 Sam 5:20). The comparison of defeating enemies to breaking waters can be read as an allusion to the defeat of the Egyptian pursuers and the separation of waters at the Exodus. Israel is formed by such breaking. But in another kind of internal rending, the kingdom is torn away from King Saul, and the metaphor is theatricalized in the story of Saul tearing Samuel's cloak in a desperate attempt to hold on to his, and hence divine, favor.

> As Samuel turned to leave, Saul caught hold of the edge of his
> cloak, and it tore. Samuel said to him, "The Lord has torn the
> kingdom of Israel from you today and has given it to one of
> your neighbors—to one better than you." (1 Sam 15:27–28)

Later, the kingdom is torn away from King Solomon as it was torn
from King Saul (1 Kings 11:11–13), but in this instance, we are told
that for the sake of King David all of it is not torn away. But if "for
David's sake" means not cutting off Israel from divine favor here,
elsewhere David is told that the sword will never be far from his
house (2 Sam 12:10). I rapidly enumerate some of the ruptures in
the story of Israel, ruptures that the language of cutting so overtly
signals,[15] because they run counter to that strong drive in biblical
scholarship to read that history as portraying a seamless development
of entities, the people and the nation.

One version of "development" that has been ascertained frequently in the books of Samuel is the "rise of David" (and with it,
the rise of the *nation* of Israel), and the corollary demise of the mad
King Saul (and with it, the dissolution of Israel's provisional status
as a prenational confederacy of tribes). Supposedly, Saul's paranoia,
ineffectuality, and estrangement from Yahweh deepen as David's political astuteness, military success, and favor from Yahweh develop.
But more sensitive biblical scholars have noted that the depiction of
Saul can be viewed as more difficult than a progressive demise, and
David is not always on the rise.[16] It is instructive to look at the curiously contradictory exchange in which David's power (i.e., Israel's)
is made secure by God: the oracle by the prophet Nathan that David
will have a secure dynasty, a permanent House. First, to set the stage:
David has been enjoying a brief period of peace, he has successfully
taken over the house of Saul, he has been made king of both the
north and the south and is at rest from his battles, and he would like
to build a house for God in Jerusalem, the city of David. Israel could
hardly be more stable, more unified, or its identity more secure. The
response comes from the Almighty: "*You* want to build *me* a house?"
(the pronouns are emphatic). David is reminded that he is not God's
patron; God is *his* patron. But then, after Yahweh corrects David on

this score, clearly *limiting* the sphere of his influence, he proceeds to *expand* his power. In this conflicting message, it sounds as though David's ambition is simultaneously rebuked and rewarded.

> The Lord says, You want to build me a house? I haven't lived in a house from the day I brought up the Israelites until this very day! Instead I've gone about in a tent wherever I happened to go throughout Israel. Did I ever speak with one of the staff-bearers of Israel whom I appointed to shepherd my people Israel and say, "Why haven't you built me a house of cedar?" . . . I took you from the sheep pasture to be prince over my people Israel. I was with you wherever you went, clearing all your enemies from your path. And I shall make you a name like the names of the nobility of the land. I shall fix a place for my people Israel and plant it, so that it will remain where it is and never again be disturbed. (2 Sam 7:5–10)

In this passage, God clearly suggests that the idea of a House, of permanence, of stability, is considerably less attractive than nomadism, than moving about in a tent, and yet he offers David a house as though it were desirable indeed. The promise of a House is far from an unequivocally welcome one. We could probably wrench our imaginations into some resolution of this conflict—certainly many scholars have separated the account into independent strands so that there is no contradiction left—but the price would be the elimination of one of those key conflicts in the Bible: the tension between, on the one hand, a nostalgia for an Israel that is not fixed and not "like the nations," nostalgia for a period of wandering, for associating tent dwelling with godliness and moral rectitude, and on the other hand, the longing for stability, for landed property, a standing army, even for a dynastic leadership, in short, for becoming a nation among the nations. This "dialectical struggle between antiroyalism and royalism persists throughout the course and formative career of the Old Testament as its structuring force. It sets the tent against the house, nomadism against agriculture, the wilderness against Canaan, wandering and exile against settlement, diaspora against the political integrity of a settled state."[17]

Only four chapters later, someone other than Yahweh will also refuse the offer from David to take up residence in a house. Israel is at war when Bathsheba's husband, Uriah the Hittite, is called back from the front by King David in an effort to cover up his adultery with the now pregnant Bathsheba. But Uriah will not sleep with his own wife. He reminds the king of Israel that

> the ark, and Israel, and Judah, dwell in tents, and my master Joab, and the servants of my master, are camping out in the open field; and I, shall I go into my house to eat and drink and to sleep with my wife? As you live and as your soul lives, I will do no such thing. (2 Sam 11:11)

No endorsement of dynasty, the passage casts a dark shadow upon the earlier promise of a stable House of Israel. Everyone else has rallied to the field to meet the enemy—only David dwells in a house.

> At the turn of the year, the time when kings go campaigning, David sent Joab and with him his own guards and the whole of Israel. They massacred the Ammonites and laid siege to Rabbah. David, however, remained in Jerusalem. (2 Sam 11:1)

And it is while he stays in that house that he commits adultery and subsequently orders the murder of Uriah, thereby, among other things, undoing that divine promise of permanence and stability to his dynasty and ultimately to Israel.

> Next morning David wrote a letter to Joab and sent it by Uriah. In the letter he wrote, "Station Uriah in the thick of the fight and then fall back behind him so that he may be struck down and die." Joab, then besieging the town, posted Uriah in a place where he knew there were fierce fighters. The men of the town sallied out and engaged Joab; the army suffered casualties, including some of David's bodyguard; and Uriah the Hittite was killed too. . . . When Uriah's wife heard that her

husband Uriah was dead, she mourned for her husband. When
the period of mourning was over, David sent to have her
brought to his house; she became his wife and bore him a son.
But what David had done displeased Yahweh. (2 Sam
11:14–27)

Cover-ups do not succeed very well when there is an omniscient
deity around. Henceforth, the nation is rent with civil strife, and the
prophet who guaranteed that David's house would be forever secure
now prophesies that the sword will never be far from David's House.
Perhaps a dynasty, a House, was a bad idea after all. Furthermore,
perhaps these narratives are not simply preoccupied with the nation
or its king *amassing* power because they are ambivalent about power.
Even as Israel tries to become "like the nations," it deplores that
very project as pernicious, for Israel depends for its identity on its
distinctiveness, on being drawn "from the nations."

DEFINING ISRAEL

Conflicting approaches to power are symptomatic of Israel's conflicting self-definitions, conflicting because what we call "the Bible"
is the site of struggles that took place between widely different fac-
tions with different political and religious interests over hundreds of
years, conflicting because corporate identity is never single or stable,
and conflicting because narratives themselves are conflicting according to everything we know about storytelling. And so, in the
course of biblical narratives, the institution of monarchy itself is presented from widely divergent points of view, often broadly drawn.
How can the narrative depict the development of the monarchy
when it is unsettled about what monarchy is, let alone what the
nation is, and what it means for this entity called a nation to be ruled
by this other entity called king, let alone what kind of power these
entities should or should not have. Rather than presupposing settled
answers, these stories seem to me to be intently interested in exploring such questions of definition. Is a king a tyrant who will
enslave the people and seize their property, as the judge/prophet/

priest Samuel (what is Samuel anyway?) warns them in his stirring testimonial against the abuses of kingship? If so, why does the same Samuel who delivers this scathing critique against monarchy anoint not one king, but two?

> He will take your sons and assign them to his chariot and cav-alry, and they will run before his chariot. He will appoint for himself captains of thousands and captains of hundreds from them. They will do his plowing, harvesting, and grape-gathering and make his weapons and the equipment of his chariotry. Your daughters he will take as perfumers and cooks and bakers. Your best fields and vineyards and olive groves he will take and give to his servants. Your seed crops and vine crops he will tithe to provide for his officers and servants. Your best slaves, maidservants, cattle, and your asses he will take and use for his own work; and your flocks too he will tithe. You yourselves will become his slaves. Then you will *cry out* because of the king you have chosen for yourselves. (1 Sam 8:11–18, my emphasis)

The Israelites had "cried out" in Egypt, groaning under slavery to Pharaoh, and the promised land was promised to offer hope of deliverance from such unbridled tyranny, certainly not to reenact their enslavement. But, at the height of Israel's peace and prosperity, when the proverbial milk and honey were flowing, King Solomon married—is it possible?—a daughter of Pharaoh. Shortly after his adultery, David himself had set a captured population to work as slave laborers—brickmaking to be precise—like the Israelites in Egyptian bondage. Is this why Israel's liberator, Moses, is a quasi-Egyptian?[18] To suggest that Israel is not simply delivered *from* Egypt, but fundamentally delivered *to* Egypt? How could Israel become Egyptianized when from its inception it is the antithesis?[19]

On yet another level, the biblical story has trouble keeping its agenda straight. If we thought it was preoccupied with the serious business of political and military history, the rise (or whatever that is) of monarchy (whatever it is), the narrative is interrupted by disturbing sex scenes like the story of David taking Bathsheba when he

spots her bathing from his roof, or Amnon raping his half-sister. Do
the struggles for Israel's definition have anything to do with these
sexual scenes? The way in which these scenes are carefully interwoven with political events would indicate that they must: the narrative about David and Bathsheba is surrounded by accounts of war
with the Ammonite enemy (2 Sam 10–12). Immediately after describing the Israelite victory over the Ammonites, the narrative turns
to the rape of Tamar, which is followed by Absalom's murder of the
rapist (his elder half-brother and heir to the throne), and civil war
rends the nation (2 Sam 10–20). Simply put, Israel is threatened from
without and within and in the very midst are acts of adultery, rape,
and incest. This is no accident. Israel's war with the Ammonites is a
war of definition, the sexual violations are tests of definition, for in
both, Israel's borders—who constitutes Israel and who does not—
are at stake.

But how can we account for the persistent figuring of national
politics in sexual terms, from the chastity of a virgin queen (Elizabe-
than England's preferred trope) to the barbarian hordes' rape of the
countryside (the Russian version of the Mongol takeover)? Is this
figuration a vestige of dynastic monarchies that were in fact constructed upon exchanges of women, of political marriages that did
historically configure and reconfigure nations and empires? Or is the
explanation less historical and more psychoanalytic, that we figure
the body politic in the image of our sexuality, and make our larger
institutions recapitulate our sexual dramas? Or is the explanation
theological? After all, the punishment that the Lord decrees against
David for his adultery returns to the crime he committed and inten-
sifies it, describing Israel's political identity by prescribing its sexual
relations.

> Thus says the Lord, "Behold, I will raise up evil against you
> out of your own house; and I will take your wives before your
> eyes, and give them to your neighbor, and he shall lie with
> your wives in the light of this sun. For you did it in secret; but
> I will do this thing before all Israel, and before the sun."
> (2 Sam 12:11–12)

That prediction is fulfilled when David's son Absalom sleeps with his father's concubines in what becomes a declaration of civil war.

Of the many kinds of explanation, certainly one is the way in which women figure in the political-economic system. There is no question that owning the sexual rights to a woman (or stealing them, as the case may be) confers power in patriarchy, and as this is overtly the case for marriage to the king's daughter or sexual intercourse with the king's concubines, it is no less the case for nonroyal sexual exchanges. Because exchanging women establishes power relations between men,[20] David's dominance over other men is signaled by both his military and his sexual conquests. Before David became king, he was a fugitive from the jealous King Saul, and he turned for provisions to a man he had previously protected, but the man refused to acknowledge his obligation to him, framing this refusal as a denial of David's very identity.

> Who is David? Who is the son of Jesse? There are many ser-
> vants nowadays who are breaking away from their masters.
> Shall I take my bread and my water and my meat that I have
> killed for my shearers, and give it to men who come from I
> do not know where? (1 Sam 25:10–11)

In an unsubtle commentary on his poor judgment, the man is named Nabal, or Fool. David decides to show him who he is by destroying Nabal and his entire household, but before he can, this test of David's identity, power, and his right to the throne takes an interesting turn. The way the story unfolds, David does not kill Nabal (who conveniently drops dead just to hear of David's threat to him); instead, David takes Nabal's wife. The power gain is presumably equivalent. Fool's wife, Abigail, readily acknowledges David's power and colludes in her own exchange, engaging in a seduction that is entirely political, or should I say, politics is her seduction?

> And when the Lord has done to my lord according to all the
> good that he has spoken concerning you, and has appointed
> you prince over Israel . . . and when the Lord has dealt well
> with my lord, then remember your handmaid. (1 Sam 25:
> 30–31)

David remembers right away and marries her.[21]

Later, when David takes another man's wife, Bathsheba, he does not need her. He is no fugitive. Rather, he is at the height of his power, king of all he surveys, including Bathsheba. She is still the property of another man, in fact, two other men have rights to her before David, as the careful inclusion of her patronym (so rare for women in the Bible) "daughter of Eliam" reminds us. Her husband, Uriah the Hittite, is a loyal servant of the king, and moreover, a loyal servant of God. His name, *'ûriyyāhû,* probably means "Yahweh is my light," and we might well wonder what a Hittite, one of Israel's Others, is doing with such a name; moreover, he is fighting Israel's holy war while David lolls about at home during "the time when kings go to war." The way King David takes Bathsheba contrasts with the way David garnered power and women as a fugitive. In fact, the roles of Nabal and David have reversed. The king is greedy as Nabal had been, and he denies his neighbor what is rightfully his, as Nabal had denied David hospitality. Now David is the fool.

When Nathan the prophet tells David a didactic parable about the rich man taking the poor man's only ewe lamb, he drives home the point that the king's adultery is also a violation of a property right: Bathsheba is compared to an animal, a favored animal, to be sure, one that is like a daughter (alluding to the Hebrew wordplay on Bathsheba's name, *bat* = daughter), and the only one the poor man has; but the polluting of his woman is analogous to the slaughter of his animal. This calls to mind the rather appalling formulation reached by Claude Lévi-Strauss that the "exchange of brides is merely the conclusion to an uninterrupted process of reciprocal gifts [from, say, wine to animals to women], which effects the transition from hostility to alliance, from anxiety to confidence, and from fear to friendship [between tribes]."[22] But when women are stolen, rather than peaceably exchanged, all of the relational directions reverse, toward fear, anxiety, and hostility. In the Bathsheba story, the consequence of stealing another's wife is the murder of a loyal servant of the king. As we have seen, chaos ensues—"you have killed with the sword so the sword will never be far from your House"—and the death of a child born of such infraction is overdetermined. The biblical division of the universe into pure and impure further suggests that we understand adultery as adulteration. A recent study makes the etymological connection explicit: "Adulteration implies pollution, contamination, a 'base admixture,' a wrong combination. . . . If society depends for its existence on certain rules governing what may be combined and what should be kept separate, then adultery, by bringing the wrong things together in the wrong places, (or the wrong people in the wrong beds) offers an attack on those rules, revealing them to be arbitrary rather than absolute."[23] Adultery not only challenges the *rules* as arbitrary, it also challenges the precarious identity of a society that depends upon them for definition. Hence, we should not be surprised that vigorous laws on adultery are invoked to police Israel's borders. According to Deuteronomy, the child of the adulterer cannot be admitted into "the Congregation of the Lord, even to the tenth generation" (Deut 23:3), that is, such a child is banned forever from the people of Israel. The rabbis even relate the Hebrew term for illegitimate child, *māmzēr,* to the adjective *zār,* "a stranger," an "alien."[24]

All of this anxiety about identity, political and sexual definition, has been succinctly summarized in that one biblical word: *nābāl.* It not only means fool, but also outcast, someone who has severed himself from society through a moral transgression, someone who has forfeited his place in society by violating taboos that define the social order. As a verb, it means "to violate," and it is used especially to indicate sexual violations: the rape of Tamar, the rape of Dinah, the rape of the Levite's woman in Judges 19, adultery in Jeremiah 23. It is also used, significantly, to indicate uttering false words, thereby disrupting the order of language. Its Akkadian stem was used to indicate breaking away (as a stone) or tearing away, and that ancient Akkadian sense of rupture is still attached to the Hebrew word used for an adulterer in ancient Israel where sexual violation signals rupturing or breaking away from the norm. A variant of *nābāl* means corpse, and in ancient Israel, a corpse represents another rupture, not only from the social order, but from the order of life itself. Death represents the strongest degree of uncleanness, an "irreparable separation from God's life-giving power and from the centre of life, the cult,"[25] and the outcast is not so very far from the corpse, for as bearers of evil, the outcasts of society not only have no home, but "no name" (Job 30:8). The Book of Job offers a Lear-like description of their pitiful undoing.

> They used to gnaw the roots of desert plants,
> and brambles from abandoned ruins;
> and plucked mallow, and brushwood leaves,
> making their meals off roots of broom.
> Outlawed from the society of men,
> who, as against thieves, raised hue and cry against them,
> they made their dwellings on ravines' steep sides,
> in caves or clefts in the rock.
> You could hear them wailing from the bushes,
> as they huddled together in the thistles.
> Their children are as worthless as they were,
> Nameless people, outcasts of society.
>   (Job 30:3–8)

Who is a *nābāl* and who is not, what makes one cast out and another not, is of course another way of asking who is an Israelite and who is not, what is Israel and what is not, for the outcasts define Israel's borders. While it is not made an explicit appellation in the Bathsheba episode, the term is most consistently used for an adulterer, and it is explicit in the episode that follows David's adultery, where his son Amnon rapes Tamar, echoing David "taking" Bathsheba. Conforming to that other sense of *nābāl*, corpse, the rapist/ adulterer/outcast Amnon is murdered, and even his death is engulfed in an ever widening circle of violence, moving from his brother (Absalom who murders him and is murdered) to the entire family (the civil war, usurpations, assassinations of the kings of Judah, and eventually the forced exile of the population). Violence attends each instance in the Bible where *nābāl* signals a sexual violation: in Genesis, the rape of Dinah causes a massacre; in Judges, the rape of the concubine precipitates war within Israel. In both cases these acts of violence are acts of definition, fought to ascertain and to kill the outcast, and thereby to define Israel.

What Tamar says of her rapist becomes an indirect indictment of David: "this is not a thing men do in Israel." At his height, when the House of David is synonymous with the nation, David behaves like an outcast. But how can the House of David both define Israel and be cast out of Israel? What happens to the promise of a House that will be stable forever when its recipient is a *nābāl*, like the no-name homeless ones?

This is not a thing men do in Israel, but David *is* Israel. Apparently, the Israelite is not only defined by the outcast; the Israelite also defends himself with such ferocity against the outcast from fear of the violator within. *Nēbālîm* is used for Israel's enemies, the generic "other," but it is also used for an Israelite tribe, the Benjaminites, when they make themselves the enemies of Israel's other tribes, and the term *outcast* is applied to all of Israel itself (Deut 32:6).

The meaning of *nābāl* deepens when we view David's act of adultery with Bathsheba not only in the light of the exchanges that characterize his other marriages or the violence set in motion by his rapist son, but in the light of the much larger issue of faithlessness that pervades biblical thought. "I am a jealous God, you will have none but me." When sexual practices are called upon to describe national politics, they pass through a third category in the Bible, *transcendence.* And this subsuming of sex and politics to divinity, along with the complex historical afterlife of that theological nexus, helps to account for their persistent association in culture. Monotheistic theology is obsessed with the possibility and actuality of betrayal, with "going astray" as the term for both faithlessness to God and sexual transgression, and it is in that context that the king of Israel goes astray. Even within the Bathsheba story itself, desire for God and human desire are made analogues of one another, with David's adultery set in stark relief—not, as we would expect, to the fidelity of Bathsheba's husband to *her*—but as a foil to Uriah's faithfulness to *God.* Under the injunctions of holy war, to sleep with his own wife would be to be faithless to God; it is that fidelity—to God—that Uriah maintains through his sexual abstinence during holy war, despite the apparent attractiveness of his wife, despite being plied with wine by the king, and it is that fidelity—to God—that he finally dies for. Meanwhile David, so very careful about idolatry, has "gone astray" from God after all.

In his act of adultery, David has violated a whole string of commandments: "You shall not kill; you shall not commit adultery; you shall not steal; you shall not bear false witness against your neighbor." And just before the commandments about not killing, not having adultery, not taking what is your neighbor's, that is, laws regulating the social order, are the commandments that insist upon the exclusive desire for God. "You shall have no gods except me." An intimate relation between the final social commands that honor the neighbor and the earlier theological ones that specify love and loyalty toward God is thereby established. When the logic of "you shall love only me, you shall not love your neighbor's God" is translated into the social sphere, it becomes "you shall love only your wife, you shall not covet your neighbor's wife," and the two spheres become inseparable. Hence, in Yahweh's response to David's adultery with Bathsheba, it is not at all clear from his rhetoric whether David's chief guilt is betrayal of her husband or betrayal of God: "A sword will never be lacking in your house, because you treated *me* with contempt and took the wife of Uriah the Hittite to be your own wife." These infidelities, to God and to a husband, are one and the same. Furthermore, the violations of adultery, rape, and the people going astray are not just violations of commandments. They are also violations of various identity constructs of "Israel," and they become tests of definition in a text that is anxious about who this story is about, and whose story it is anyway.

Sexual fidelity and divine fidelity, monogamy and monotheism, are preoccupations of a narrative that tends to construct identity as someone or some people set apart, with boundaries that could be mapped, ownership that could be titled. But if, as I have been arguing, the parameters of Israel's identity are always very much at issue, if which God is allowed and which is not, and which woman is allowed and which is not is forever being contested, then the identity of the nation and the people is not already mapped, but in the process of being anxiously drawn and redrawn. We must then address the prior question: which people are outside and which are inside the boundaries of the community of Israel? *Is* this people set apart? Or is their hankering to "go astray" an effort to cross boundaries, or at least to blur them by being God's and being someone else's too.

The biblical narrative's effort to construct Israel's past may well be an effort to construct Israel, but this is not a German historian's project, not a construction in the sense of building a building, or a national spirit unfolding, or an organic personality flowering. Instead, the notion of "Israel" is an inconsistent, fractured, and multiple concept: a people who are bound by a law that they refuse to obey, a people who are defined by their nomadism but who are promised a land to settle in and embark on its conquest, a people who remember (or adopt) a shared history only to constantly forget it, a people who promise fidelity to their God only to go astray. And even these formulations are misleadingly stable, for each presupposes "a people" when defining them is very much a part of the task of this history. A Bible that suggests that identity is a question rather than an answer, provisional and not reified, fails to underwrite nationalism, imperialism, and persecutions of the Other, in part because it fails to make any clear claims about who the Other is. But if I have offered a more politically congenial Bible (for some) than the one the heirs of German historicism have given us, it is not an invitation to authorize it, for to seek such authority—even for the insight that history is ruptured and collective identity provisional—is, as I have tried to show, to seek foundations in shifting sand.

Chapter Five

INSCRIBING IDENTITY

MEMORY

I remember the time I knew what happiness was
Let the memory live again.
—Trevor Nunn and Andrew Lloyd Webber

Whenever I bring clouds over the earth and the bow appears in
the clouds, I will remember my Covenant between myself and
you and every living creature of every kind. And so the waters
shall never again become a flood to destroy all life.
—Genesis 9:14–15

Memory constructs identity. The biblical preoccupation with
memory (the various declensions of *zakhar* appear 169 times
in the Hebrew Bible),[1] the proliferation of narratives that record memories and the numerous explicit injunctions to remember
are all in the service of forging a community through the creation
of collective memory. In contrast to other group identity formations,

like the naturalism of kinship or the ownership of land, collective memory readily acknowledges its invented character. The coexistence of different versions of one narrative and of the varied, even conflicting, memories they purport to record make it futile to even pretend that there is a single verifiable "accurate" memory.

In practice, then, how do multiple narratives and their multiple memories generate communities? In his study of the transmission of memory, the social theorist Paul Connerton notes that "there is a striking disparity between the pervasiveness of social memory in the conduct of everyday life and the relatively scant attention . . . that has been paid to specifically *social* memory."[2] If memory is a conduit through time, how are collective memories passed on in social groups from one generation to the next? How are the borders of communities determined by means of memories, and what are the consequences for communities of determining, even fixing, the store of memories? Conversely, what causes memories to change, and how do these fluid memories alter the shape of communities? What impact do disparate memories have on a community when "it is an implicit rule that participants in any social order must presuppose a shared memory," and "to the extent that their memories of a society's past diverge, to that extent its members can share neither experiences nor assumptions."[3] What happens when the memories change, as they inevitably do? The Bible offers an unusual opportunity to explore these questions because it preserves the variations of oral traditions—fluid multiple memories—but it has also inscribed selected memories on scrolls and even tried to fix them in a canon. In short, the Bible has both proliferated memories and made claims to limit memories, and throughout, communities have been defined by these inclusions and exclusions.

First, the question of fixity. The past can either inspire or inhibit innovation in the present. When energy is devoted primarily to conservation of the past, it becomes a museum, a place where a bygone time is gawked at with alien eyes, or a mausoleum, a monument to the dead. When efforts are made to repeat the past identically, it becomes the object of parody; imitated in an inevitably changed context, the past becomes "retro." On the one hand, this means that the present is imperiled by efforts to fix time, and on the other hand, the past is treated with irreverence, converted to dust by the conservative instinct that would maintain it unchanged (like the crumbling wedding dress of Dickens's Miss Havisham, who demands that time stop, or the apple in hell that turns to ashes, which Milton's Satan, denying change, is condemned to reach for forever). In the end, efforts to fix memories violate the past rather than pay homage to it. We cannot do as our ancestors did because we are not our ancestors. To do as they did, we would need to displace them, in yet another form of violence toward the past. Although Heraclitus cautioned long ago that we cannot step in the same river twice, we continue to dam the river and to destroy it as flowing water.

While all this may seem obvious enough, it also seems logical that an impulse to defend the borders of a community would be accompanied by efforts to fix its memories. Surely, defining a group would entail isolating a set of its memories, possibly even refusing to add further ones that would confuse the group identity, and then making those select memories authoritative. Simply put, to define a group is to delimit its story. The more rigid the group identity, the more rigid its memories. Such a process would be more likely to take place when anxiety about group identity is at its height, either at its inception as it tries to separate and distinguish itself from parent identities or when the fear becomes palpable that its identity is threatened by outsiders. The process of biblical canonization took place in the latter climate: when ancient Israel had lost its national identity, it created a fixed narrative from what had been a fluid, evolving set of memories.

Exile induced a crisis, and one result of that crisis was that authority became attached to a set of narratives rather than to a geopolitical configuration. Thereafter the narratives, instead of the nation, became identity-defining. While this account greatly oversimplifies the process of the Bible's codification—a complex process that occurred in stages—scholars do concur that each time the biblical narratives assumed some definitive shape, it was in response to a devastating crisis. The first block of material came together at the Babylonian Exile, the next at the destruction of the Jerusalem Temple in

A.D. 70. Israel's efforts to consolidate its identity through narratives were defenses against, respectively, assimilation by Babylonia and absorption by Hellenization. Inevitably, then, the movement toward creating a canon entailed forging identity agonistically, against Others' memories and other memories. Like alternative identity formations that also prescribe inclusions by means of exclusions, the process was marked by a kind of violence. Because different communities authorized different books, leaving certain books out of the official store meant that the communities attached to them were left out, too.

The biblical canon, that is, should not be understood as the product of a peaceful consensus, but as the result of protracted struggles for authority between competing communities.[4] "Other Jewish parties in the first century had recognized other collections . . . but after the destruction of Jerusalem in 70 the Pharisaic party gradually won out and its collection came to be generally accepted."[5] The formation of the Christian biblical canon was equally contentious and even more protracted, with the status of Revelation and the Apocrypha under fierce debate as late as the Reformation. To judge from the frequency with which the question has been reopened, it seems that canonization, the delimiting of biblical narratives that was intended to separate the endorsed, official memories from others in order to demarcate the community, courted a palpable risk: closing the text against not just contemporary Others but the Others of the future, that is, of excluding future generations and their own (future) memories. Memories will not be fixed, and because they will not, when any community claims that "this is our memory and thou shalt have no other memories" it must do so coercively.

If efforts to fix the store of memories entail violence, allowing memories to change and to be fluid should, in theory, dissipate violence. Such fluidity suggests a plenitude of communal narratives rather than a limited supply, a "substantial archive" rather than a "closed corpus" as one scholar put it.[6] A closer look at the canonization process shows that revisions continued to be made and commentary continued to be inserted long after the supposedly definitive biblical canon was set. Debates continued into the second century about the canonicity of the Book of Esther, the Song of Songs, Ecclesiastes, Proverbs, and the Book of Ezekiel. The discovery of whole libraries at Qumran and Nag Hammadi demonstrates that no single collection had emerged as authoritative for all communities. Remarkably enough, in light of how frequently we use the term *Bible* as though it had a definitive meaning, no single collection has emerged as authoritative for all communities to this day: in broad terms, the Protestant, Catholic, and Jewish Bibles still differ, and in the practices of smaller communities, whole passages are discretely omitted from the store of available selections for Bible reading in liturgy. Further additions to Scripture are mandated by the idea of ongoing revelation: the Reformation included a call to reform the Scriptures; Mormonism added the *Book of Mormon,* Christian Scientists added *Science and Health.* When the game plan includes such ongoing adjustments to authentic inclusions, it becomes less clear who the winner is.

While one scholar argues that an antique historiographer and his school composed most of the biblical narrative after the exile,[7] many others concur that a span of more than a thousand years encompassed the complicated process of the development and interrelation of sources, adaptation, amalgamation, and editing, a process that, in turn, has been the subject of intensive study for more than two hundred years. As a distinguished Israeli scholar of the Qumran texts wrote, "A major problem to be investigated with regard to the history of the Bible text is not so much the existence of a limited plurality of text types, but rather the loss of other presumably more numerous textual traditions."[8] The multitude of books considered sacred along with the fluidity of books entering and exiting that status suggests that, as another has phrased it, "canon understood as process valorizes biblical pluralism."[9] If for some strands of postexilic Judaism the "biblical period" was considered a completed chapter in the history of Israel, there is evidence that at least one community, at Qumran, did not see it that way.

The Qumran Covenanters did not subscribe to the idea that the biblical era had been terminated, nor did they accept the

concomitant notion that "biblical" literature and literary standards had been superseded or replaced by new conceptions. It
appears that the very concept of a "canon of biblical writings"
never took root in their world of ideas, whatever way the term
"canon" is defined. Ergo, the very notion of a closing of the
canon was not relevant. This applies to the completion of the
canon of Scriptures as a whole, and also to the closure of its
major components. . . . Prophetic or quasi-prophetic "inspiration" continued to inform the leaders of the Qumran community, who did not subscribe to the rabbinic dictum that with
"the demise of the last prophets Haggai, Zechariah and Ma-
lachi inspiration had departed from Israel."[10]

This self-understanding as part of a continuum in an open line of
inspiration is not unique to the Qumran community. Inspiration did
not depart with the demise of the last biblical prophets, for there
were more prophets. Some have even argued that mainstream rabbinic Judaism did not make a clear-cut distinction between the authority of the Book and its subsequent interpretation, with the term
Torah referring both to the written and the ongoing oral law.[11] Illu-
mination became "a new mode of access to God for a new type
of community—formed around teachers and the texts which they
authoritatively interpret."[12] And in early Christianity, the teacher
who authoritatively interpreted the text was Jesus Christ.

REMEMBERING THE EXODUS

If, in theory, canonization was an effort to fix the boundaries of the
community, in practice both the community and its memories resisted such fixity. Furthermore, the very process of canonization was
at odds with the way even so-called canonized narratives assumed
shape: with their multiple and conflicting versions of memories, they
mock the notion of a single authoritative one. For instance, here is
an account of an "official" memory from the Hebrew Bible, one
that members of the community were explicitly asked to accept as
their own narrative in a ritual of bringing the offering of first fruits
to the sanctuary.

My father was a wandering Aramean. He went down into Egypt to find refuge there, few in numbers; but there he became a nation, great, mighty, strong. The Egyptians ill-treated us, they gave us no peace and inflicted harsh slavery on us. But we called on Yahweh the God of our fathers. Yahweh heard our voice and saw our misery, our toil and our oppression; and Yahweh brought us out of Egypt with a mighty hand and outstretched arm, with great terror, and with signs and wonders. He brought us here and gave us this land, a land where milk and honey flow. Here then I bring the first fruits of the produce of the soil that you, Yahweh, have given me. (Deut 26:5–10)

But this Deuteronomic version of the Exodus is only one among many. The Bible proliferates exodus memories, not privileging the version of just one community or even one generation. It includes the memory productions of disparate communities over many generations. The Exodus is remembered by those in exile, by those who return from exile to Jerusalem, by those in the Diaspora; and in the institution of the Passover, it is remembered by communities all over the world even today. While the Exodus is remembered as the familiar liberation from slavery in the passage above, elsewhere in the Bible, memories of escaping from Egypt blur into conquering Canaan. The exodus from bondage is remembered as a conquest of a new land.[13] The opening chapters of the Book of Joshua reawaken the memory of the exodus explicitly, casting it in that context of conquest. Instead of the Sea of Reeds, the waters of the river Jordan are now parted, and instead of the Israelites fleeing their oppressors on the dry ground, here the priests carry the ark of the covenant through the Jordan on dry ground. Throughout, the passage is self-consciously shaping a new memory that is intended to be rehearsed to future generations. Joshua tells twelve men:

"Pass on before the ark of Yahweh your God into mid-Jordan, and each of you take one stone on his shoulder . . . to make a memorial of this in your midst." . . . Then he said to the Israelites, "When your children in days to come ask their fathers,

'What is the meaning of these stones?' tell them this, 'You see the Jordan. Israel crossed over it dry-shod, because Yahweh our God dried up the waters of the Jordan in front of you until you had crossed just as Yahweh your God had done with the Sea of Reeds, which he dried up before us till we had crossed it; so that all the peoples of the earth may recognize how mighty the hand of Yahweh is, and that you yourselves may always stand in awe of Yahweh your God.'" (Josh 4:5–6, 21–24)

The emphasis in this memory is less on a flight to freedom than on attaining authority and power, qualities that are conferred upon Joshua as they were, not incidentally, upon Moses. Yahweh said to Joshua, "This very day I will begin to make you a great man in the eyes of all Israel, to let them be sure that I am going to be with you even as I was with Moses" (Josh 3:7). This memory insists that, both at the Jordan and at the Sea of Reeds, the might of Yahweh is the chief lesson to be told to future generations.

Jeremiah is as explicit as Joshua about forging a new memory. Faced with the destruction of the nation of Israel by the Assyrians, Jeremiah returns to the old emphasis on freedom from oppressors, but he is anxious to change the identity of the oppressors, to make the exodus less a memory of an event in the past, before Israel was a nation, than of an event taking place in his time, in which his people are saved from their current enemy. From his time forth, he insists, the exodus will be remembered as liberation from the north. Ironically, even as he advocates that a new narrative (of the present) replace the old one (of the past), he must invoke the resonance of the past to lend its power to his rhetoric.

So, then, the days are coming—it is Yahweh who speaks— when people will no longer say, "As Yahweh lives who brought the sons of Israel out of the land of Egypt!" but, "As Yahweh lives who led back and brought home the descendants of the house of Israel out of the land of the north and from all the countries to which he had dispersed them, to live on their own soil." (Jer 23:7–8)

In the first instance of the memory of the exodus that the Bible reader encounters, this preoccupation—not so much with the *event* of the Exodus as with how to *remember* it—is foregrounded. In the Book of Exodus, Moses asks Pharaoh to allow the Israelites to go, and Pharaoh responds by doubling their labor. But in turn Yahweh responds with plagues.

> I myself will harden Pharaoh's heart, and perform many a sign and wonder in the land of Egypt. Pharaoh will not listen to you and so I will smite Egypt and lead out my armies, my people, the sons of Israel, from the land of Egypt. (Ex 7:3–4)

Nine such "smitings" or plagues follow, escalating in intensity, but before the tenth and final plague, the death of the firstborn throughout Egypt—that is, before the decisive terror that inspires Pharaoh to relent—the narrative pauses in the midst of this suspenseful drama to prescribe the ritual of the Passover.[14] The Israelites have not yet crossed the Sea of Reeds in their escape from Egypt when the "memory" of that subsequent event is created.

> Keep this day in remembrance, the day you came out of Egypt, from the house of slavery, for it was by sheer power that Yahweh brought you out of it; not-leavened bread must be eaten. On this day, in the month of Abib, you are leaving Egypt. And so, in this same month, when Yahweh brings you to the land of the Canaanites, the Hittites, the Amorites, the Hivites, the Jebusites, the land he swore to your fathers he would give you, a land where milk and honey flow, you are to hold this service. . . . And on that day you will explain to your son, "This is because of what Yahweh did for me when I came out of Egypt." The rite will serve as a sign on your hand would serve, or a memento on your forehead, and in that way the law of Yahweh will be ever on your lips, for Yahweh brought you out of Egypt with a mighty hand. You will observe this ordinance each year at its appointed time. (Ex 13:3–5, 8–10)

Only then do the plagues resume, only then are the firstborn of Egypt killed, only then do the Israelites depart through the Sea of

Reeds (Ex 14). So pivotal is the place of memory in this narrative that a tradition about an event is fully elaborated before the event itself takes place. While the ritual that commemorates the event includes the resolution to fix each of its features in order to fix the memory, nonetheless, the exodus memory clearly remains open to innovations—for biblical writers, for later biblical interpreters, and for the living liturgy that continually commemorates it in a new key.

"Where the old ways are alive, traditions need be neither revived nor invented."[15] Perhaps the most stunning example of how very alive the exodus memory is for biblical writers can be found in Isaiah, where it is the *Egyptians* who are saved from oppression and subsequently become faithful followers of Yahweh.

> When in oppression the Egyptians cry to Yahweh he will send them a savior to protect and deliver them. Yahweh will reveal himself to them, and that day the Egyptians will acknowledge Yahweh and worship him. . . . Then, though Yahweh has struck the Egyptians harshly, he will heal them. They will turn to Yahweh who will listen to them and heal them. . . . That day, Israel, making the third with Egypt and Assyria, will be blessed in the center of the world. Yahweh Sabaoth will give his blessing in the words, "Blessed be my people Egypt, Assyria my creation, and Israel my heritage." (Is 19:20–25)

While such a triumph of Yahwism may not be so attractive from the Egyptian point of view, from the Israelite perspective the memory of an exodus filled with victims and victimizers is supplanted here by a projected new memory of universal blessings, complete harmony of vision and purpose, with all the attendant attractions and dangers of universalism.

How then is the exodus remembered? Which is the definitive account? Because this memory is not standardized, it has been reconfigured, adapted, and rewritten not only within disparate contexts in Judaism, but also in Christianity, where the transfiguration in Mark 9 depicts Moses with Elijah and Jesus on a mountaintop and the ritual of the "Lord's Supper" elaborates the Passover ritual (Mark 14). Later, Puritans would allude to the Exodus when they described crossing the sea to the New World; African-Americans would invoke the exodus as a paradigm for their quest for freedom from slavery; liberation theologians in Latin America would see their project as an exodus; and black South Africans would remember the exodus as a prophecy of liberation from white colonization.[16]

THE POLITICS OF MEMORY

Not only do politicians and theologians reconstruct these exodus memories, so too do critics and historians.[17] Their variations on the exodus theme are no more random than the biblical ones; each serves the distinctive political purposes of its appropriator. In his brief but powerful critique of the biblical stories of exodus and conquest, Robert Allen Warrior confesses that as a member of the Osage Nation of Native Americans who stands in solidarity with other tribal people around the world, he reads the exodus stories with Canaanite eyes, and he observes that the Canaanite side of the story has been largely overlooked by those seeking to articulate theologies of liberation—"especially ignored are those parts of the story that describe Yahweh's command to mercilessly annihilate the indigenous population."[18] Parts like the following:

> But you shalt utterly destroy them; namely, the Hittites and the Amorites, the Canaanites and the Perizzites, the Hivites and the Jebusites; as the Lord thy God hath commanded thee, that they teach you not to do after all their abominations. (Deut 20:17–18)

Edward Said has voiced a similar complaint in a review tellingly entitled "Michael Walzer's Exodus and Revolution: A Canaanite Reading." Walzer, he charges, barely mentions the Canaanites, and given his emphasis on the continuing political relevance of the exodus model, that omission serves to reinforce the invisibility of the Palestinians. Walzer, in turn, has his own ax to grind: expounding the exodus as a paradigm for revolutionary politics, he is grounding Labor Zionism in exodus thinking (in contrast to the right-wing fundamentalism grounded in messianism).

The political life of these biblical narratives is nothing new. When Oliver Cromwell addressed the first Parliament of his protectorate, he described the exodus as the "only parallel of God's dealing with us that I know in the world." Benjamin Franklin wanted the Great Seal of the United States to depict Moses, rod lifted, with the Egyptian army (British redcoats) drowning in the Red Sea (Atlantic). The question, then, is not can contemporary political life be forged with ancient memories? but *how* and *why?*[19] What are the echoes that those old memories carry with them into their contemporary setting? Must an allusion to the exodus inevitably invoke the specter of victims and victimizers or of freedom from oppression or of conquest, or the kind of uneasy universalism we find in Isaiah that imagines oppressors as converts—or none of the above? Can the memory be fully refigured? When Jeremiah advocates that the Exodus should be remembered, not as a defeat of Egypt, but a defeat of the enemy of the north, are we to understand that all new memories work like Jeremiah's, recalling the old ones despite themselves? After his own breathless survey of the exodus tradition, Jonathan Boyarin concludes insightfully that "the Exodus narrative is susceptible to both colonizing and liberationist readings, that the two variations are not often identified as such and that they are frequently mingled in the minds of readers. . . . Exodus was inherited by the shapers of modern imperialism and liberationism, used by many in their own projects and thereby passed on as their heritage to us."[20]

Meanwhile, biblical scholars have taken considerable trouble to uncover the history of the Israelite conquest/settlement in Canaan, that is, to uncover what really happened, historically, rather than simply accept the biblical narrative's account of things. And some of their accounts are considerably less odious. Most oppressed peoples would take heart, for instance, in the description of a revolution against oppressive overlords that has been elaborated by the biblical scholar Norman Gottwald.[21] And the attention being paid to "peaceful settlement" theories has its own attractions: in this version of the past, there is no violence at all, for the Israelites did not "arise in violent opposition to the culture of that age either by invasion or revolution."[22] Rather, the emphasis in this theory is on the religious and cultural continuity between Canaanites and Israelites.[23] For these "peaceful settlement" scholars, seeing the Israelites as really (that is, historically) Canaanites seems to make the narrative about their engaging in a massacre less troubling. But does it?

What does happen when a pivotal memory from an authoritative text is refigured by historians to tell either (1) a story of outsiders' peaceful settlement and intermingling, or (2) of an indigenous people's revolt against overlords, rather than the biblical story of conquering a people by outside invaders? There are problems implicit in posing that question. First, how was the real (historical) story— whatever it was—so completely misremembered in the biblical narrative? Why was it covered up? Why weren't the ways in which Canaanites were really Israelites made more explicit, or the success of the revolutionaries recorded, instead of the stories that have been handed down to us of the bloody conquest of one people by another? And if the process was so peaceful, how did this story of violent invasion come to be? Whom did it serve, when and why? Let us presume that answers to these questions were available, *definitively* available as the mysteries that are shrouded in the past can never be. But let us just surmise that some day some excavation will uncover documents that tell the true story of how the conquest story came about. We would learn why biblical traditions invented an account of seizing and murdering, we would see evidence of that invention—perhaps an earlier account that gave historical witness—and we would be given some rationale for this ideology of conquering, some reason why Israelites (or are they Canaanites?) would want to imagine themselves as external to the land, external to the Canaanites, and want to imagine slaughtering them (even though they were Canaanites themselves).[24] What then? If we did uncover the true story of Israel's "settlement" in Canaan—and notice how that phrase whitewashes the harsher language of "conquest theory"—and if we even unveiled the process by which it was distorted into the biblical story we have, how would that discovery alter our thinking? Here is one example of the complexity elaborated by Warrior: "If indeed the Canaanites were integral to Israel's early history, the Exodus narratives could reflect a situation in which indigenous peoples put their hope in a god from outside, were liberated from their oppressors, and then saw their story of oppression revised out of the new nation's history of salvation. They were assimilated into another people's identity and the history of their ancestors came to be regarded as suspect and a danger to the safety of Israel. In short, they were betrayed."[25]

What is really at stake here is the relation between history, politics, and culture. And that relation can never be transparent. Oppressed peoples write utopian myths of conquest. Peoples in exile write fantastic tales of land acquisition. But conquerors also celebrate their conquests, and empires describe their subject peoples as indeed subjected. If historical events give rise to narratives in complex ways, the historical afterlife of a given narrative is equally convoluted. The exodus has served two opposite rhetorical and political strategies: Cromwell's description of England's rebellion against monarchy and Dryden's justification for the restoration of monarchy. Just as a story's ideology is never discrete from its interpretations, so its interpretations are never separable from the events of history. One narrative (literary) blurs into another narrative (history). These narratives rewrite one another, altering emphases, changing contexts, shifting focus, substituting characters, times, and places. If from one perspective biblical typology opens its vast maw to ingest all the events of history, from another the ancient text is dismembered, rewritten, rethought, and relived in conditions that are distinct from one another and so utterly contingent upon their historical specificity that the mind reels at their comparison. Canaanites become Native Americans and Palestinians (but wait, Native Americans are not Palestinians); ancient Israelites (who were really Canaanites) become British Puritans, Black Africans, and Latin Americans. In practice, it seems that the narratives of history (and the agents driving them) adopt a particular version of a narrative of biblical literature with a particular political purpose. Christian crusaders against Islamic peoples may have adjusted the conquest of the Holy Land narrative to narratives about papal legitimacy and then forged identifications to serve preestablished political ends; for instance, the Muslim infidels became Canaanites. Puritans invoked the Exodus when they wanted to identify with oppressed Israelites, but then they used the conquest story to justify heartlessness toward Native Americans. But this account of the political uses of literature barely acknowledges the reverse causality: the way the narratives-in-literature have a decisive impact on the narratives-of-history. Our politics are not hammered out ex nihilo, but in the context of an entire cultural/political/historical inheritance.[26] The process of selecting, of legitimizing and identifying with narratives is itself part of the life and afterlife of narrative. As Steven Knapp has so aptly said, "Beyond the *causal* role they play in influencing people's dispositions, the narratives preserved by collective memory sometimes play a *normative* role—that is, they may in various ways provide criteria, implicit or explicit, by which contemporary models of action can be shaped or corrected, or even by which particular ethical or political proposals can be authorized or criticized."[27] The narratives forged by literature are brought to the table of ideological formations to negotiate, so to speak, with the narratives of history, and eventually the distinction between the narratives of literature and the narratives of history collapses.[28]

Note how ill-defined the relation between ideology and a theory of history is in the following remarks about the "peaceful settlement" theory: "What will be biblical theology's shape, as we now try to articulate it, and how will it affect our contemporary theology, ethics, [and politics]? Older models with stress on conflict and Israelite distinction *in some way undergirded* a salvation history biblical theology, which in turn *resonated with* dialectical theology" (my emphasis).[29]

In this wide wilderness of effects—stories spawning events, events distorted into stories *reflecting* some historical events and *forging* others (but how to discern which is which?)—we choose our focus. And amid this endless refracting, we might do well to pause and look again, not at historical clues to the historical narrative concerning the conquest—the Israelite four-room house, the collar-rimmed jar, or distinctive terracing—but at the biblical narratives of conquest and their political afterlife. Here is one such narrative.

> Yahweh your God will deliver them over to you and you will
> conquer them. You must lay them under ban. You must make

no covenant with them nor show them any pity. You must not marry with them: you must not give a daughter of yours to a son of theirs. . . . instead, deal with them like this: tear down their altars, smash their standing-stones, cut down their sacred poles, and set fire to their idols. (Deut 7:2–5)

This certainly sounds like Cowboys against Indians, Israel against Canaan, Us against Them, and it also sounds like a recommendation that the solution to the conflict is to murder the inhabitants and settle their land.

Undoubtedly, passages like this are more widely known and read, and hence they enjoy a broader political afterlife than any (albeit brilliant) biblical scholar's arcane theory, however politically palatable or historically plausible. But because biblical narratives have been granted authority, rewriting the historical story, whether as revolt, infiltration, or peaceful settlement, or nuancing the conquest itself may be too subtle to change its political effect in light of the vast influence the literary narratives of conquest have wielded and continue to wield. Perhaps instead of rewriting the *historical* narrative with versions that may allow us to feel better about it, we should reopen and rewrite the *biblical* narrative. This disturbing bit of our cultural inheritance alone has done powerful ideological work, reflecting and spawning a way of thinking about identity, about territory, about the Other, and about violence. But it never is alone. The narrative of conquest has been elaborated in Christianity, where it has been universalized and spiritualized; in Islam, where it has been fundamentalized; it has been coopted by nationalism, where it has been secularized; and it has moved recently into the sphere of identity politics, where it has been politically correctized.

All this is to say that memories are not only fluid, they are also deeply political. They are forged to further some agenda even as they forge agendas. That truism holds during the long biblical period, when Hosea's objectives in recalling the conquest were different from Isaiah's, and both diverged from those of the Joshua narrative, as in its varied afterlife. That is, a "poetics of biblical narrative"[30] creates a "politics of communities." And if memories are not revised in those communities, if instead they are frozen, their constituents are forced either to assent to them in conformity, or to disavow them in isolation. Abraham came to be remembered as father not only of the ancient Hebrews, but also of Christians and Muslims. It could have been one community. Sadly enough, these revisions succumbed to competition for the status of the true children of Abraham, to the scarcity principle.[31] The myth of common humankind—the sons of Adam—splintered all too quickly into the terrors of Cain and Abel and their legacy of ethnic, national, and religious hatred.

FORGETTING

Understanding collective memories as closed and collective identities as fixed is not uniformly endorsed in the Bible.[32] Many biblical stories have made not only remembering the past but forgetting and reinventing it their explicit theme, and as they tell it, forgetting offers more of an opportunity than a threat to the community. Refashioning their story can open the borders of their identity configuration. The most graphic example of this recreation is the fate of the Book of Jeremiah. In his prophecy, Jeremiah foretells Israel's bondage to Babylonia, and he blames that bondage on social injustices promulgated within Israel that flout divine law. But it was not enough for him to declaim the abuses of Israelites (at such pointed places as the steps to the Temple of Jerusalem), Jeremiah also needed his prophecy to be recorded, for an inscription that would fix his words would make them binding, would make his prophecy come true. Sensing this power of inscription, the king resolved to obliterate Jeremiah's words of condemnation, hoping thereby to nullify his prediction of doom. According to Jeremiah 36, as the scroll of Jeremiah's prophecy was read to the king, he tore it off and burned it in the warming fire of his winter apartments. But then, at Yahweh's behest, Jeremiah ordered his scribe to begin again, and the Book of Jeremiah was rewritten.

And then the word of Yahweh was addressed to Jeremiah, after the king had burnt the scroll containing the words Baruch had

written at the dictation of Jeremiah, "Take another scroll and
write down all the words that were written on the first scroll
burnt by Jehoiakim king of Judah." (Jer 36:27–28)

Quite apart from the question of all the mediations, all the room for
slippage and creativity as the word of Yahweh is translated to Jeremiah and thence to his scribe Baruch, and whether the words written are the same as the ones dictated, we might wonder if this second
inscription is identical to the first. This time we are given an answer
to that question: the words that are written again turn out to be *not*
identical to the ones in the burned scroll.

> Jeremiah then took another scroll and gave it to the scribe Bar-
> uch son of Neriah, and at the dictation of Jeremiah he wrote
> down all the words of the book that Jehoiakim king of Judah
> had burnt, with many similar words in addition. (Jer 36:32)

The pretense of identical repetition is dropped; there are "similar
words in addition." This little narrative is meant to underscore the
nature of prophecy—that it will not be silenced, that the word of
God conveyed through the prophet is impervious to the ravages of
kings or fires. And so it is all the more striking that the word of God
is not fixed, that it accommodates "similar words in addition" in a
nonidentical repetition, a re-creation. Here is an invitation to add
more stories even as the old ones were retained. There is a method
to this madness, for the coexistence of multiple memories allows
both a retention of the past and innovation, without understanding
these impulses as conflicting.

The phenomenon of destroying and re-creating a text, and
thereby losing and reinventing memories, recurs in the Law. When
Moses is given the tablets of the Law, before he even has had a
chance to promulgate it, he dashes the tablets to pieces. The Law
that the people are constantly urged to remember is lost. The Torah
itself must be rewritten. The one we have is a copy; in turn, it proliferates further copies: whatever was rewritten was apparently not the
last word, for there are numerous codes of law in the Bible and they
are never identical. As we have seen, the rabbis asserted that this

proliferation of the Law was not confined to the written law; they insisted that the oral law continues in tradition. And it is this law—multiple, fluid, and proliferating—that constitutes a fluid identity of Israel, an Israel fluid enough to include widely diverse peoples in far-flung places over a long span of time, fluid enough to include, among others, England's Puritans, colonial America's revolutionaries, South Africa's freedom seekers, French nationalists, and German nationalists.

This dialectic of loss and re-creation, of forgetting and remembering, is so frequent in the Bible that it comes to inform each of the scenes of writing the Bible depicts. Deuteronomy rehearses another version of the Exodus and the Law, with its version of Moses enjoining his hearers to remember and retell the story themselves.

> Do not then forget Yahweh your God who brought you out of the land of Egypt, out of the house of slavery: who guided you through this vast and dreadful wilderness, . . . who in this wilderness fed you with manna that your fathers had not known. . . . Remember Yahweh your God: it was he who gave you this strength. (Deut 8:14–18)

The demand to remember is expressed in the requirement to make inscriptions on virtually every space, interior and exterior, private and public, on the heart and on the gate.

> Let these words which I urge on you today be written on your heart. You shall repeat them to your children and say them over to them whether at rest in your house or walking abroad, at your lying down or at your rising; you shall fasten them on your hand as a sign and on your forehead as a circlet; you shall write them on the doorposts of your house and on your gates. (Deut 6:6–9)

Somehow these reminders of Deuteronomy are also forgotten. When that text is lost, with it even the reminder to remember is forgotten. But then the narrative goes on to tell a remarkable story about this forgetting and the way it enables the re-membering of the community. Many years later, after the Israelites inherit the land of

Canaan and establish a dynasty, they go astray, forgetting all the words Moses asked them to remember, and their continued existence is in grave danger. In that context, a religious reform takes place that includes the restoration of the Temple, and there, among the debris, the long-forgotten book is found.[33] The community repents and is reconstituted. Logically, because communities are forged by their collective memories of the past, forgetting should pose a threat to them, but in that brief suggestive narrative, both memory and community depend upon forgetting. Rather than dissolving community, forgetting allows the building of new memories. Ironically, communities only survive because their stories of the past are forgotten so that they must be remembered (or misremembered), that is, re-created in the present. Nonidentical repetition is a way out of the violence of congealing the past. When memories are nonidentical, they do not coerce all stories into one story, and in theory, they do not coerce all members of a community into assenting to that one story. In theory.

JOSEPH (HE ADDS)

All of the varieties of repression that the texts of Jeremiah, Ezra, Deuteronomy, and the tablets of the Law, seem to suffer—destroying, forgetting, and losing—have a role in the story of Joseph. But here the story focuses on a person who is destroyed, forgotten, and lost. At least, Joseph's father assumes that he has been destroyed, torn to pieces by a wild animal, and his brothers do forget him. "Our brother is no more," they tell the harsh-speaking stranger they do not recognize, not knowing that they speak to this one who "is no more" (Gen 42:13). But here too, the loss and repression described in the narrative—the losing and finding of Joseph and his brothers— are paradigmatic of the fate of the narrative. Losing an object is not so very different from forgetting it, from forgetting where we have put it, from forgetting all about it, and while destroying is characterized by an act of aggression that may not attend misplacing or forgetting, it does issue in the same result: the object is gone. Part of the thrust of the Joseph story is to equate these kinds of losses. To forget

Joseph is to lose him, in essence, to destroy him: "Our brother is no more." To remember him is to find him, to, in effect, give him back his life. Furthermore, in the Joseph story, to be remembered by him is to survive.

Throughout the various forgettings and rememberings, losses and recoveries, Joseph interprets. He interprets the dreams of his fellow prisoners and of Pharaoh. He interprets the fact that his brothers sold him into slavery. He interprets the behavior of his brothers when they appear in Egypt. And throughout, the very ordeal of losing and finding, of forgetting and remembering, also characterizes the process of interpretation. Our modern dream interpreter, Freud, wrote that descriptively speaking, interpretation fills in gaps in memory; dynamically speaking, interpretation overcomes resistances due to repression.[34] And he was to further explain that interpretation does not simply overcome repression; rather, the two are subtly and thoroughly interdependent.[35] That is, a simplistic version of psychoanalysis, which understands the future as dependent upon our recovery of a repressed past, may create more problems than it solves. Freud himself reminisced about the early days of analysis when the "old technique" of hypnosis prevailed. "In these hypnotic treatments the process of remembering took a very simple form. The patient put himself back into an earlier situation, which he seemed never to confuse with the present one, and gave an account of the mental processes belonging to it."[36] But Freud insisted that such reversions to the past must be replaced by another approach, that is, transference, in which the process of interpreting the past is carried on in the conscious present. In transference, the past can never be retrieved identically. We cannot speak of an "accurate" memory, as though memory could recover the contents of the past. All we have, all we *can* have are reconstructions, re-, and we must include that hyphen, memberings. "The dream as nocturnal spectacle is unknown to us," explains one of Freud's most astute interpreters, Paul Ricoeur. "It is accessible only through the account of the waking hours. The analyst interprets this account, substituting for it another text which is, in his eye, the thought-content of desire." He concludes, not surprisingly, that "it must be assumed . . . that dreams in themselves border on language, since they can be told, analyzed, interpreted."[37] The inaccessible dream gives rise to elaborations, to "accounts" and accounts of accounts. And so, in the end, repression not only invites interpretation, it enables it, and the "accounts of accounts" become re-creations rather than a recovery of a definitive truth. "When Freud made the unconscious the key to our psychic life, he made the repressed material—or, the very act of repression however voluntary or involuntary—a key to interpretation."[38] So does Joseph. While the Bible sometimes seems to depict its moments of loss as failures, it also insists upon them as necessary.

In the Bible, the preoccupation with forgetting and remembering is explicitly joined to the familiar one about scarcity and plenty. The Joseph story depicts seven long years of famine in Egypt that alternate with equal numbers of years of abundance, dreams of lean cows and fat cows, dreams of bread that is wasted and of wine conserved. A famine ravages Israel, threatening to starve Joseph's family. Sibling rivalry emerges from parental favoritism—why don't all the sons receive a special coat from their father? Time itself is scarce. That scarcity also erupts into efforts either to renounce the past altogether or to repeat it identically; both extreme responses presuppose that the past, or "parts of it," can be delimited. All of this scarcity is punctuated by violence. But when the past inspires innovations and repetitions with a difference, a discrete and delimited past opens its boundaries and pours into the living present. The Joseph story ties all of these threads together. It is the reawakening of the repressed past, recalling his abandonment by his brothers but reinterpreting it, that allows Joseph to be the harbinger of plenty and the rightful heir of his name, *Joseph,* "he adds": "Do not be distressed and do not be angry with yourselves for selling me here, because it was to save lives that God sent me ahead of you" (Gen 45:5). Scarcity will give way to plenty. Violence will give way to reconciliation. If Joseph names his firstborn Manasseh, saying, "It is because God has made me forget all my trouble and all my father's household," he names his second Ephraim, saying, "It is because God has made me fruitful in the land of my suffering" (Gen 41:51–52).

Like the Exodus stories, there are conflicting accounts of Joseph's story, with little effort to harmonize these multiple memories. They deserve sustained attention because these varied accounts offer a challenge to the Bible's singular monotheism, an alternative vision in which difference does not collapse into the Same, a heterogeneity that defies the message of singular Identity. First, Joseph's disappearance. What happened to him? Can we discern what happened? The scene of abandonment is a complicated business, marked by deflections and displacements (Gen 37). The brothers plot to kill Joseph, but one, Reuben, intervenes to save him: "Let us have no bloodshed. . . . Throw him into this pit in the wilderness, but do him no bodily harm." They agree, but then later another brother, Judah, speaks up with no indication that he has heard another defender: "What shall we gain by killing our brother and concealing his death? Why not sell him to the Ishmaelites?" The sale is similarly confusing. After Judah's suggestion that the brothers sell him to the Ishmaelites, it is the Midianites—not the brothers or the Ishmaelites—who come along and draw Joseph from the pit and sell him to the Ishmaelites for twenty pieces of silver and it is the Ishmaelites—not the Midianites—who take him to Egypt. (But then we learn that the *Midianites* sell him, not to the Ishmaelites but to the Egyptian Potiphar). Even a summary is confusing. Historical-critical scholars found a ready solution to the contradiction in the documentary hypothesis: "all of this narrative confusion is dissipated automatically once the narrative is broken up into two originally independent versions."[39] Nonetheless, they cannot explain why the editor let these explicit contradictions stand, with the result that there is no single, accurate account of what happened to Joseph. But what is an apparent lapse by an otherwise painstaking editor/writer may be instead an invitation— to read the event as a memory. Memories cannot claim complete accuracy. However much we try to reconstruct a coherent account from memory, details elude us, some are lost altogether, others displaced, and they tend to proliferate variegated versions.

In contrast, Joseph's response to the event is not at all confusing: Joseph the dreamer and interpreter of dreams will make every effort to repress his waking nightmare. Once his fortunes have reversed and he prospers in Egypt, he names his firstborn Manasseh (forget-

ful), saying, "It is because God has made me forget all my trouble
and all my father's household." Only seven verses later, the narrative
begins to describe the return of that household and the instigators of
his trouble. One senses that the brothers will not let Joseph forget.
When they stand before him to seek grain from the now-powerful
vizier of Egypt (his Israelite identity concealed), they provoke a fascinating response: "When Joseph saw his brothers he recognized them
but he made himself a stranger to them. . . . Although Joseph recognized his brothers, they did not recognize him" (Gen 42:7–8). Their
forgetfulness is emphasized with a pun on "recognize"—whose root
nkr also alludes to the root of "stranger"—to forget Joseph is to
make him a stranger. Nonetheless, according to the narrator, the
appearance of his brothers instantly reminds Joseph, not of their cru-
elty, but of his own dreams: "then he remembered his dreams about
them"—dreams of sheaves bowing down to a sheaf and of the sun,
moon, and eleven stars. But the dreams are not construed as an arro-
gant youthful sign of hegemony over his brothers. Now the dreams
come to signal his responsibility to save them.[40]

In what follows, Joseph acts out fragments from his repressed past
with substitutes. He imprisons his brothers as he was imprisoned, he
separates one from the others, and then he insists on separating another from his father. Repeating rather than remembering his pain,
Joseph compulsively tries to master it. When he demands that Benjamin be brought to Egypt, taken away from his father before he will
sell his brothers grain—thereby demanding that the brothers sell another brother into Egypt—the prospect of losing another brother
provokes their memory of Joseph.

> They said to one another, "Surely we are being punished be-
> cause of our brother. We saw how distressed he was when he
> pleaded with us for his life, but we would not listen; that's why
> this distress has come upon us." (Gen 42:21)

Instead of a grand reunion, Joseph finds his brothers and is found by
them in long drawn-out stages, each marked by losses, if only temporary, and each provoking memories. It soon becomes clear that
separations enable reunions and forgetting is the precondition for

remembering that, in turn, enables survival. Joseph will not punish his brothers. Rather, he will educate them in their moral responsibility, encouraging them to revisit and reinterpret their past in order to ensure their future. Only when they achieve the awareness that they must be their brothers' keepers, the insight Cain so dramatically denied, are they qualified to forge a community—in peace, not in violence. And so while Cain is condemned to exile, Joseph's brothers become the Sons of Israel.[41]

TYPOLOGY AND TOTALITY

I have explored how memories are really inventions, and re-creations are really creations, but there is another way of interpreting the Bible that has had a long and illustrious history: biblical typology. Typology does not fix the borders of community by fixing memory. Nor does it proliferate multiple and nonidentical accounts of the past that agree to differ without recourse to some hidden ultimate truth. It has another agenda, one more analogous to the universalistic side of monotheism, a kind of interpretive imperialism. There is little room for genuine innovation in typology, not because the canon is closed—typology promiscuously welcomes virtually all variations— but because all of these variations are reducible to one story. All events, biblical and postbiblical, all narratives, biblical and extrabiblical, are simply shadows of the real story, the fall of man and his redemption by Christ. A procedure that looks proliferating is instead totalizing, cramming all memories into its vast interpretive maw. And while typology never closes the text in the way that canonization does (no events can be excluded), it does presuppose the special closure of complete incorporation rather than exclusion.

Typology takes up the center of Northrop Frye's book on the Bible, *The Great Code*.[42] His scheme describes a U-shaped structure of descent and ascent: ancient Israel descends into apostasy and bondage, proceeds to repent, and then begins its ascent to deliverance and the promised land. Frye tells us that this structure encompasses the Bible as a whole, a "divine comedy" characterized by a final restoration after an initial loss. The garden in Eden is denied us, to be replaced by a "paradise happier far" if not within the hearts of men, then above, in the heavens. Exodus is the type of this deliverance. As Frye so wonderfully puts it, "Mythically, the Exodus is the only thing that really happens in the Old Testament."[43] The descent into Egypt, into captivity and idolatry, repentance, and finally the deliverance at the Sea of Reeds offer the complete structure. And all of these events foreshadow the narrative of Christ's life, which fits the same pattern, with the descent of the incarnation and ascent of the resurrection. In this sense, the resurrection is the only thing that really happens in the New Testament. The "double mirroring" of the testaments creates a lucid structure: the entirety of the Bible boils down to the resurrection as the fulfillment or "antitype" of the exodus. Luke uses just that term, *exodos,* to describe the life of Jesus that culminates in his death and resurrection, his exodus.[44]

But here is where Frye's drive to perceive (or create) patterns glosses over a stubborn difference, glosses over all difference, for his analytical model is not tuned to the music of distinctions. When the Israelites emerge from the wilderness, it is not to attain anything like the final triumph of a resurrection. He does acknowledge, in an aside, that at what he deems the sixth stage in this story, deliverance, the Hebraic and Christian patterns diverge. However muted, that aside tells it all: "For Christianity Jesus achieved a definitive deliverance for all mankind with his revelation that the ideal kingdom of Israel was a spiritual kingdom; for Judaism, the expulsion from their homeland by the edict of Hadrian in 135 A.D. began a renewed exile which in many respects still endures."[45]

In order to conclude, the New Testament must launch its structure into a new and separate plane, an ideal realm, a heaven. Vertical metaphors are often invoked to describe this move: a literary critic speaks of the "right angle" of biblical history in order to separate the horizontal, this-world domain of the Hebrew Bible from the cataclysmic turn vertically at the incarnation and resurrection.[46] Typology "points to future events that are often thought of as transcending time, so that they contain a vertical lift as well as a horizontal move forward."[47] Most recently, Michael Walzer has argued that the very idea of the exodus stands as an alternative to such verticality. For in the Book of Exodus, the promised land is a nation with a political configuration, not an Eden in the heavens. The deliverance it depicts is from human oppressors, not from the bondage of the flesh. "Exodus thinking" implies future revolutions and future redemptions. "The Exodus did not happen once and for all. . . . in fact, the return to Egypt is part of the story, though it exists in the text only as a possibility: that's why the story can be retold so often."[48] There is no definitive conclusion in the Hebrew pattern. The drama of exile and exodus persists.

How, then, are we to read those patterns that have proved such a rich resource for typological thinkers, without invoking typology? Joseph's story is an especially apt example because, if on the one hand it invites a typological reading, on the other it is also given to nonidentical repetition. It offers essentially a text case to distinguish biblical repetition from typology. For a typological thinker like Frye—and what follows is a hypothetical reading—the Joseph story would constitute a biblical romance, fitting the descent-ascent structure. Joseph is thrown down into a pit, from there he is sold into bondage, into Egypt, a deeper pit yet, and lands in the pit of a prison (he makes the comparison between that first pit and his imprisonment explicit to his brothers). Joseph rises from his first pit to become the aid of the Egyptian Potiphar, rises from his pit/prison to become first the adviser to Pharaoh and then overseer of the land, and ultimately rises to save Egypt and his family from a world famine. In addition to Joseph's enduring a series of descents and ascents, he makes his brothers repeat them: they come down to Egypt and before he allows them to go up to Israel, he re-creates the experience of his own captivity in the person of his younger brother, Benjamin. The Joseph narrative is punctuated by dreams, oaths, testimonies, tokens of recognition (all hallmarks of the literary genre, romance); the famous image of a coat, used as false witness of Joseph's death, is also used to indict him for a staged seduction of Potiphar's wife, yet he is awarded, and awards his brothers, festal garments in the end. In other words, the symbolic coat itself follows the pattern of descent and ascent: torn and bloodied, it will be made whole. To read Joseph's descent into the pit as a descent into the underworld is not at all strained. When his father, Jacob, mourns for Joseph, he speaks of going down to Sheol in grief where he will mourn his son. The Hebrew term used for descent throughout the narrative, *yrd,* is also the psalter's term of choice for a descent into the underworld. And so the temptation to see Joseph as prefiguring or shadowing other descents, culminating in the final one of the incarnation, was not to be resisted—by the New Testament, the Fathers, or Frye.[49]

"The Jews wandering in the wilderness did not know that manna prefigured the Eucharist, nor did Joshua know that in leading his people into the Promised Land he was a type of Jesus leading His people into Heaven. . . . Hence, the meaning of a type cannot be known until it has been fulfilled in its antitype."[50] In typological thinking, meaning is conferred retrospectively: the early instances have a provisional status until, at last, a last one fulfills it. As the sixteenth-century divine Lancelot Andrewes shows, the meaning of these "Old" Testament events becomes apparent with knowledge of their New Testament sequel. His Christmas sermon of 1620 offers an exemplary statement of this logic: "That which was thus promised to, and by the Patriarchs, shadowed forth in the figures of the Law, the Temple, and the Tabernacle; that which was foresaid by the Prophets, and foresung of in the Psalms, that was this day fulfilled."[51] This term, *fulfillment,* appears in most discussions of typology. For instance, Andrewes's Christmas sermon of 1609: "And well also might it be called the fulness of time in another regard. For till then all was but in promise, in shadows and figures and prophecies only, which fill not, God knows. But when the performance of these promises, the body of these shadows, the substance of those figures, the fulfilling or filling full of all those prophecies came, then came 'the fulness of time' truly so called. Till then it came not; then it came."[52] One church father, Irenaeus, isolated what he called the consummative nature of typological thinking, its drive to formalize and complete. God's plan for the Hebrew nation is consummated in typology, that is, it is concluded and perfected by Christ. Irenaeus wrote that "the Son of God became the son of David and son of Abraham, perfecting and summing up this in himself, that he might enable us to possess life."[53] He could turn to a text like Matthew 5:17 for corroboration: "Do not imagine that I have come to abolish the law or the prophets. I have come not to abolish but to complete them."

That same urge to conclude gives rise to the corollary feature of typology: its provisional meanings. The very notion of fulfillment suggests that things must *be* fulfilled, and are not yet. Again, the language is telling: Paul refers in Corinthians to the Hebrews in the desert as *typoi hemon*, "figures of ourselves"; to early biblical events as *skia*, or "shadows" of the coming of Christ (1 Cor 10:6, 11); in Romans, Adam is the *typos*, or "figure," of Christ (5:14); and the classic image for partial understanding, for a glimpse of meaning, is that of a veil: Corinthians refers to the *kalymnos*, or "veil," that covers scripture when the Jews read it (2 Cor 3:14).[54] On another level, the work of typologists is necessarily incomplete, for the definitive event has not yet arrived. The interpretive activity itself mocks the very totality it presupposes, adding shadows to shadows, veils to veils.

In practice, the conclusions and definitive meanings suggested by typology do not foreclose the opportunity for invention. On the contrary, the cast of characters who comprise types is ever changing because the system is large enough to incorporate everyone. Another British Renaissance divine, Edwin Sandys, left no one out of his Christmas sermon. He refers to Christ:

This is that seed of the woman which breaketh the serpent's head, that meek Abel murdered by his brother for our sin, that true Isaac whom his father hath offered up to be sacrifice of pacification and atonement between him and us. This is that Melchisedech, both a King and a Priest that liveth forever, without father or mother, beginning or ending. This is that Joseph that was sold for thirty pieces of silver. This is that Samson full of strength and courage, who to save his people and destroy his enemies hath brought death upon his own head.

171

... This is that Bridegroom in the canticle. ... This is that Lamb of God, pointed at by John. ... This is the child that is born for us.[55]

Governed by the logic of similitude, but with no laws to legislate what constitutes "the similar," typological thinking can, with enough ingenuity, make anything fit anything else.

But to return to Joseph, let us note some differences. While Joseph may parallel Jesus in his descent, he does not rise in the same way. No tomb is left empty. There is no resurrection. Instead, Joseph's dying words—and a last testament confers special power on them in the Bible—stipulate a provision about his bones. "I am about to die," he says. "God will surely remember you and take you up from this land to the land that he promised on oath to Abraham, Isaac, and Jacob" (Gen 50:24). Paul asks, Who will deliver me from this body of death? Joseph asks that his body *be delivered,* not that he be delivered from it: then Joseph put the sons of Israel under oath, saying, "When God remembers you, be sure to take up my bones from here." And then Joseph is embalmed and laid in his coffin. Joseph is buried in the ground, bound to that horizontal plane; and while he will be carried to the promised land, he will be trans*plant*ed to another burial plot and not translated to the upper realm. The detail is underscored: we learn that at the exodus Moses takes with him the bones of Joseph, and the Book of Joshua ends with the burial of those bones in the promised land. This emphasis on burial is reinforced in the account of Jacob's extensive funeral. Militating against any hint of an ascension, the narrator offers rich detail concerning his place of burial.

> Thus Jacob's sons did for him as he had instructed them. His sons bore him to the land of Canaan and buried him in the cave of the field of Machpelah, facing on Mamre, the field that Abraham had bought from Ephron the Hittite for a burial site. (Gen 50:12–13)

The burial plot of Jacob is, significantly, the only piece of land that Abraham, the first to be blessed with the promise of land, acquired in his lifetime. And the cave of Machpelah is full—not empty. We can discern patterns in the Joseph narrative, but instead of partial meanings that become conclusive, dim apprehensions that become definitive understanding, they are better described in categories that suggest an unending and proliferating process: forgetting and remembering.

When truth is multiple instead of single, when memories are plentiful instead of scarce, what happens to the idea of contradiction? How can conflicting interpretations and memories coexist? Stories are competing, with one that emerges as right, another as wrong, only when there is one truth. But when Truth itself is reconceived, understood as proliferating, it becomes truths, or better, stories, that illuminate and enrich each other with their variety and multiplicity rather than being partial installments on the one true story. Multiple accounts become compatible instead of competing, and difference is not agonistic because it is not fixed. Conflict is only generated by the familiar commitment to One. Creativity is generated by the Many. In Genesis, there are two very different creation narratives: in one, after a vast cosmos has been delineated, humankind is created; in the other, humans are created first and the cosmos has shrunk to a garden that suits their needs. Together, these accounts tell that humankind is both the periphery and the center, that the universe is both incomprehensibly vast and intimate. And what is to prevent further creation narratives, not just these two? What indeed? The prophets rehearse the creation again and again, in a chorus of differences—now the God who created the heavens and earth measures everything and punishes the sinner, now the God who created the heavens and earth strengthens the weary, now the creation is a rebuke to Job's inquiry into divine justice, now creation is invoked in a prayer of thanksgiving uttered by Jonah in the belly of the whale.

LIVING MEMORY

Remembering is persistently linked to the survival of the community. Joseph asks a fellow prisoner to remember him trapped in prison after he has been released: the implication is clear that to be so re-

membered is to be freed. The prisoner forgets Joseph, only to remember later. Joseph's brothers slowly recall their brother. Acknowledging their guilt, they are rewarded for their recollection with grain
during a time of famine. The next installment in the Bible after the
Joseph narrative, Exodus, begins with a pharaoh who knew nothing
of Joseph, and his poor memory issues in an extermination policy
for the descendants of the forgotten one. But when we say that remembering is the condition of survival in the Bible, we cannot mean
it in any naive sense. With no such thing as accurate memory possible, dependence on such memory would enable no future at all.
Rather, it is the innovative interpretation that becomes the ground
of continuity, a future that is enabled by forgetting and reinventing
the past.

If this is a deliverance, it is not the glorious and final deliverance
that resurrection holds; Joseph instigates something far more modest:
"It was not you who sold me into Egypt," explains Joseph. "God
sent me before you to ensure for you a remnant on earth, and to
save your lives" (Gen 45:7). A remnant that survives destruction,
like Noah from the Flood; Lot from the destruction of Sodom; the
generation who survive the wilderness; the tottering hut of David
that survives the exile; survivors of a famine; and texts that survive
as remnants, like Deuteronomy, Jeremiah, and the Torah itself. Like
typology, memory reconfigures events from the past, but its motive
is more humble. It is not a drive to interpret authoritatively; the
motive of memory is simply to preserve, and preservation, by its
very nature, does not end. Once a type is fulfilled, there is no need
to remember. Once we incorporate the body of Christ, there is no
need to recall the text.

Modern psychoanalytic theory teaches us that fictions of closure
are linked to the death drive, that, as the end of desire, fulfillment is
tantamount to death. Desire itself, however, perpetual desire, assures
textuality, in our parlance script-uality. The Bible complicates this
picture, for it gives us at once desire (the promised land is, after all,
promised) and nostalgia (Eden, the original paradisal home, is forever
lost). As to re-member presupposes that something has been dismembered, or lost, or forgotten, so too, to repeat suggests that what

is repeated is discrete in some sense, and hence repeatable instead of a mere continuation. One of the ironies that inheres in the notion of repetition is that only those things that are finished in some sense can be repeated. The documents that are lost and found in the Bible, including the Bible, *are* documents; they have integrity, with beginnings and endings. But writing persists in another sense, as perpetual rewriting. Biblical repetition, then, suggests at once discontinuity and continuity: discontinuity, because there must be a break in order for something to be repeated, just as something must be lost to be recovered, forgotten to be remembered; and continuity, because the fact of repetition, recovery, memory, assures a living-on. In this sense, the idea of death and resurrection is not so much alien to the Hebrew Bible as it is terribly familiar. "Only because man has lost does he write about it, must he write about it, can he only write about it."[56] There are many dyings and risings rather than a single resurrection.

Thus, there are more bones. In Ezekiel, the bones of the army of Israel come to life. In Genesis, God creates from bones: Eve is made from a rib. Jacob's bones are buried at Machpelah, Joseph's lie in Canaan, but no one knows where the bones of Moses lie. For a typologist, those missing bones suggest the possibility of ascension. The absent grave is powerful testimony that Moses is the type of a resurrected Christ. To someone who subscribes to a less completing hermeneutics, the missing bones of Moses point to infinite Moseses, and suggest that we, like Moses, will never reach the promised land of a definitive truth. In John Milton's allegory, the body of Truth was hewn in a thousand pieces and scattered to the four winds; "from that time ever since, the sad friends of Truth, such as durst appear, went up and down gathering up limb by limb still as they could find them." With Milton, we can only hope to re-member her torn body.[57]

To open the biblical canon is my concluding call, and by that I do not mean some partial commentary of sanctified unalterable authoritative texts, but a genuine rewriting of traditions: new creation stories, new exoduses, new losses, and new recoveries of what is lost. Despite the intransigent and tragic scarcities that are part of our condition in the world, at least memories need not be in short supply. While there can be no easy causation between the proliferation of memories and the politics of communities, nonetheless, the fact that the communities that identify themselves with Judaism, Christianity, and Islam all claim versions of these stories, adding to them, revising them, and that other communities continue to re-write them in a secular vernacular, suggests that we may not be able to completely escape biblical myths as our cultural inheritance, and so the best we can do is rewrite them in a new key. And so here I have offered my small contribution to that far more illustrious history of rewritings, one in which Luther read all of the Bible through his belief that faith is the promise of redemption, in which Milton read the Bible as asserting individual moral victories in the face of constant struggles against the chaos of sin, in which Blake read the Bible through the lenses of an oppressed imagination trying to free itself from the chains of creation's order, and in which Freud read the Bible as a drama of a primal horde's ambivalent struggle with patricidal urges. My re-vision would produce an alternative Bible that subverts the dominant vision of violence and scarcity with an ideal of plenitude and its corollary ethical imperative of generosity. It would be a Bible embracing multiplicity instead of monotheism. And I hope that this description of the Bible will also serve to describe its future, that it will not only tell of proliferation, but that new versions, decrying the violence of monotheism, will proliferate. When I began this project, I anticipated concluding with the injunction from Augustine to "close the Book." For him, faith had superseded it; for me, its ancient agonistic values are far too dangerous to continue authorizing. But I have come to understand that same urge in a new light. The old "monotheistic" Book must be closed so that the new books may be fruitful and multiply. After all, that was the first commandment.

Notes

ACKNOWLEDGMENTS

1. Even when violence has erupted in the climate of Eastern religions, it often reflects an importation of Western understandings of collective identity. See Stanley Jeyaraja Tambiah, *Buddhism Betrayed? Religion, Politics, and Violence in Sri Lanka* (Chicago: University of Chicago Press, 1992). In *The Color of Violence* (Chicago: University of Chicago Press, 1996), Sudhir Kakar turns to a psychological grounding for violent conflict, one that transcends religious differences; I have just read this fascinating study in manuscript.

2. While my chief focus in this book is on the narratives of the Hebrew Bible, ones that were appropriated by Christianity as the Old Testament, the five ways in which discrete group identity is constituted—by covenant, kinship, nation, territory, and collective memory—also linger in the New Testament. Despite the dominant emphasis on a community of converts, the genealogies of Matthew suggest that for him the category of kinship still has the power to define who is in and who is out, for he goes to considerable trouble to legitimize Jesus as a blood descendant of David. In the New Testament, territorialized identity is not made irrelevant either; rather, it is made transcendent as the heavenly Jerusalem even as the earthly Holy Land still remains a goal, one

sought literally in the Crusades. A collective memory is also forged by means of the New Testament—first, by binding the "old" testament with the "new," thereby claiming a continuous memory with the ancient Israelites, then by offering the witness accounts of the Gospels, and by canonizing Paul's letters as part of The Book. The differences between the two testaments widen over the "nation." Marginalized in the Roman Empire, early Christian communities did not think of themselves as forging a nation, and when they did come to express ambitions of temporal power, it was not as a nation among nations but, like their oppressors, as an empire. On the other hand, the Kingdom of God knows no boundaries. Paul's emphasis on the covenant of grace and his understanding that a community is bound chiefly by a common faith created a different understanding of group identity in the New Testament, a community that constitutes the "body of Christ." The fascinating debates about the way that collective identity is forged through the Eucharist in Christianity is the subject of my next book.

INTRODUCTION

1. *Remembering and Repeating: On Milton's Theology and Poetics* (Cambridge: Cambridge University Press, 1988; reprint, Chicago: University of Chicago Press, 1993) was my effort to come to terms with an influential figure who grappled with suffering in the context of the biblical myth. I concluded that Milton delineated a force of destruction greater than Adam and Eve's single disobedience, a (moral) chaos that perpetually threatens us and can only be countered by repeated acts of creation and renewal.

2. Many a commentator has noted that the story dramatizes a victory of the sower over the shepherd, but with a clear bias against the agriculturalist (Cain) and in favor of the pastoralist (Abel). While the sociological explanation may help to mitigate the impression of an arbitrary deity, it does not explain it away completely: a certain group tells its own tale (of murdered pastoralist or cursed agriculturalist?—whose tale is this anyway?) in its own interests (an explanation of the superiority of pastoral economy or of the difficulty of agriculture?). But there is compelling evidence that pastoral and agricultural economies were deeply interdependent in the ancient world: herders needed grain as planters needed meat; grazing herds and growing crops alternated land use with benefits similar to modern crop rotation. Why, then, would the story depict the deity preferring one group to the other? See Norman K. Gottwald, "Were the Early Israelites Pastoral Nomads?" in *Rhetorical Criticism: Essays in Honor of James Muilenburg,* ed. Jared J. Jackson and Martin Kessler,

Pittsburgh Theological Monograph Series 1 (Pittsburgh: Pickwick Press, 1974), 223–55.

3. *The Rights of Minority Cultures,* ed. Will Kymlicka (Oxford: Oxford University Press, 1995), is one such important collection, discussing the rights of different minority groups thoughtfully.

4. In *The Color of Violence* (189), Sudhir Kakar describes the process of collective identity formation in psychological terms: "The self-assertion of 'We are,' with its potential for confrontation with the 'We are' of other groups, is *inherently* a carrier of aggression, together with the consequent fears of persecution, and is thus always attended by a sense of risk and potential for violence." I find it fascinating that, with very different approaches, we arrived at this conclusion independently and simultaneously.

5. Carl Schmitt, *Political Theology,* trans. George Schwab (Cambridge: MIT Press, 1988), originally published as *Politische Theologie: Vier Kapital zur Lehre von der Souveränitat* (Munich: Duncker und Humblot, 1922), 36.

6. Benedict Anderson, *Imagined Communities: Reflections on the Origin and Spread of Nationalism* (New York: Verso, 1983), 19–20.

7. Ibid., 43; see Lucien Febvre and Henri-Jean Martin, *The Coming of the Book: The Impact of Printing, 1450–1800,* trans. David Gerard (London: NLB, 1976), 289–95.

8. Exceptions are predominantly within the rubric of theology, especially newer currents in theology that attend to social theory and liberation theology. See John Milbank, *Theology and Social Theory: Beyond Secular Reason* (Oxford: Basil Blackwell, 1990); Itumeleng J. Mosala, *Biblical and Black Theology in South Africa* (Grand Rapids, MI: Eerdmans, 1989); Cornel West, *Prophesy Deliverance: An Afro-American Revolutionary Christianity* (Philadelphia: Westminster, 1982); Cain Hope Felder, ed., *Stony the Road We Trod: African American Biblical Interpretation* (Minneapolis: Augsburg Fortress, 1991). In political studies the notable exceptions are the penetrating study by Garry Wills, *Under God: Religion and American Politics* (New York: Simon and Schuster, 1990), and Michael Walzer, *Exodus and Revolution* (New York: Basic Books, 1984).

9. Historically, Judaism never had enough temporal power to put its authorized text to service as an instrument of widespread oppression. Even in its original setting, the Bible did not function in that way. While biblical historians continue to debate the precise details, most conclude that the bulk of biblical narratives were composed by a dispossessed people; hence, their myths of conquest were fantasies of victory over the oppressor.

10. See Hans Frei, *The Eclipse of Biblical Narrative: A Study in Eigh-*

teenth and Nineteenth Century Hermeneutics (New Haven: Yale University Press, 1988); Regina Schwartz, "Introduction: On Biblical Criticism," in *The Book and the Text: The Bible and Literary Theory,* ed. Regina Schwartz (Oxford: Basil Blackwell, 1990), 1–15.

11. While it is generally conceded that the birthplace of European nationalism was France (and by the way, the physician to Louis XV, Jean Astruc, who noted two separate names for God in Genesis, Yahweh and Elohim, and posited that two separate documents had been joined, offered really the first intimations of biblical source criticism), it was in nineteenth-century Germany that a thoroughgoing nationalist theory was developed to justify the creation of a nation-state, the setting where higher criticism flourished.

12. George Mosse, *Nationalization of the Masses: Political Symbolism and Mass Movements in Germany from the Napoleonic Wars through the Third Reich* (New York: H. Fertig, 1975), 14.

13. Ibid., 81.

14. F. A. Aulard, *Le Culte de la raison et le culte de l'Être supreme* (Paris: F. Alcan, 1892), 35, cited in Carlton J. H. Hayes, *Essays on Nationalism* (New York: Russell and Russell, 1966), 103.

15. Anderson, *Imagined Communities,* 20–28.

16. Hayes, *Essays on Nationalism,* 104–5.

17. Schmitt, *Political Theology,* 39.

18. In the impassioned rhetoric of antiroyalists, God's will underwrote the very different revolutions of England, France, and America.

19. Peter Alter, *Nationalism,* trans. Stuart McKinnin-Evans (London: E. Arnold, 1989), 9–10.

20. Ibid., 10.

21. My students at Duke University are pursuing the larger project with fascinating results. They are studying the ways in which biblical notions of identity become entangled in specific forms of nationalism, spanning vastly different cultural and political settings, in the poet Edmund Spenser's work on Ireland, in the missionary Guaman Poma's account of colonization in Peru, in the political vision of the English radical Puritan Winstanley, in John Ireland's vision of Catholicism in America, in Theodore Dreiser's *American Tragedy.* Their work will be published in a collection called *Nationalism and Religion.*

CHAPTER ONE

1. Friedrich Carl von Moser in Gerhard Kaiser, *Pietismus und Patriotismus im literarischen Deutschland* (Wiesbaden, 1961), 41, cited in George Mosse, *Nationalization of the Masses: Political Symbolism and Mass Move-*

ments in Germany from the Napoleonic Wars through the Third Reich (New York: H. Fertig, 1975), 14.

2. Everett Emerson, *John Cotton* (Boston: Twayne Publishers, 1990), 113.

3. While Christian and Islamic sacred texts both disseminated materials derived from the Hebrew Bible, they did it in very different ways, since Christianity incorporated the whole Hebrew Bible intact (adding some books that Judaism rejected) into its Scripture, while Islam repudiated both the Hebrew Bible and the New Testament as false versions of the true word. The Qur'an contains different versions of some of the stories in the Bible, along with material not found in either testament.

4. There are about twenty-five allusions in all of the Hebrew Bible to the effect that there are no other gods but Israel's. Moshe Halbertal and Avishai Margolit, *Idolatry*, trans. Naomit Goldblum (Cambridge: Harvard University Press, 1992), takes up the question of idolatry, examining its varied political and philosophical aspects.

5. In *God: A Biography* (New York: Knopf, 1995), 72, Jack Miles writes: "The emergence of monotheism from polytheism is a matter of selective inclusion as well as wholesale exclusion. . . . In fact, the most coherent way to imagine the Lord God of Israel is as the inclusion of the content of several ancient divine personalities in a single character."

6. In "The Lie of the Land: The Text beyond Canaan," *Representations* 25 (winter 1989): 119–38, Harry Berger Jr. has observed astutely that "the more centralized hierarchic power is, the more its thrust beyond history toward nature strives to be absolute. Its assertion of totality is presented as the whole truth and nothing but the truth."

7. Others have felt this dynamism in the Hebrew Bible, regarding it as a self-critical tendency. See especially Herbert Schneidau, *Sacred Discontent: The Bible and Western Tradition* (Berkeley: University of California Press, 1977); Robert Alter, *The Art of Biblical Narrative* (New York: Basic Books, 1981); Mieke Bal, *Death and Dissymmetry: The Politics of Coherence in the Book of Judges* (Chicago: University of Chicago Press, 1988).

8. Here the verb root for incising letters in stone is *ḥqq* and not *krt*.

9. The blazing torch is generally considered to be a theophany (God also appears in fire in Exodus). The implication is that God is binding himself in an oath to Abraham to confirm his promise of offspring. This oath is referred to later in the narrative (Gen 50:24) and in the prophets. Here, in an inversion, Israel is constituted under the explicit threat of violence against *God*. Perhaps the entire oath ceremony is being parodied, as David Noel Freedman has suggested.

10. Rene Girard, *Violence and the Sacred* (Baltimore: Johns Hopkins

University Press, 1977), 8, originally published as *La Violence et la sacre* (Paris: Bernard Grasset, 1972).

11. Jeremiah promises that the penalty of the oath/curse will be exacted from Jerusalem in the destruction of the city, which Nebuchadrezzar will execute in the immediate future.

12. Barbara Johnson has insightfully written, "Difference is not engendered in the space between identities; it is what makes all totalization of identity . . . impossible. . . . Far from constituting unique identity, it is that which subverts the very idea of identity" (*The Critical Difference: Essays in the Contemporary Rhetoric of Reading* [Baltimore: Johns Hopkins University Press, 1981], 4–5).

13. The historian Donald Harmon Akenson has recently observed, "That the bedrock beliefs of the ancient Hebrews were laid down even before they became an iron-using people, and that these beliefs (however gentled and tidied up by later redactors) not only survive in our own time, but continue to be an independent and formative force in the history of nations, can only make one stop in awe" (*God's Peoples: Covenant and Land in South Africa, Israel, and Ulster* [Ithaca: Cornell University Press, 1992], 349).

14. Diego de Landa, *Yucatan before and after the Conquest* (Baltimore: Maya Society, 1937), 160.

15. Quoted in Delbert R. Hillers, *Covenant: The History of a Biblical Idea* (Baltimore: Johns Hopkins University Press, 1969), 30, 31. See also Dennis McCarthy, *Treaty and Covenant* (Rome: Pontifical Biblical Institute, 1963); Dennis McCarthy, *Old Testament Covenant: A Survey of Current Opinions* (Louisville, KY: John Knox Press, 1972); Jakob Jocz, *The Covenant: A Theology of Human Destiny* (Grand Rapids, MI: Eerdmans, 1968).

16. In the ancient annals, kings alluded to these pacts, not as "our treaty," but as "my treaty." "It is the great king's pact, not in the sense that he is the one expected to obey it but that he is the one who granted it" (Hillers, *Covenant,* 30).

17. Gerhard von Rad, *Old Testament Theology* (New York: Harper and Row, 1962), 1:190; originally published as *Theologie des Alten Testaments* (Munich: Chr. Kaiser Verlag, 1957).

18. Norman K. Gottwald, *The Tribes of Yahweh: A Sociology of the Religion of Liberated Israel, 1250–1050 B.C.E.* (Maryknoll, NY: Orbis, 1979); George Mendenhall, *The Tenth Generation: The Origins of the Biblical Tradition* (Baltimore: Johns Hopkins University Press, 1973); George Mendenhall, "The Hebrew Conquest of Palestine," *Biblical Archaeologist* 25 (1962): 66–87.

19. The ancient treaty was "essentially an elaborate oath," according

to Hillers (*Covenant,* 28), with two fundamental components: what was to be performed, and the invoking of divine vengeance in case the requirement was not met; both parts made up its deep structure.

20. Quoted in ibid., 37.

21. Morton Smith, *Palestinian Parties and Politics That Shaped the Old Testament* (New York: Columbia University Press, 1971).

22. Gilles Deleuze, "A Philosophical Concept," in *Who Comes after the Subject,* ed. Eduardo Cadava, Peter Connor, and Jean-Luc Nancy (New York: Routledge, 1991), 94–95.

CHAPTER TWO

1. Phyllis Trible, Carol Meyers, and Mieke Bal have all been deliberate about their various translations of the term for the original earth-creature, *'ādām,* as neuter. However it is translated, it must be distinguished from the gendered *ish/ishah* terms for man and woman. See Trible, *God and the Rhetoric of Sexuality* (Philadelphia: Fortress Press, 1978); Meyers, *Discovering Eve: Ancient Israelite Women in Context* (New York: Oxford University Press, 1988); Bal, *Lethal Love: Feminist Literary Readings of Biblical Love Stories* (Bloomington: Indiana University Press, 1987).

2. There is extensive literature on Israel and the wilderness traditions. See especially Herbert Schneidau, "The Hebrews against the High Cultures," in *Sacred Discontent: The Bible and Western Tradition* (Berkeley: University of California Press, 1977); Shemaryahu Talmon, "The 'Desert Motif' in the Bible and in Qumran Literature," in *Biblical Motifs,* ed. Alexander Altmann (Cambridge: Harvard University Press, 1966), 31–63; W. D. Davies, *The Territorial Dimension of Judaism* (Berkeley: University of California Press, 1982).

3. Davies, *Territorial Dimension of Judaism,* 15–19; Gerhard von Rad, *The Problem of the Hexateuch and Other Essays,* trans. E. W. T. Dicken (New York: McGraw-Hill, 1966), 85–93.

4. Freud made similar observations in *The Future of an Illusion* (trans. James Strachey [New York: Norton, 1961]) about the comforts of religion in an existential world. He later revised his understanding of religion and considerably nuanced it in *Moses and Monotheism* (trans. Katherine Jones [New York: Knopf, 1937]). See my "Freud's God: Moses and Polytheism" in *Post- Secular Philosophy,* ed. Philip Blond (New York: Routledge, 1996).

5. The question of Israel's early nomadism is a vexed one for historians of the period. For a century, the model of Israel as a "pastoral nomadic people who penetrated Canaan from the desert, and who, in the

course of settling down on the land, underwent massive transition to an agriculture economy and, more slowly and unevenly, through village organization toward urbanization" prevailed (Norman K. Gottwald, "Were the Early Israelites Pastoral Nomads?" in *Rhetorical Criticism: Essays in Honor of James Muilenburg,* ed. Jared J. Jackson and Martin Kessler, Pittsburgh Theological Monograph Series 1 [Pittsburgh: Pickwick Press, 1974], 224). However, the evidence for early Israelites as pastoral nomads has been questioned by John T. Luke, *Pastoralism and Politics in the Mari Period: A Re-examination of the Character and Political Significance of the Major West Semitic Tribal Groups in the Middle Euphrates* (Ann Arbor, MI: University Microfilms, 1965); and by Gottwald in the above essay. Gottwald is eager to demonstrate that nomadism was interdependent upon the dominant agriculturalism, that pastoralists and agriculturalists were together aligned against urbanism.

6. Herbert Schneidau, *Sacred Discontent: The Bible and Western Tradition* (Berkeley: University of California Press, 1977); Harry Berger Jr., "The Lie of the Land: The Text beyond Canaan," *Representations* 25 (winter 1989): 119–38, a deeply insightful essay.

7. In Jeremiah, this critique of agriculture is entangled with the familiar emphasis on obedience. Nomadism is not represented as an alternative to monotheism—"We have no vineyard or field or seed; but we have lived in tents, and have obeyed and done all our ancestor Jonadab commanded of us" (Jer 35:8–10)— and Yahweh complains that "[t]he descendants of Jonadab son of Rechab have carried out the command that their ancestor gave them, but this people has not obeyed me" (Jer 35:16).

8. As Berger ("Lie of the Land," 134) eloquently put it: "A phantom double of the Pharoah . . . traveled with the fugitive Israelites, stored its potency within their early image of Yahweh, and waited for the time when they would inevitably return to spiritual Egypt, not as slaves who had been betrayed or been forced into captivity but as the captors and the victors themselves. . . . the seeds of Egypt are carried within it and will sprout . . . when sown in any new land."

9. Davies, *Territorial Dimension of Judaism,* 15–19.

10. Walter Brueggemann, "Land: Fertility and Justice," in *Theology of the Land,* ed. Leonard Weber, Bernard F. Evans, and Gregory D. Cusack (Collegeville, MN: Liturgical Press, 1987), 46. See also Walter Brueggemann, *The Land: Place as Gift, Promise, and Challenge in Biblical Faith* (Philadelphia: Fortress Press, 1977).

11. Brueggemann, "Land: Fertility and Justice," 47.

12. See also Is 10:13 and Deut 19:14 on boundary markers being moved and patrimony.

13. Brueggemann, "Land: Fertility and Justice," 49.

14. See von Rad, *Problem of the Hexateuch,* 89.

15. Steven Knapp has written a provocative essay on the relationship between memory and the actual past, "Collective Memory and the Actual Past," *Representations* 26 (spring 1989): 123–49.

16. John Dryden, *Absalom and Achitophel* (London: printed for J. T., 1681).

17. Robert Allen Warrior, "Canaanites, Cowboys, and Indians: Deliverance, Conquest, and Liberation Theology Today," *Christianity and Crisis* 49 (1989): 264.

18. According to most biblical scholars, the Priestly writer identified the god of exodus with El, the god of Abraham, the Egyptian origin myth with the Babylonian origin myth. The Yahwist calls this God Yhwh from the beginning of Genesis on (most scholars assign Ex 6:2–3 to the Priestly writer).

19. See Norman K. Gottwald, *Hebrew Bible: A Socio-Literary Introduction* (Philadelphia: Fortress Press, 1985), 261–88; Robert Gnuse, "Israelite Settlement of Canaan: A Peaceful Internal Process: Part 1," *Biblical Theology Bulletin* 21 (1991): 56–66.

20. R. S. Sugirth-arajah, ed., *Voices from the Margin: Interpreting the Bible in the Third World* (London: SPCK, 1991), 290.

21. Warrior, "Canaanites, Cowboys, and Indians," 264.

22. Mary Douglas, *Purity and Danger* (London: Routledge and Kegan Paul, 1966), 41. See also Julia Kristeva, *The Powers of Horror: An Essay on Abjection,* trans. Leon S. Roudiez (New York: Columbia University Press, 1982).

23. See Davies, *Territorial Dimension of Judaism,* 19–21. He summarizes the prohibitions that would pollute the land of Israel and notes that the concept of protecting totality governs all these rules. "There is a Yahweh-given order to the cosmos; a division is made between the sacred and the profane. And it can safely be asserted that each of the prohibitions singled out here is directed against the violation of that order and the mixing of the sacred and profane which leads to the disintegration and profanation of the whole cosmos" (20). The prohibitions are (1) against harlotry, (2) against shedding blood, (3) against allowing a corpse to remain hanging on a tree, and (4) against remarriage with a former wife, who has remarried after her divorce.

24. Ibid., 20.

25. Claudia Camp, *Wisdom and the Feminine in the Book of Proverbs* (Decatur, GA: Almond Press, 1985), 118–19.

26. Ibid., 119.

27. Renita J. Weems has explored abuse and violence in *Battered*

Love: Marriage, Sex, and Violence in the Hebrew Prophets (Minneapolis: Fortress Press, 1995), 58–64.

28. Sandra Gravett has written a superb dissertation on the violence against women in Ezekiel, "That All Women May Be Worn: Reading the Sexual and Ethnic Violence in Ezekiel 16 and 23," Duke University, 1995.

29. Carol Delaney, *The Seed and the Soil: Gender and Cosmology in Turkish Village Society* (Berkeley: University of California Press, 1991), 30.

30. Ibid., 38.

31. Ibid., 40.

32. Ibid., 39 n. 14.

33. Howard Eilberg-Schwartz, *The Savage in Judaism* (Bloomington: Indiana University Press, 1990).

34. Ibid., 178.

35. Douglas, *Purity and Danger,* 124.

36. Eilberg-Schwartz, *Savage in Judaism,* 191.

37. John Donne, "Batter My Heart," in *The Divine Poems,* ed. Helen Gardner (New York: Oxford University Press, 1978), 11.

38. *Achor* means misfortune.

39. See, for example, the note in *The Jerusalem Bible* ([Garden City, NY: Doubleday, 1966], 1454), explaining that when *ḥěsěd* is used for human relationships, it means friendship, union, loyalty; used of God, the term signals his faithfulness to his covenant; used by Hosea "in the context of married love, the word assumes and from then on retains a still warmer significance: it means the tender love God has for his people. . . . this divine *hesed* calls for corresponding *hesed* in man, a love which is a joyful submission to the will of God and an active charity to fellow men."

CHAPTER THREE

1. On descent and inheritance, see Mara E. Donaldson, "Kinship Theory in the Patriarchal Narratives: The Case of the Barren Wife," *Journal of the American Academy of Religion* 49, no. 1 (1981): 77–87; Zafrira Ben-Barak, "Inheritance by Daughters in the Ancient Near East," *Journal of Semitic Studies* 25 (1980): 22–33; Millar Burrows, "The Ancient Oriental Background of Hebrew Levirate Marriage," *Bulletin of the American Schools of Oriental Research* 77 (1940): 2–15; Terry J. Prewitt, "Kinship Structures and the Genesis Genealogies," *Journal of Near Eastern Studies* 40 (1981): 87–98; Shaye J. D. Cohen et al., "The Issue of Patrilineal Descent: A Symposium," *Judaism* 34, no. 1 (1985): 3–135; Naomi

Steinberg, *Kinship and Marriage in Genesis: A Household Economics Perspective* (Minneapolis: Fortress Press, 1993); David R. Mace, *Hebrew Marriage: A Sociological Study* (London: Epworth Press, 1953).

2. David Schneider, *A Critique of the Study of Kinship* (Ann Arbor: University of Michigan Press, 1984).

3. Julian Pitt-Rivers has written an analysis of the Genesis narratives that asks many of the key questions: "How closely related must you be in order to be one people and how other must you be in order to be a spouse? Other sex? Other family? Other lineage? Other tribe? Other nation? The limits of endogamy and exogamy are debated throughout the length of Genesis" (*The Fate of Shechem, or the Politics of Sex* [Cambridge: Cambridge University Press, 1977], 154). His answers pursue a different direction, one marked by his own version of structuralism (he is no slavish follower of Lévi-Strauss). His chief debt, in turn, is to Edmund Leach, *Genesis as Myth and Other Essays* (London: Cape, 1969), a work that has been criticized by biblical scholarship for its small mistakes but whose depth of insights into the key biblical quandaries will doubtless endure.

4. Christiana van Houten's *The Alien in Israelite Law* (Sheffield, England: JSOT Press, 1991) carefully delineates how varied the concept and even the use of the term *ger* is in the biblical legal collections, ranging from "resident alien" to convert.

5. This pattern of a rejected son prevails in each generation in the patriarchal saga. The divine blessing and promise conferred on Abraham is not conferred equally by him on his sons Ishmael and Isaac. Ishmael is to be an outcast. The pattern is disrupted, significantly, in another account about Ishmael, progenitor of the Arabs: "I will establish my covenant with him [Isaac] as an everlasting covenant for his descendants after him. And as for Ishmael, I have heard you: I will surely bless him; I will make him fruitful and will greatly increase his numbers. He will be the father of twelve rulers, and I will make him into a great nation. But my covenant I will establish with Isaac" (Gen 17:19–20).

6. Norman K. Gottwald, *The Tribes of Yahweh: A Sociology of the Religion of Liberated Israel, 1250–1050 B.C.E.* (Maryknoll, NY: Orbis, 1979); John Van Seters, *Abraham in History and Tradition* (New Haven: Yale University Press, 1975).

7. Because Isaac/Ishmael and Jacob/Esau are eponymous ancestors, their fraternal rivalry signals hostility between peoples.

8. A legal tradition frames all of the stories about the children's inheritance: the favored son, often but not necessarily the oldest, will receive a special portion over and above the others, and the other sons will not be excluded from the inheritance but will share equally with

each other. This sets the exclusions of Ishmael and Esau in high relief. The pattern is broken by Joseph, who shares the inheritance with his brothers and thereby the twelve-brother nation of Israel can come into being.

9. Rebekah, born to Bethuel son of Milcah, the wife of Nahor, Abraham's brother.

10. Nancy Jay offers a fresh reading of patrilineal descent in the Genesis narratives in *Throughout Your Generations Forever: Sacrifice, Religion, and Paternity* (Chicago: University of Chicago Press, 1992). James Nohrnberg also pursues the intricacies of genealogy in Genesis in "The Keeping of Nahor: The Etiology of Biblical Election," in *The Book and the Text: The Bible and Literary Theory*, ed. Regina Schwartz (Oxford: Basil Blackwell, 1990), 161–88.

11. Lot's daughters seduce him, but that incest issues in the birth of the foreigners, the Ammonites and Moabites. Judah's daughter-in-law seduces him, and that incest issues in the birth of Perez, the progenitor of King David of Israel.

12. Robert A. Oden Jr., "Jacob as Father, Husband, and Nephew: Kinship Studies and the Patriarchal Narratives," *Journal of Biblical Literature* 102, no. 2 (1983): 189–205. Jacob and his wives are actually double cross-cousins, related on both sides.

13. See Howard Eilberg-Schwartz, *The Savage in Judaism* (Bloomington: Indiana University Press, 1990), 177–94, for a fine discussion of leaking bodies and pollution.

14. Unsurprisingly, biblical scholars have not been able to agree on the referent; their proposals have ranged from non-Jewish inhabitants of the territory, Jewish and non-Jewish inhabitants outside the territory, and non-Jewish or part-Jewish descendants of peoples like the Moabites and Edomites, whether living within the territory of Judea or not. I am indebted in my discussion of Ezra to F. Volker Greifenhagen's unpublished seminar paper, "Intermarriage as a Theme and Social Problem of Post-exilic Judah: Reading the 'Evidence' of Ezra and Nehemiah."

15. Ironically, most of these peoples (the exceptions are the Ammonites, Moabites, and Egyptians) no longer existed in Ezra's day, in post-exilic times. In fact, the "others" we would anticipate Ezra wanting the Israelites to separate themselves from are the conquerors with whom they have assimilated during the exile—the Persians and Babylonians—but he makes no mention of them.

16. The related question, in whose interest is it to categorize the foreigner—historically, who gains and who loses— is one that consigns us to speculation. My strategy is to seek out ideologies that are compati-

ble and conflicting, to ask if the narratives isolate consistent winners and losers in this deadly game of insiders and outsiders, and to critique that game, rather than to enter into the perilous business of dating the text and assigning definite cultural contexts to those dates only to have them revised repeatedly by biblical archeologists.

17. Mary Douglas in *Purity and Danger* (London: Routledge and Kegan Paul, 1966) and the recent study "Atonement in Leviticus," *Jewish Studies Quarterly* 1 (1993/94): 109–30, which revises her earlier thesis, explore biblical thought on purity in detail. Julia Kristeva's *Powers of Horror: An Essay on Abjection* (New York: Columbia University Press, 1982) is a brilliantly provocative rumination on abjection, and I am generally inspired by her thinking.

18. On the whole, the Deuteronomistic narrative that spans Judges through 2 Kings does not condemn intermarriage. Solomon is a notable exception: he had many foreign wives—among them a daughter of Pharaoh—about which the narrator is disapproving, blaming the idolatry of the entire kingdom on them. Joseph married a daughter of Pharaoh, and their children Manasseh and Ephraim are formally adopted by his father, Jacob, to be included among the tribes of Israel. Deuteronomy 23 specifies that no Ammonite or Moabite or any of their descendants may enter the "assembly of the Lord" (that is, be counted among the Israelites) "even down to the tenth generation. . . . Do not seek peace or good relations with them as long as you live." But when Ruth the Moabite gave birth to the progenitor of David, she and her illustrious descendants were, we are assured, admitted to the "assembly of the Lord." See Oden, "Jacob"; Athalya Brenner, *The Israelite Woman: Social Role and Literary Type in Biblical Narrative* (Sheffield, England: JSOT Press, 1985).

19. Marc Shell, "Marranos (Pigs), or From Coexistence to Toleration," *Critical Inquiry* 17 (1991): 307. Shell concludes that the rarity of the category of a nonsibling human, an other who is not a brother, in Christian discourse is the source of intolerance. See also Daniel Boyarin and Jonathan Boyarin, "Diaspora: Generation and the Ground of Jewish Identity," *Critical Inquiry* 19 (1993): 693–725.

20. Phyllis Trible, "Two Women in a Man's World: A Reading of the Book of Ruth," *Soundings* 59 (1976): 215–79.

21. Ibid.

22. Claude Lévi-Strauss, *The Elementary Structures of Kinship* (1949), trans. James Harle Bell and John Richard von Sturmer (Boston: Beacon Press, 1969).

23. See Robert Alter, *The Art of Biblical Narrative* (New York: Basic

Books, 1981); Meir Sternberg, *The Poetics of Biblical Narrative: Ideological Literature and the Drama of Reading* (Bloomington: Indiana University Press, 1985), 316.

24. Much work has been done on the wife-as-sister motif in its cultural context: Nuzi documents attest to adoptions of wives as sisters in vestiges of fratriarchal society where women had higher status than men in the ancient world. Discussions of these episodes include those of E. A. Speiser, *The Anchor Bible Commentary on Genesis* (Garden City, NY: Doubleday, 1964); Robert Polzin, "'The Ancestresses of Israel in Danger' in Danger?" *Semeia* 3 (1975): 81–98; John Van Seters, *Abraham in History and Tradition* (New Haven: Yale University Press, 1975); Michael Fishbane, "Composition and Structure in the Jacob Cycle," *Journal of Jewish Studies* 26 (1975): 15–38; and Naomi Steinberg, *Kinship and Marriage in Genesis.* The wife-as-sister motif in the context of depictions of the patriarchal wives was the subject of my thesis in religious studies under the direction of James S. Ackerman.

25. The patriarchal narratives are inconsistent about incest. In contrast to Abraham, Lot's incest with his daughters gives rise to the foreigners, the Ammonites and Moabites. The parallel story in which Judah sleeps with his daughter-in-law gives rise to the Israelite line of David, but there is evidence that this daughter-in-law is a foreigner. While the Bible legislates against incest and attaches it to the foreigner in the case of Lot, no easy generalizations hold.

26. Lévi-Strauss, *Elementary Structures of Kinship.*

27. However improbable we may find such rapid inversion from hatred/violence to love, Leviticus legislates that the rapist must either marry his victim or pay the bride-price for her, seeing her as violated property.

28. Despite the outrage of the sons of Jacob, in theory the Shechemites' behavior was within Israelite legal definition: under Israelite law if a man rapes the daughter of another man the offense can be settled by having the rapist marry her.

29. See Meir Sternberg's nuanced and detailed discussion of the episode of the rape of Dinah, *Poetics of Biblical Narrative,* 445–75. With Sternberg, I am reading the story against the grain of the interpretive tradition that asserts that the Shechemites are portrayed as morally superior to the Israelites in this encounter, and that therefore the behavior of the sons of Jacob, who use an excuse to kill and rob the people whose land they coveted, is all the more reprehensible—as Jacob himself condemns it.

30. Robert Alter has explored the dynamics of how type scenes work in the Hebrew Bible in "Biblical Type Scenes and the Uses of Convention," in *The Art of Biblical Narrative* (New York: Basic Books, 1981), 47–62.

31. David Noel Freedman, "Dinah and Shechem, Tamar and Amnon," *Austin Seminary Bulletin* 105 (spring 1990): 51–63. Freedman sees the two stories as forming "book-ends or two parentheses around the story of Israel from the time of the patriarch until the establishment of the united kingdoms by David and Solomon" (51). He draws the insightful conclusion that the stories suggest "the immorality rampant throughout the body politic," foreshadowing the decline and fall of the nation, and serve as a warning that the restoration of Israel must depend upon keeping the standards of the covenant that have been violated (62–63).

32. While Tamar is the daughter of Amnon's father but not his mother, and hence she is a half-sister like Abraham's wife Sarah, the narrative insists on calling them brother and sister throughout; here the category "sister" clearly encompasses a sibling by one parent.

33. Why the abhorrence of incest in Israelite law when there is a corollary recoiling from exogamy? This is a question that also struck Edmund Leach in *Genesis as Myth and Other Essays* (London: Cape, 1969). His response (indebted to Lévi-Strauss) is that the biblical narratives were written to "mediate these contraries." It is difficult to quarrel with such a generalized claim, but it may be too broad to be very helpful. Unfortunately, my interest, in the way exogamous and endogamous marriage figures in the understanding of the foreigner and the insider, is not addressed by Leach.

34. Jack Goody, *Comparative Studies in Kinship* (Stanford: Stanford University Press, 1969), 13–38.

35. Leach, *Genesis as Myth*, 7–23.

36. See Albert C. Sundberg Jr., *The Old Testament of the Early Church,* Harvard Theological Studies 20 (Cambridge: Harvard University Press, 1964). "Christians received their collection of holy writings from Judaism before a restricted collection of Writings and a closed canon was formulated in Judaism" (82).

37. The distortions begin with mislabeling the curse on Canaan; biblical historians believe that the Canaanites were difficult to distinguish linguistically, culturally, or ethnically from the Israelites.

38. Canaan is depicted as the youngest son of Ham; for much of the second millennium B.C.E., Canaan was a province of the Egyptian empire, and the Egyptians were grouped with the children of Ham. But

the substitution, the "curse of Ham," implies a causal logic the story does not offer explicitly, for Ham looks in on his father's nakedness even though Canaan is the one who is cursed.

39. Philological arguments were also marshaled. In his *Dictionary of the Holy Bible,* ed. Charles Taylor (London: W. Stratford, Crown-Court, Temple-Bar, 1801), Augustin Calmet translated the name Ham as "burnt, swarthy," and "black" and said that Noah had given him Africa for his inheritance.

40. Josiah Priest, *Slavery, as It Relates to the Negro, or African Race, Examined in the Light of Circumstances, History, and the Holy Scriptures; with an Account of the Origin of the Black Man's Color, Causes of His State of Servitude and Traces of His Character as Well in Ancient and in Modern Times* (Albany: C. Van Benthuysen and Co., 1843), 15, 27–28, cited in Thomas Virgil Peterson, *Ham and Japheth: The Mythic World of Whites in the Antebellum South* (Metuchen, NJ: Scarecrow Press, 1978), 42. Josiah Priest was a New York harness maker whose book was reprinted five times in eight years.

41. Peterson, *Ham and Japheth,* 42–43.

42. *Dred Scott v Sanders,* 1857, cited in Don E. Fehrenbacker, *The Dred Scott Case: Its Significance in American Law and Politics* (New York: Oxford University Press, 1978), 341–43.

43. Etienne Balibar writes: "In the space of the world-economy, which has effectively become that of world politics and world ideology, the division between subhumans and super-humans is a structural but violently unstable one. Previously, the notion of humanity was merely an abstraction. But, to the question, 'What is man?' which—however aberrant its forms may appear to us—is insistently present in racist thought, there is today no response in which this split is not at work" (Etienne Balibar and Immanuel Wallerstein, *Race, Nation, Class: Ambiguous Identities,* translation of Balibar by Chris Turner [London: Verso, 1991], 44).

44. The traditional answer, that homosexuality is against the injunction of procreation, is irresponsible at best; cultures that celebrate homosexuality also bear children from heterosexual relations.

45. Sigmund Freud, *Totem and Taboo* (1950), trans. James Strachey (London: Routledge, 1960), 142.

46. Ibid., 49.

47. The story of the curse of Canaan is regarded as a conflation of two separate stories, which now encompasses three generations, that of Noah, Ham, and Canaan, instead of two. See Speiser, *Genesis,* 60–63; John Skinner, *The International Critical Commentary: A Critical and Exeget-*

ical Commentary on Genesis (New York: Charles Scribner's Sons, 1910), 181–87.

48. Freud, *Totem and Taboo,* 141.

49. Freud insisted upon his intuition that incest and other taboos were interconnected, but the relation he constructs seems forced. For Freud, no one can have the women once hoarded by the father; the incest taboo is born of guilt for parricide. But I would argue that the incest taboo is not predicated upon desire for women at all, but on the son's desire for the father, and the incest taboo against women is a displacement of the injunction not to have the father.

50. For a longer discussion, see Regina Schwartz, "Freud's God: Moses and Polytheism," in *Post-Secular Philosophy,* ed. Philip Blond (New York: Routledge, 1996); see also Susan Handelman, *The Slayers of Moses: The Emergence of Rabbinic Interpretation in Modern Literary Theory* (Albany: State University of New York Press, 1982); Yosef Hayim Yerushalmi, *Freud's Moses: Judaism Terminable and Interminable* (New Haven: Yale University Press, 1991).

51. Freud, *Totem and Taboo,* xi, 144.

52. Ibid., 145.

53. Sigmund Freud, *Future of an Illusion* (New York: Norton, 1961), 19.

54. In this, as in most things, the Bible is inconsistent. In Ex 34:27–35, when Moses is in the presence of God, his face lights up. In Ex 33:11, we are told that Moses and Yahweh talk to each other as a man talks to his companion, that is, probably face to face.

CHAPTER FOUR

1. F. Volker Greifenhagen, "'That You May Know That the Lord Makes a Distinction between Egypt and Israel': The Plagues and Israelite Identity in the Pentateuch," a paper delivered at the American Academy of Religion, Chicago, November 1995.

2. Yitzhak Shamir, speech at the Middle East Peace Conference, Madrid, 31 October 1991, from Reuters transcripts.

3. Wilhelm de Wette, quoted in Hans-Joachim Kraus, *Geschichte der historisch-kritischen Erforschung des Alten Testaments,* 2d edition (Neukirchen-Vluyn: Neukirchener Verlag, 1969), 176–77. Like any discipline, biblical scholarship is not monolithic. In particular, recent interest in literary questions is beginning to make headway into the dominant methodology I characterize. See especially the sensitive readings of David Gunn, in *The Story of King David* (Sheffield, England: JSOT Press,

1978), who argues that the so-called succession narrative is not best described as history writing; J. P. Fokkelman, *Narrative Art and Poetry in the Books of Samuel,* 2 vols. (Assen, The Netherlands: Van Gorcum, 1981, 1986); Robert Polzin, *Samuel and the Deuteronomist* (New York: Harper and Row, 1989), especially 1–17, who is explicitly bracketing the concerns that preoccupy traditional biblical scholars; Meir Sternberg, *The Poetics of Biblical Narrative* (Bloomington: Indiana University Press, 1985); Peter Miscall, *I Samuel: A Literary Reading* (Bloomington: Indiana University Press, 1986).

Furthermore, not all traditional biblical scholars who are interested in sources depict a developmental vision of history for the Samuel narratives. Among the notable exceptions is R. N. Whybray (*The Succession Narrative,* Studies in Biblical Theology 2d Series, 9 [Naperville, IL: A. R. Allenson, 1968]), who points out that there are too many personal scenes for this narrative to be characterized as history; instead, he regards it as political propaganda. His account of this so-called political propaganda produces a far more coherent ideology than any I detect: "Every incident in the story without exception is a necessary link in a chain of narrative which shows how, by the steady elimination of the alternative possibilities, it came about that it was Solomon who succeeded his father on the throne of Israel" (20–21).

4. A brief survey recently published of the major positions held by biblical scholars in this century shows how consistent their presuppositions are despite their different conclusions, for these theories take different stands on the same issue: the nature and extent of two layers of redacted material in the biblical text and on how those two layers came together. The two layers are the Dtr and non-Dtr. Dtr means the Deuteronomic and/or Deuteronomistic, the distinction being part of the dispute about the "nature and extent of the sources." A summary of the positions is in Suzanne Boorer, "The Importance of a Diachronic Approach: The Case of Genesis-Kings," *Catholic Biblical Quarterly* 51 (1989): 195–208.

5. I pursue the question of biblical repetition versus fulfillment further in "Joseph's Bones and the Resurrection of the Text," *PMLA* 103 (1988): 114–24, and in chapter 5 below.

6. Robert A. Oden Jr., *The Bible without Theology* (New York: Harper and Row, 1987), 6. I am greatly indebted to Oden's chapter 1 for bringing to the fore the role of German historicism in biblical scholarship.

7. Johann Gustav Droysen, *Outline of the Principles of History,* trans. and introduced by E. Benjamin Andrews (Boston: Ginn and Co., 1893), partial translation of *Historik: Vorlesungen über Enzyklopadie und Methodo-*

logie der Geschichte (1857), 8th edition, ed. R. Hubner (Munich: R. Old-ernbourg, 1977).

8. In his *Geschichte de preussischen Politik* (1868–86)—which he worked on for decades, leaving it unfinished at his death—Droysen tried to argue that, ever since the fifteenth century Prussian rulers (ever conscious of Prussia's German mission) followed a consistent plan of action, a plan still unfolding in Germany. See the discussion of Droysen in Georg G. Iggers, *The German Conception of History: The National Tradition of Historical Thought from Herder to the Present* (Middletown, CT: Wesleyan University Press, 1968), 106.

9. Wilhelm von Humboldt, "Über die Aufgabe des Geschichtschreibers," in *Gesammelte Schriften,* 17 vols. (Berlin: B. Behr, 1903–36), 4:35. This does not necessarily mean the historian is an empiricist. Events are "only in part accessible to the senses. The rest has to be felt *(empfunden),* inferred *(geschlossen),* or divined *(errathen)*" (as cited and translated in Iggers, *German Conception of History,* 60).

10. Julius Wellhausen, *Prolegomena to the History of Ancient Israel* (1878; reprint, Cleveland: Meridian, 1957), 12.

11. Ibid., 228.

12. While my focus here is the influence of German historicism on biblical study, classical philology had an equally formative role, and it too was made to serve the principles of consistency and development.

13. Martin Noth, *The Deuteronomistic History* (1967), trans. J. Doull et al. (Sheffield, England: JSOT Press, 1981), 80–81. This thesis of Martin Noth was considerably revised by Gerhard von Rad and Frank Cross, who noted the positive elements in the Deuteronomistic history that conflicted with this sweeping principle. This critical history is summarized in P. Kyle McCarter Jr., *The Anchor Bible Commentary on II Samuel* (Garden City, NY: Doubleday, 1984), 4–8.

14. Michel Foucault, "Nietzsche, Genealogy, History," in *Language, Counter-Memory, Practice: Selected Essays and Interviews,* ed. D. F. Bouchard (Ithaca: Cornell University Press, 1977), 139–64.

15. Mieke Bal has explored the provocative relation between speech acts, cutting, and violence against women in the Book of Judges; see especially her discussion of the sacrifice of Jephthah's daughter and the dismemberment of the concubine (*Death and Dissymmetry: The Politics of Coherence in the Book of Judges* [Chicago: University of Chicago Press, 1988], 129–68).

16. Gunn, *Story of King David;* David M. Gunn, "David and the Gift of the Kingdom," *Semeia* 3 (1975): 14–45; David M. Gunn, "In Security: The David of Biblical Narrative," in *Signs and Wonders: Biblical Texts in Literary Focus,* ed. J. Cheryl Exum (Atlanta: Scholars Press, 1989), 133–51.

17. Harry Berger Jr., "The Lie of the Land: The Text beyond Canaan," *Representations* 25 (winter 1989): 123.

18. On Moses, see James Nohrnberg, "Moses," in *Images of Man and God: Old Testament Short Stories in Literary Focus,* ed. Burke O. Long (Sheffield, England: Almond Press, 1981), 35–57. He has another book on Moses currently in press.

19. Again, Harry Berger Jr. has described this phenomenon of the return to Egypt emerging from the competition between royalist and priest: "To build the sanctuary is to return to Egypt. To build the temple is to return to Egypt. To rebuild the temple is to return to Egypt" ("Lie of the Land," 129). Richard E. Friedman, in *Who Wrote the Bible* (Englewood Cliffs, NJ: Prentice Hall, 1987), also notes that combining the Deuteronomistic history with Jeremiah yields a story of leaving Egypt and returning to Egypt. In the closing chapters of Jeremiah, the remnant left in Jerusalem after the capture of the city and destruction of the Temple also depart—to go back to Egypt.

20. Claude Lévi-Strauss, *The Elementary Structures of Kinship* (Boston: Beacon Press, 1969), originally published as *Les Structures élémentaires de la parente* (Paris: Presses Universitaires de France, 1949).

21. Sexual and political power are so completely fused again in the story of Saul's concubine that it is not quite right to claim that one is a metaphor for the other; they are not distinct enough to stand in for one another. Upon the death of Saul, his general, Abner, sleeps with one of the deceased king's concubines, Rizpah. When the king's son learns of it, he is incensed; the act is clearly a sign of pretension to the throne, for the competition over who will succeed Saul—his son or his general—is fought symbolically over sexual ownership of the concubine. The king's general does not like competition from the king's son: "Am I a dog's head? Here I am full of goodwill toward the house of Saul your father, and you find fault with me about a woman!" (2 Sam 2:8). Abner is sufficiently incensed over the contest about "the woman" to vow to betray Saul's son by joining the enemy David in a treaty. Needless to say, his betrayal is cast in the same terms—traffic in women—for the condition David sets to enter into any agreement with Abner ups the ante: David will take, not one of Saul's concubines, but Saul's *daughter,* Michal, thereby crushing all hopes for succession for both Abner and Saul's son.

22. Lévi-Strauss, *Elementary Structures of Kinship,* 68.

23. Tony Tanner, *Adultery in the Novel: Contract and Transgression* (Baltimore: Johns Hopkins University Press, 1979), 12, 13.

24. See Joseph Levitsky, "The Illegitimate Child in Jewish Law," *Jewish Biblical Quarterly* 18 (fall 1989): 6–12. In the Bible, *māmzēr* also means

illegitimate as a product of an incestuous union, as the children of Lot by his daughters.

25. Wolfgang M. W. Roth, "NBL," *Vetus Testamentum* 10 (1960): 401.

CHAPTER FIVE

1. Yosef Hayim Yerushalmi, *Zakhor: Jewish History and Jewish Memory* (Seattle: University of Washington Press, 1982), 5, a book that celebrates the achievement of biblical historiography.

2. Paul Connerton, *How Societies Remember* (Cambridge: Cambridge University Press, 1989), 21.

3. Ibid., 3.

4. Philip R. Davies, *In Search of "Ancient Israel,"* JSOT Supplement Series 148 (Sheffield, England: Sheffield Academic Press, 1992). In this penetrating study, he writes of this winning party: "The establishment of a temple and priesthood, a sacrificial system, a caste system . . . and an ideology of holiness to support it were not separable as religious 'characteristics' from other means of political control. To characterize, let alone glorify, these mechanisms as products of religious zeal would be bordering on the ludicrous. . . . Negatively, the 'people of the land' who have *prima facie* a more secure right to the land will be denied that right unless they conform to cultic and ethnic definition" (117–18).

5. Morton Smith, *Palestinian Parties and Politics That Shaped the Old Testament* (New York: Columbia University Press, 1971), 1. See also James A. Sanders, *From Sacred Story to Sacred Text* (Philadelphia: Fortress Press, 1987), 11–30; Bernhard Lang, *Monotheism and the Prophetic Minority* (Sheffield, England: Almond Press, 1983).

6. Davies, *In Search of "Ancient Israel,"* 133.

7. John Van Seters, *In Search of History: Historiography in the Ancient World and the Origins of Biblical History* (New Haven: Yale University Press, 1983).

8. Shemaryahu Talmon, "Textual Study of the Bible: A New Outlook," in *Qumran and the History of the Biblical Text,* ed. Shemaryahu Talmon and Frank Moore Cross (Cambridge: Harvard University Press, 1975), 327.

9. Harry Y. Gamble, *Anchor Bible Dictionary,* ed. David Noel Freedman (New York: Doubleday, 1992), s.v. "canon," 847.

10. Talmon, "Textual Study of the Bible," 379.

11. "Complementing the divine revelation now embodied in a written Torah, the sage seeks from God the grace of an ongoing revelation through the words of Scripture itself—as mediated through exegesis"

(Michael Fishbane, "From Scribalism to Rabbinism," in *The Garments of Torah* [Bloomington: Indiana University Press, 1989], 67).

12. Ibid., 69.

13. See Exodus 15. In the following discussion of Exodus, I am closely indebted to Michael Fishbane's excellent discussion of the motif in one of the best studies to date of biblical literature, *Biblical Interpretation in Ancient Israel* (Oxford: Clarendon Press, 1985), 358–68.

14. John Milton was the astute reader who first pointed this out to me. See my *Remembering and Repeating: On Milton's Theology and Poetics* (Cambridge: Cambridge University Press, 1988; reprint, Chicago: Chicago University Press, 1993).

15. Eric Hobsbawm, *The Invention of Tradition,* ed. Eric Hobsbawm and Terence Ranger (Cambridge: Cambridge University Press, 1983), 8.

16. Bible and Culture Collective, *The Postmodern Bible* (New Haven: Yale University Press, 1995), 282–93.

17. See Jonathan Boyarin, "Reading Exodus into History," *New Literary History* 23 (1992): 523–54, a penetrating study especially sensitive to the "shaping force of a history of readings on the latest in their sequence" (524) that discusses Said's and Walzer's exodus readings at length; Michael Walzer, whose *Exodus and Revolution* (New York: Basic Books, 1984) focuses on the radical political echoes throughout Western history; and Edward Said, "Michael Walzer's Exodus and Revolution: A Canaanite Reading," *Grand Street* 5 (winter 1986): 86–106. For a different approach, see Norman K. Gottwald, *The Tribes of Yahweh: A Sociology of the Religion of Liberated Israel* (Maryknoll, NY: Orbis, 1979).

18. Robert Allen Warrior, "Canaanites, Cowboys, and Indians: Deliverance, Conquest, and Liberation Theology Today," *Christianity and Crisis* 49 (1989): 264.

19. See Steven Knapp ("Collective Memory and the Actual Past," *Representations* 26 [spring 1989]: 123–49), who asks, "Why should it ever matter, if it does, that an authoritative narrative correspond to historical actuality?" and how does the truth about the actual past have relevance for ethical and political action in the present (123–24).

20. Boyarin, "Reading Exodus into History," 543.

21. Gottwald, *Tribes of Yahweh*. See also George Mendenhall, "The Hebrew Conquest of Palestine," *Biblical Archaeologist* 25 (1962): 66–87, where the revolt model was introduced.

22. The scholarship is summarized by Robert Gnuse in "Israelite Settlement of Canaan: A Peaceful Internal Process, Parts 1 and 2," *Biblical Theology Bulletin* 21 (1991): 56–66, 109–17. A chief proponent of continuity between the Canaanites and the Israelites is Niels Peter Lemche, *Ancient History: A New History of Israelite Society* (Sheffield, England:

JSOT Press, 1988) and *The Canaanites and Their Land: The Tradition of the Canaanites,* JSOTS 110 (Sheffield, England: JSOT Press, 1990).

23. Gnuse, "Israelite Settlement of Canaan," 116.

24. Keith Whitelam, "Israel's Traditions of Origin: Reclaiming the Land," *Journal for the Study of the Old Testament* 44 (1989): 19–42.

25. Warrior, "Canaanites, Cowboys, and Indians," 264.

26. Here I concur with Jonathan Boyarin.

27. Knapp, "Collective Memory and the Actual Past," 123.

28. See Pierre Bourdieu, *Outline of a Theory of Practice,* trans. Richard Nice (Cambridge: Cambridge University Press, 1977); Pierre Bourdieu, *Reproduction in Education, Society, and Culture,* trans. Richard Nice (London: Sage Publications, 1977); John Guillory, *Cultural Capital* (Chicago: University of Chicago Press, 1993).

29. Gnuse, "Israelite Settlement of Canaan, Part 2," 116.

30. This poetics of repetition has been richly explored by Robert Alter, *The Art of Biblical Narrative* (New York: Basic Books, 1981); Fishbane, *Biblical Interpretation;* and Meir Sternberg, *The Poetics of Biblical Narrative* (Bloomington: Indiana University Press, 1985).

31. There is a glimmer in the biblical narrative of longing for plenitude even in the story of Abraham's sons, for Ishmael will be the patriarch of a league of twelve tribes (Gen 17:20). This vision is compromised by Sarah's categorical rejection of Hagar and her offspring.

32. My ensuing observations about memory largely follow the argument I made in "Joseph's Bones and the Resurrection of the Text," *PMLA* 103 (March 1988): 114–24, which in turn reflects the paper I delivered at the Colorado Conference on the Bible and Literary Theory in May 1986 (along with helpful suggestions from the audience). To my immense delight, in the same year that "Joseph's Bones" appeared, Gabriel Josipovici published *The Book of God* (New Haven: Yale University Press, 1988), where I discovered corroboration for many of my instincts; working independently (but as two literature professors on two different continents), we had arrived at remarkably similar conclusions about the importance of an ongoing, open memory in the Bible. In the end, his excellent discussion (135–52) turns to liturgy and to Proust while mine turns to typology and Irenaeus.

33. See Gerald Bruns's discussion in "Canon and Power in the Hebrew Scriptures," *Critical Inquiry* 10 (March 1984): 462–80; reprint, *Canons,* ed. Robert von Hallberg (Chicago: University of Chicago Press, 1984), 65–83.

34. Sigmund Freud, *Standard Edition of the Complete Psychological Works* (London: Hogarth, 1953–74), 12:148. See Meir Sternberg's discussion of gap filling in the Bible, *Poetics of Biblical Narrative,* 186–263.

35. I invoke Freud, and will often, because *he* invokes Joseph at the very opening of his great project of dream interpretation, *Die Traumdeutung,* calling up the ancient authority of dream interpretation to clear the ground: Joseph was wrong to interpret thus, Freud will interpret so. But he himself taught us to read such denials as affirmations, as a debt admitted only to be denied only to be admitted. Perhaps his relation to Joseph the dream interpreter is similarly complex. There may be a deeper affinity in their technique than Freud wanted to be fully aware of: Joseph may not only simplistically substitute one code, a predictive one, for another, the dream (as Freud would have it); perhaps Joseph also demonstrates that interpretation is bound to repression.

36. Freud, *Standard Edition,* 12:148.

37. Paul Ricoeur, *Freud and Philosophy: An Essay on Interpretation,* trans. Denis Savage (New Haven: Yale University Press, 1970), 15.

38. Harold Bloom, *A Map of Misreading* (New York: Oxford University Press, 1975).

39. E. A. Speiser, *The Anchor Bible Commentary on Genesis,* (Garden City, NY: Doubleday, 1964), 293. In one version, Joseph's defender is Reuben and the traders are the Midianites; in the other, Joseph's defender is Judah and the traders are the Ishmaelites.

40. See James S. Ackerman, "Joseph, Judah, and Jacob," in *Literary Interpretations of Biblical Narratives,* vol. 2, ed. K. R. R. Gros Louis (Nashville: Abingdon, 1974), 85–113.

41. Even the condemned Cain is given a glimmer of hope for a future. He founds the first city (Gen 4:17), and his descendants are the founders of civilization (Gen 4:20–22); moreover, in the composite story of the Flood (Gen 6–9), a latent tradition, silenced, has left traces that Cain's son Lamech, instead of Noah, survived the Flood with his three artificer sons, thereby preserving essential arts and crafts for humanity. Needless to say, the Noah tradition won out. See Speiser, *Genesis,* 41–43, 54–56.

42. Northrop Frye, *The Great Code: The Bible and Literature* (New York: Harcourt, Brace, Jovanovich, 1982), "Typology I" and "Typology II," 78–138.

43. Ibid., 171.

44. Joseph A. Fitzmyer, *The Anchor Bible,* vol. 28, *The Gospel according to Luke* (Garden City, NY: Doubleday, 1981), 167.

45. Frye, *Great Code,* 171.

46. M. H. Abrams, *Natural Supernaturalism* (New York: Norton, 1971), 36.

47. Frye, *Great Code,* 82.

48. Michael Walzer, *Exodus and Revolution* (New York: Basic Books, 1984), 5.

49. Frye does apply the descent structure to Joseph explicitly, but briefly. "The Incarnation was a voluntary descent into the lower world repeated in the creation of Adam, hence Paul characterizes Jesus as a second Adam (I Corinthians 15:45). There is in Genesis a type of such a descent, not wholly voluntary, in the story of Joseph, whose 'coat of many colors' suggests fertility-god imagery, and who, like Burns' John Barleycorn, is thrown into a pit" (*Great Code,* 176). Frye's own associative methods are not so very different from Tertullian: "Joseph likewise was a type of Christ, not indeed on this ground . . . that he suffered persecution for the cause of God from his brethren, as Christ did from His brethren after the flesh, the Jews; but when he is blessed by his father in these words: 'His glory is that of a bullock; his horns are the horns of a unicorn; with them shall he push the nations to the very ends of the earth,' (Deut. 33:17), he was not, of course, designated as a mere unicorn with its one horn, or a minotaur with two; but Christ was indicated in him—a bullock in respect of both His characteristics: to some as severe as a Judge, to others gentle as a Saviour, whose horns were the extremities of His cross. For the antenna, which is a part of a cross, the ends are called horns; while the midway stake of the whole frame is the unicorn" (Tertullian, "The Five Books against Marcion," in *The Ante-Nicene Fathers* [Grand Rapids, MI: Eerdmans, 1980], 3:336). Clearly, typology does not foreclose invention. Even Joseph's seduction by Potiphar's wife has been seen typologically, for Joseph was Christlike "because he flourished as the flower of chastity in a gross and carnal age" ("The Testaments of the Twelve Patriarchs," in *The Ante-Nicene Fathers,* ed. Alexander Roberts and James Donaldson, revised by A. Cleveland Coxe [New York: Scribner's, 1906], 8:4).

50. Jean Danielou, "The Problem of Symbolism," *Thought* 25 (1950): 423–40.

51. Lancelot Andrewes, *Sermons on the Nativity* (Grand Rapids, MI: Baker House, 1955), 237.

52. Ibid., 48.

53. Irenaeus, *Demonstratio* 37 SPCK, 103. See also K. J. Woollcombe, "The Biblical Origins and Patristic Development of Typology," in *Essays in Typology,* Studies in Biblical Theology, 22 (Naperville, IL: Allenson, 1957), 42.

54. Erich Auerbach, "Figura," in *Scenes from the Drama of European Literature* (New York: Meridian Books, 1959), 49–51.

55. Edwin Sandys, *Sermons Made by the Most Reverend Father in God,*

Edwin, Archbishop of York, Primate of England and Metropolitan at London (1585), ed. John Ayre (Cambridge: Cambridge University Press, 1841), 7–8.

56. Edward Said, *Beginnings: Intention and Method* (New York: Basic Books, 1975), 280.

57. John Milton, "Areopagitica," in *The Complete Prose Works of John Milton,* ed. Don Wolfe et al. (New Haven: Yale University Press, 1959), 2:549.

Index

Index

Bible (continued)
terpreting, 9–11, 17–18; as a manual
for politics, 8, 58–62, 102–6, 123;
plenitude in, xi, 34–37, 119; presumption of scarcity in, xi, 2–4,
88–90; remembering in, 127–28,
143–45, 159–62, 173–76; understanding of identity in, x, 6–7, 83–
87, 138–42. See also Biblical narratives; Christian Bible; Named books of
the Bible
Biblical narratives: about adultery, 18,
62–75, 137, 140–42; about conquest,
59–60; defining the foreigner, 78–79,
83–95, 100; of the exodus, 148–53,
169; fixing of, 145–47; as forgetting
and reinventing the past, 159, 162–
67, 173–74; idea of nation in, 38,
120–22, 145–46, 133–42; idea of nomadism in, 41, 43–44, 50–52, 131;
idea of plenitude in, 19, 34–37, 117–
19, 164, 173; as identity defining,
145–48; about incest, 83–84, 99–
101, 107; about land, 41–43, 49–50,
55–60, 62–69. See also Bible; Canonization
Biblical scholarship: dealing with Bible's
contradictions, 127–28, 165; exodus/
conquest myth in, 60–62, 153–59;
on history of Israelite conquest/settle-
ment, 154–58; nationalism and
10–11; in nineteenth-century German historicism, 10–11, 123–28;
projects on origins and sources, 8,
123–28. See also Elohist (E) writer;
Yahwist (J) writer
Blake, William, 176
Blond, Philip, 183n.4, 193n.50
Bloom, Harold, 200n.38
Boaz, 90
Boorer, Suzanne, 194n.4
Bouchard, D. F., 195n.14
Boundaries: defining and defending, 4–5;
fixing community boundaries,
146–48; of land, 53–54
Bourdieu, Pierre, 199n.28
Boyarin, Daniel, 189n.19
Boyarin, Jonathan, 154, 189n.19, 198nn.
17, 20, 199n.26
Brenner, Athalya, 189n.18

Brueggemann, Walter, 53, 184nn.10, 11,
185n.13
Bruns, Gerald, 19n.33
Burrows, Millar, 186n.1

Cadava, Eduardo, 183n.22
Cain: depicted as agriculturalist, 178n.2;
exiled, 52; rejection by God, 2–3; in
rivalry with Abel, 2–3, 82–83, 114
Calmet, Augustin, 192n.39
Camp, Claudia, 185nn. 25, 26
Canaanites, ix–xi, 61, 153–56
Canonization: Christian biblical, 146;
closing of text by, 146–48, 167; opening the canon, 175–76
Chénier, Marie-Joseph-Blaise, 12
Christian Bible: collective identity/mem-
ory in, 177n.2; contents of, 181n.3;
interpretation of Old Testament narratives, 104–6; remembrance of the
Exodus, 152
Cohen, Shaye J. D., 186n.1
Collective identity: Bible's role in forging, 5–13; as corporeal, 78, 97; covenantal, 25–26; as created and maintained through violence, x–xi, 2–5, 9,
22–25, 37, 79–80, 87–97, 139–40;
defining and defending borders of,
4–5, 140–42; and difference, 25, 31;
forged through negation of the
Other, 4–5, 16, 18–25, 79–80, 94;
and kinship, 79–119; monotheism
and, x–xi, 15–25, 72, 176; myth of,
6; nation and nationalism and, 6–7,
120–21; in New Testament, 177n.2;
role of scarcity in, 20; secular and religious notions of, 10–13, 16, 25–27,
121–22; shared memories as defining,
43–44, 143–53; as territorially based,
39–55; toleration and multiplicity in,
19–20, 31–38
Collective memory: communities
formed by, 143–46, 162; identity of
Israel formed by, 32–33; in New Testament, 177n.2
Community. See Collective identity
Competition: absence of motive for, 117;
between Cain and Abel, 2–4; for inheritance, 83–91; of sons with father,
110–11. See also Scarcity

204

Index